SCRIPTURAL TRACES: CRITICAL PERSPECTIVES ON
THE RECEPTION AND INFLUENCE OF THE BIBLE

23

Published under

LIBRARY OF NEW TESTAMENT STUDIES

622

Formerly Journal for the Study of the Old Testament Supplement Series

THE BIBLE ON TELEVISION

Edited by

Helen K. Bond and Edward Adams

LONDON • NEW YORK • OXFORD • NEW DELHI • SYDNEY

T&T CLARK

Bloomsbury Publishing Plc

50 Bedford Square, London, WC1B 3DP, UK

1385 Broadway, New York, NY 10018, USA

BLOOMSBURY, T&T CLARK and the T&T Clark logo
are trademarks of Bloomsbury Publishing Plc

First published in Great Britain 2020

A catalogue record for this book is available from the British Library.
A catalog record for this book is available from the Library of Congress.

ISBN: HB: 978-0-5676-7399-2
         ePDF: 978-0-5676-7400-5
         ePUB: 978-0-5676-9333-4
         XML: 978-0-5676-7401-2

Series: Library of New Testament Studies, ISSN 2513-8790, volume 622
Scriptural Traces, volume 23

Typeset by: Forthcoming Publications Ltd

To find out more about our authors and books visit www.bloomsbury.com and sign up for our
newsletters.

CONTENTS

CONTRIBUTORS

Edward Adams is Professor of New Testament Studies at King's College London. He has written several books including *Parallel Lives of Jesus: Four Gospels, One Story* (Westminster John Knox, 2011), and *The Earliest Christian Meeting Places: Almost Exclusively Houses?* (Bloomsbury, 2015). He has given many radio and TV interviews, and was academic consultant to *David Suchet: In the Footsteps of St Paul* (2012) and *David Suchet: In the Footsteps of St Peter* (2015).

David Batty has been producing and directing films for more than 25 years. He cut his teeth on Channel 4's award-winning *Cutting Edge* series. Since then he has made a wide range of major films and series for broadcasters all over the world (BBC, Channel 4, PBS, NHK, Discovery etc.). He directed two of the award-winning S*econd World War in Colour* series and his documentary *Cult of the Suicide Bomber* was nominated for an International Emmy in 2005 and *Variety* described it as 'remarkable, incisive…controversial'. More recently he has completed highly acclaimed award-winning films about Dickie Attenborough and Ian Paisley. He has also directed four feature film versions (collectively known as The Lumo Project) of the Four Gospels, the first – *The Gospel of John* – premiered on US Netflix in December 2014 and was broadcast on the BBC over Easter 2015. His most recent feature documentary about the social revolution of the 1960s called *MY GENERATION* with Michael Caine and written by Dick Clement and Ian La Frenais, produced by Simon Fuller at XIX Entertainment, was premiered at the 2017 Venice Film Festival and released in the UK in 2018. Earlier this autumn he had a two-part series on BBC 4 called *Lost Films of World War Two*.

Robert Beckford is Professor of Theology at the Queen's Foundation in Birmingham. He has research interests in African and African Caribbean history, religion and popular culture; he interrogates the intersection(s) of social history, religious experience and cultural politics. Robert researches across a range of media and has written a number of books, including *Jesus Is Dread: Black Theology and Black Culture in Britain* (Darton, Longman & Todd, 1998), *Jesus Dub: Theology, Music and Social Change* (Routledge, 2006), and *Documentary as Exorcism: Resisting the Bewitchment* *of Colonial Christianity* (Bloomsbury, 2014). He also explores theology in black urban music(s) and has written and produced the studio album, *The Jamaican Bible Remix* (5AM Records, 2017). Robert is a BAFTA award-winning television presenter, and has presented over twenty-five television documentaries, including Channel 4's *Who Wrote the Bible?* (2004), *The Nativity Decoded* (2008) and BBC's *The Battle for Christianity* (2016).

Helen K. Bond is Professor of Christian Origins at the University of Edinburgh and is interested in all aspects of the history, culture and religious beliefs of first-century Judaea. She has written a number of books, including *Pontius Pilate in History and Interpretation* (Cambridge University Press, 1998), *Caiaphas: Friend of Rome and Judge of Jesus?* (Westminster John Knox, 2004) and *The Historical Jesus: A Guide for the Perplexed* (Bloomsbury, 2012). She has contributed to over 50 TV and radio documentaries (BBC, Channel 4, Discovery, National Geographic, etc.), both as an on-screen 'talking head' and presenter. She was historical consultant to History Channel's *The Bible* (2012), BBC's *The Nativity* (2010) and RTE's *Countdown to Calvary* (2018). Most recently, she co-presented *Jesus' Female Disciples* (Channel 4, 2018), with Joan Taylor.

Jean-Claude Bragard is Creative Director of Minerva Media, a British TV production company specializing in programmes about religion, history and archaeology. Previously he was Executive Producer and Head of Documentaries in BBC Religion & Ethics. As producer/director, series producer and executive producer he has made more than a hundred films for several broadcasters, including ITV, Channel 4, BBC 1, 2 and 4, Discovery Channel, TLC, ZDF, France 2, AHC, Discovery Health and Travel Channel. In the past three decades he has been the creative force behind many award-winning documentaries about the Bible, Christianity and religion generally, including *Son of God*, *Evil*, *A History of Christianity* and *Around the World in 80 Faiths*. This is his first academic paper since the bright lights of television lured him away from the ivory towers.

Ray Bruce is an internationally acclaimed and multi-award-winning documentary producer with credits across a range of films focusing on religion, history and archaeology. His particular interest is the Abrahamic traditions, which has inevitably drawn him to work extensively in Israel/ Palestine and the Mediterranean world, acquiring extensive knowledge and expertise in the process. He is a passionate advocate of promoting religious literacy through TV and film. Exploring Christian origins and the Jesus story has been a major part of his documentary output for both UK and international broadcasters, including *Bible Hunters*; *Secrets of the Cross*; *Who Wrote The Dead Sea Scrolls?*; *Jesus Christ Movie Star*;

The Secret Family of Jesus; and *The Story of Jesus and Battle for the Holy Land.* Recently, he was theological and historical consultant on the ground-breaking and critically acclaimed Lumo Project, a series of four feature films based on the word-for-word accounts of the four Gospels. He has developed a highly successful collaboration with David Suchet, producing two series for BBC 1: *David Suchet: In the Footsteps of St Paul* and *David Suchet: In the Footsteps of St Peter.* Ray formerly was Head of Production and Executive Producer for CTVC and now has his own consultancy company.

Mark Harris is Professor in Science and Religion at the University of Edinburgh. Working originally in earth sciences and then in physics at the Rutherford Appleton Laboratory, with S. Bramwell he discovered 'spin ice', a model system that has revolutionized research into magnetism. In more recent years he has turned to biblical studies in his research and teaching, and he is particularly interested in the ways that the natural sciences have changed how the Bible is perceived and read today. He is the author of *The Nature of Creation: Examining the Bible and Science* (Acumen, 2013), and is working on a long-term project on the impact of science on the miracle stories in the book of Exodus.

Cherryl Hunt is currently Academic Registrar and an Associate Tutor with South West Ministry Training Course. A molecular biologist who metamorphosed into a theologian, she previously studied, researched and taught in the biosciences, and then theology at the University of Exeter. Her chapter on the Bible on TV draws partly on her Bible Society-sponsored doctoral thesis in theology, which examined strategies by which 'ordinary' Christians (those with little or no academic theological education) might be enabled to engage with the ancient texts comprising the Bible; the resources employed included biblically focused television programmes.

Margaret (Meg) E. Ramey (PhD, University of St. Andrews) is the Director of Education Abroad for Tutku Educational Travel, where she enjoys working with professors in the development of education abroad programs across the Mediterranean, Middle East, and Europe as well as lecturing on biblical studies during many of Tutku's adult education programs. Formerly, she was Associate Professor of Biblical Studies at Messiah College, Grantham, Pennsylvania, USA, where, in addition to teaching classes on the Bible and cross-cultural studies, she also offered a course on Jesus in Fiction and Film. She currently edits the "Bible in Fiction" project for *Oxford Biblical Studies Online* and has written several articles on the reception of the Bible in popular culture, particularly focusing on the portrayal of Jesus in modern novels, movies and television. Her first monograph, entitled *The Quest for the Fictional Jesus: Gospel Rewrites, Gospel (Re)Interpretation, and Christological Portraits within Jesus Novels* (Pickwick Publications), was published in 2013. In her free time, she serves on the board of YesLiberia, a non-profit that seeks to empower young people in Liberia through meaningful service learning opportunities in education, healthcare, and technology.

Joan E. Taylor is Professor of Christian Origins and Second Temple Judaism at King's College London. After a BA at Auckland University and a period working for New Zealand's National Film Unit, she completed postgraduate studies at the University of Otago and then went to the British School of Archaeology in Jerusalem (Kenyon Institute) as Annual Scholar in 1986. She undertook a PhD at New College, Edinburgh University, as a Commonwealth Scholar, and was appointed in 1992 to a position of lecturer (subsequently senior lecturer) at the University of Waikato, New Zealand, in the departments of both Religious Studies and History. She has been at King's since 2009. Publishing mainly in the fields of biblical studies, Second Temple Judaism and early Christianity, her special focus is on history, archaeology and women/gender. She has worked in television and radio as an interviewee, interviewer, historical consultant and script consultant. She recently co-presented *Jesus' Female Disciples* (Channel 4, 2018) with Helen Bond.

David Tollerton is Senior Lecturer in Jewish Studies and Contemporary Religion at the University of Exeter. He is the author of *The Book of Job in Post-Holocaust Thought* (Sheffield Phoenix Press, 2012) and the editor of *A New Hollywood Moses: On the Spectacle and Reception of Exodus: Gods and Kings* (Bloomsbury, 2017). He is currently writing a book on public Holocaust memory in contemporary Britain. He has written on Holocaust memory and contemporary politics for *The Guardian, The Times Higher Education* and *The Conversation*, and spoken on this subject on radio and at public events.

Richard Wallis is Principal Academic in the Faculty of Media & Communication, Bournemouth University. His research interests include media literacy, media policy, the nature and experience of work within media industries, media representations of religion and the public understanding of religion. Richard was previously Head of Twofour Learning (part of the Twofour Group) and served on the Board of Twofour Communications. He has variously been an adviser, presenter, director, and producer, for a range of religious programmes across both the BBC and ITV.

PREFACE

There has been a lot of academic activity in recent years in the area of the Bible in film, but relatively little work has been done on the Bible on television. This volume, which arose out of a conversation between the editors, is an attempt to bring together programme-makers and academics who have a special interest in the use of the Bible on television to reflect critically on the subject from their own perspectives. Contributors include producers and directors of biblically focused programming, academics who have contributed to such shows (as presenters, consultants or interviewees), and scholarly analysts who work on religion in the media. As far as the editors are aware, this is the first volume of its kind, and their hope is that it helps to open up a new field of research at the intersection of biblical and television studies. The editors are grateful to their universities for supporting this endeavour. They would also like to thank David Clines at Sheffield Phoenix Press for his encouragement of the project, and more recently Dominic Mattos and Sarah Blake at Bloomsbury for seeing the book through to publication.

Helen K. Bond and Edward Adams
October 2019

INTRODUCTION

Helen K. Bond

In the run-up to Easter 1984, a newly established TV channel aired the most provocative and challenging biblical documentary ever seen on British screens. *Jesus the Evidence* was a three-part miniseries which brought the fledgling 'third quest' for the historical Jesus to sitting rooms throughout the land. Although the ideas contained in the documentary were already well known within theology faculties, the film caused public outrage. Churches were up in arms, accusing the broadcasters not only of a lack of balance but of deliberately attempting to undermine Christian faith and tradition.[1]

Writing in *The Times*, Clifford Longley described the new Channel 4 as 'the first swallow heralding the broadcasting pluralism of cable and satellite'.[2] And indeed it was. By the 1980s, the cosy relationship between Christian churches and British broadcasters could no longer be relied upon. Religious programming had become dull and uninspiring, and new channels had no intention of making their output reflective of mainstream

---

1. The series was produced and directed by David W. Rolfe for London Weekend Television and aired on Channel 4; the researcher was Jean-Claude Bragard, the author of Chapter 2 in this volume. The series is now available on YouTube at https://www.youtube.com/watch?v=D_-zsoUjqjU. For one contributor's experience of both the programme and the following outcry, see G. Vermes, 'A Television Documentary on Christ and the British Press: Channel 4's Jesus the Evidence', in *Searching for the Real Jesus* (London: SCM, 2010), 63–70. One of the editors of this collection (Adams) remembers writing in to complain about the programme, while Professor Mark Goodacre of Duke University made his first TV appearance as a teenager on an episode of *Right to Reply* devoted to the episode.

2. I owe this quotation to the excellent analysis of the programme (and the furore surrounding it) by Robert Wallis, 'Channel 4 and the Declining Influence of Organised Religion on UK Television: The Case of Jesus: The Evidence', *Historical Journal of Film Radio and TV* 36 (2016): 668–88 (683).

Christian views (even if such a thing were entirely possible). Channel 4 had been launched in November 1982 with a specific mandate to cater for minority groups and to offer alternative points of view. Within religious programming this included not only catering to a variety of faiths, but commissioning a different type of more intellectual programme with a mandate to question accepted Christian presuppositions. When churches complained about the latter type of programming, TV executives could point out that they were simply conveying the findings of biblical scholarship to a wider audience, and could also claim (with some justification) that they were only attempting to bridge the gap between academia and ordinary folk which the clergy themselves had so badly failed to do.

Watching the programme now, it all seems innocuous enough. The three episodes chart biblical scholarship from the eighteenth century to the present day; they present Jesus as a popular charismatic holy man and healer, emphatically rejecting any suggestion he thought of himself as the Jewish Messiah, let alone God; and conclude by tracing varying forms of Christian belief as far as the Nicene Creed. The programme exudes an eighties feel: the dramatizations are overly theatrical; the suited (male) scholars read their lines directly into the camera; and an unseen authoritative narrator (Jeremy Kemp) links sections together in clipped BBC English. Most bizarre of all are a series of Pythonesque touches – an exploding Jesus (which is used twice), an awkward musical score and the words 'Excommunicated', which stamp out the faces of scholars whose work got them into trouble with the Catholic Church.

In many respects, the programme stands as a monument to biblical studies, or at least certain branches of the discipline, in the early eighties. The work of Geza Vermes features prominently: his research on the Dead Sea Scrolls and Josephus provides the general setting for events, and his identification of Jesus as a Jewish *hasid* (or charismatic holy man) is a major element of the film. Rather more controversially, the programme reports Morton Smith's views on *Secret Mark* and his theory that the lost text reflects clandestine naked initiation rituals (though the hypothetical nature of this is noted). Helmut Koester appears at length in the third episode, where he outlines his explanation for the empty tomb traditions and presents 'Gnostic Christianity' as a vibrant third strand of early Jesus-devotion (alongside Jewish and Gentile branches of the new faith). Few scholars would share these views today, but the programme offers a unique opportunity for modern researchers to see an earlier generation in action.[3]

3. Other highlights are a short film of Albert Schweitzer receiving his Nobel prize, and interviews with Werner Kümmel (Marburg), Dennis Nineham (Bristol), Howard Marshall (Aberdeen), Anthony Harvey (Westminster Abbey) and Gilles Quispel

One of the most striking aspects of the film is the level at which it is pitched: viewers are introduced to a vast sweep of biblical scholarship and bombarded by names and theories from Strauss and Wrede to form criticism and the synoptic problem. Despite the dramatic episodes, the finished product has the air of an illustrated lecture; it demands a high level of engagement from its audience, with no concessions to late-comers.

Over the last three and half decades, biblical film makers have not had to look far for content or controversy. The same year that *Jesus the Evidence* aired, two other Anglican clergymen found themselves at the centre of media storms. The Bishop of Durham, David Jenkins, was propelled into the spotlight after he queried the literal truth of the 'virgin birth' and Jesus' bodily resurrection, and Don Cupitt's BBC series *The Sea of Faith* popularized his unconventional theology.[4] In the early 1990s, the growing demand in the US for the publication of the Dead Sea Scrolls and the high-profile work of the Jesus Seminar began to make an impact on UK media, and the same decade saw the Church of England wrestle with the question of women's ordination. Dan Brown's 2003 bestseller, *The Da Vinci Code*, raised the question of whether Jesus had a wife (a topic seemingly of perennial interest[5]), and suggested that other gospels, specifically those of a Gnostic outlook, had been deliberately excluded from the Christian canon. The spate of 'Swords and Sandals' films over the last few years – notably Mel Gibson's *The Passion of the Christ* (2004) and *Exodus*, *Noah*, *Son of God* and *Mary, Mother of Christ* (all 2014) and most recently *Mary Magdalene* (2018) – have also kept the Bible in the public view.

Yet biblical documentaries have not stood still in the intervening 35 years. Some of this may well be down to changes in the discipline itself: a greater interest in social history and archaeology (which always works well on camera), an appreciation for the dramatic quality of the texts (which invites costumed reconstructions) and an interest in the characters that make up the biblical story. The greatest change, however, has been

(Utrecht). Airing a year before E. P. Sanders's highly influential *Jesus and Judaism* (Philadelphia: Fortress, 1985), the programme makes little of Jesus' demonstration in the Temple, regarding it as a critique of the Jewish authorities' economic activity rather than a prophecy of the building's destruction (as would be more common nowadays).

4. Bishop Jenkins's ideas were first aired on ITV's *Credo*, then reported in a number of newspapers. We use the popular term 'virgin birth' to refer to the virginal conception, of course.

5. More recently, consider the fuss over the publication in 2012 of the so-called 'Jesus' wife' papyrus; http://gospelofjesuswife.hds.harvard.edu/.

the loss of biblical literacy within British culture. When the producers sat down to plan *Jesus the Evidence* they could be assured that the majority of their audience had at least a general knowledge of the biblical texts, particularly the gospels. The same is by no means true today. Knowledge of the Bible and the story it has to tell is much less prevalent in the early twenty-first century than it was in the early 1980s, and it cannot be assumed that potential viewers know even the general story. In fact, in an age where declining numbers of people go to church and read their Bibles, information about the biblical story tends to come from a variety of alternative sources: the internet, popular spirituality, podcasts, YouTube videos and novels. Steig Larssen's *The Girl with the Dragon Tattoo*, for example, may well provide the only introduction to Leviticus that some people might ever have (and for this reason can provide an interesting starting point in a classroom discussion[6]). And many people unconsciously absorb what they know of Christian symbolism and allegory from popular TV shows such as *Doctor Who*.[7] In this new climate, documentaries are themselves often the means by which certain people gain their biblical knowledge. What these people make of a biblical story may to a large extent be a question of how compelling they found a related documentary.

Television culture has also continued to change greatly over the last 35 years. The advent of cable, satellite and digital TV has produced an apparently infinite number of channels, all competing for a share of the audience. Programmes with advertising breaks need to package their information in 'bite-size' chunks, always aware that they may not hold a viewer's attention for long. Shows can be downloaded on TV 'playback' facilities, or watched through a laptop on the journey into work or in a lunchbreak. Viewers might decide to flick over to emails or Facebook when things get dull, to speed along to the next section or to switch off altogether. A kaleidoscope of images and emotive scenes replaces linear argument, and TV programmers are required to provide entertainment rather than information (or perhaps better, 'infotainment').[8] In an attempt

---

6. See C. A. Blyth, 'Lisbeth and Leviticus: Biblical Literacy and The Girl with the Dragon Tattoo', in *Rethinking Biblical Literacy*, ed. Katie Edwards (London: Bloomsbury/T&T Clark, 2015), 165–86. More generally, see A. Bach, *Religion, Politics, Media in the Broadband Era* (Sheffield: Sheffield Phoenix, 2004).

7. So S. Balstrup, 'Doctor Who: Christianity, Atheism, and the Source of Sacredeness in the Davies Years', *Journal of Religion and Popular Culture* 26 (2014): 145–56.

8. See B. D. Forbes, 'Why Clergy Should Not Ignore Television', *Word and World* 18 (1998): 34–43.

to hold our gaze, many Bible documentaries quite openly cater to a modern love of mystery, of cover-ups and conspiracy theories (particularly when they can be connected to the Catholic Church); it is almost mandatory nowadays for biblical documentaries to promise to reveal 'Mysteries', 'Buried Secrets' or the 'Bible Unearthed'. Viewers are taken on fast-paced trips to famous sites around the eastern Mediterranean and the Middle East, or into dark museum vaults and previously unexplored archaeological sites. Presenters are no longer straight from the lecture theatre, but are often well-known actors, journalists or politicians, friendly guides on a joint journey of discovery.

And the 'experts' have also changed: now they tend to be younger, as likely to be female as male, and most of all passionate about their research. Suits have been jettisoned in favour of jeans, and authoritative mini-lectures are replaced by chatty soundbites. Some producers prefer local experts to imported academics: field archaeologists, museum curators, local priests. Novelists and self-taught 'historians' also appear, not only in the more sensational pieces but also in those wanting a more 'creative' edge – much to the chagrin of university professors. In this brave new world it is almost impossible for viewers to tell the difference between what we might call 'mainstream scholars' and mavericks. A respectable university scholar might briefly appear on the screen, perhaps along with an academic title, but the format is often to present a range of views and simply to allow the observer to select whichever has most appeal.[9]

One of the side-effects of the digital age is that the division between 'expert' and viewer is almost dissolved. No longer are academics shut up in ivory towers with impenetrable walls. With a couple of clicks, anyone can find an email address, and within seconds it is possible to send a thought to the person you are watching on the screen. 'Are you a Christian yourself?' 'Do you think Jesus really existed?' 'Is that your natural hair colour?' 'Are you single?' From the point of view of an academic taking part in a documentary, reaction can be almost instantaneous, and critics/admirers often do not pull their punches.

All of this has paid off. Bible documentaries are clearly popular and regularly enjoy high viewing figures. The Hebrew Bible has its own cast of favourites: the 'real' stories of Moses, Samson, or King David; programmes offering to 'explain' the flood or the parting of the Red Sea,

---

9. Also noted by G. J. Brooke, 'The Scrolls in the British Media (1987–2002)', *Dead Sea Discoveries* 12 (2005): 38–51, here 48 and L. H. Schiffman, 'Inverting Reality: The Dead Sea Scrolls in the Popular Media', *Dead Sea Discoveries* 12 (2005): 24–34, especially 25–9.

or the contribution of archaeology to the story of Jericho. In the New
Testament, it is unsurprisingly Jesus who assumes top billing, with apparently every aspect of his life held up to scrutiny by curious TV viewers:
the circumstances of his birth, his relationship to Mary Magdalene and
the reasons for his execution. A host of related phenomena have been
scrutinized: the star of Bethlehem, the so-called Tomb of Jesus and the
Turin Shroud. The life of Paul, too, has proved fertile ground, along with
a wealth of other biblical characters – King Herod, Pontius Pilate, the
disciples and Mary the mother of Jesus. Taking a broader perspective, the
whole issue of which books became canonical and which were 'banned
from the Bible' has also become popular lately. So, too, are the Dead Sea
Scrolls, which for many people contain secret revelations of Christian
origins.[10]

Documentaries, of course, come in all different types. Some researchers
take their work seriously, reading up on the subject, talking to reputable
scholars (on camera and off), and looking for consensus positions. The
programmes they produce tend to be balanced, serious attempts to convey
the latest scholarship to an interested public. Others are rather more
crafty; they will do their research reasonably thoroughly, but will tend
to use a rather maverick view to reel in the audience. Even if this view
is completely discredited by the programme, it can leave its mark on the
audience's memory (and is often the subject of controversy both before
and after the programme airs). A third group, however, are the televisual
equivalent of the tabloid press. This type refuses to let research get in
the way of a good story; researchers seek out writers with eccentric and
outlandish views in an attempt to piece together a sensational account.
The resulting programme might be entertaining, but has virtually no
educational value whatsoever.[11] All three of these categories will be
discussed in this book.

In many respects, Bible documentaries occupy an ambiguous place
in modern TV scheduling. In broad terms, they tend to come under
the heading of 'religious programming', yet many viewers would be
reluctant to call them 'religious' programmes. This is largely because the
documentary genre itself generally aims to be neutral, to offer information
to the viewer to make up his or her own mind. Many Bible documentaries
make this quite clear from the start: it is common to have a presenter

---

10. On the popular perception of the Dead Sea Scrolls, see Schiffman, 'Inverting
Reality', and M. L. Grossmann, 'Mystery or History: The Dead Sea Scrolls as Popular
Phenomena', *Dead Sea Discoveries* 12 (2005): 68–86.

11. For these broad categorizations, see Schiffman, 'Inverting Reality', 33–7.

who might admit to having been brought up a Christian but who has now lost that faith and is ready to embark on a journey as an interested observer, but not one of faith. This of course fits the demographic of most viewers and offers a non-threatening disclaimer from the start. Yet there is clearly an audience for Bible documentaries amongst religious Jews and Christians, people who are interested in knowing more about what biblical scholars are saying about the texts at the centre of their faith. Most thoughtful believers will welcome a well-made piece; some churches and synagogues might even use a documentary as the basis of a study group, or to bring the text to life. But there are clearly some Christians who seem opposed to any probing of the biblical story on the TV screen, however gentle; and Jews may, with some reason, resent the 'Christianizing' of the Hebrew Bible (a case in point is the History Channel's epic ten-hour dramatization of *The Bible*, which is really a life of Jesus with a few key 'Old Testament' pointers to precede it). To some, the very notion of 'neutrality' in the religious sphere is offensive: all religious dialogue requires a personal response, and to remain neutral is to align oneself with the forces of darkness.[12] This is a dynamic which seems to be unique to religious broadcasting. It is hard to imagine anyone objecting to a documentary on Chaucer or Henry V, particularly when the programme draws on established scholars from respectable universities. In the case of Bible documentaries, there is a suspicion amongst a small minority of Christian groups that biblical scholarship in general, and the BBC in particular, has a deliberate anti-faith agenda. So entrenched is this suspicion that many prefer to complain about a documentary rather than to watch it.

The documentaries that form the basis of this volume, then, are expressions of the reception of the Bible in the late twentieth and early twenty-first centuries. The questions they ask, the narratives they weave, and the way they present the material all reflect the demands and complexities of modern TV audiences, themselves shaped by contemporary

---

12. For discussion, see A. Tilby, 'The Bible and Television', in *Using the Bible Today: Contemporary Interpretations of Scripture*, ed. D. Cohn-Sherbok (London: Bellew Publishing, 1991), 38–46, here 42. This assumption seems to underlie James W. Voelz's critique of Peter Jennings's three-hour ABC special, *Jesus and Paul*, 'The Beginnings of Christianity Are Not on Television', *Concordia Journal* 30 (2004): 122–3. Commenting on another of Peter Jennings's works (this time *Reporting: The Search for Jesus*), D. Bock also complains of a 'misguided sense of journalistic detachment [which] limited the special's goal to Jesus the man', 'No More Hollow Jesus', *Christianity Today* 44 (2000): 73.

culture and expectations. The way that these documentaries draw on biblical scholarship, too, says something about the role of the 'expert' in modern culture, and the way that they are received - by religious groups in particular – illustrates the complicated relationship between faith and academia in our time.

This book has three main purposes. The first is to subject Bible documentaries to scrutiny. Although Bible films have been analyzed in academia for some time now, documentaries, perhaps because of their more ephemeral nature, have not been given the attention they deserve.[13] To our knowledge, only programmes relating to the Dead Sea Scrolls and the Apocalypse have been the subject of scholarly scrutiny, and even here the bibliography is sparse.[14] In the following chapters, we take 'documentaries' in a fairly broad manner: most of what is discussed will fit the general convention of a factual piece which, through a combination of presenters/narrators and/or talking heads, aims to elucidate some aspect of the biblical story. It is increasingly common nowadays for documentaries to intersperse comment with dramatic reconstructions of events, as was already apparent in *Jesus the Evidence*, so the exact line of demarcation between the factual and the reconstructed/imaginative becomes blurred. As extreme examples of this, we have included the BBC's *The Nativity* (2010) and the History Channel's epic *The Bible* (2012). Although both of

---

13. There is a large and growing bibliography concerned with the Bible and film; some examples are L. J. Kreitzer, *The New Testament in Fiction and Film: On Reversing the Hermeneutical Flow* (Sheffield: Sheffield Academic, 1993); R. C. Stern, C. N. Jefford and G. Debona, *Savior of the Silver Screen* (New York: Paulist, 1999); A. Reinhartz, *Jesus of Hollywood* (Oxford: Oxford University Press, 2007); A. Reinhartz, *Bible and Cinema: An Introduction* (London: Routledge, 2013); D. J. Shepherd, *The Bible on Silent Film: Spectacle, Story and Scripture in the Early Cinema* (Cambridge: Cambridge University Press, 2013). Volumes have also been devoted to specific films, e.g. K. E. Corley and R. L. Webb, *Jesus and Mel Gibson's The Passion of the Christ: The Film, the Gospels and the Claims of History* (London: Continuum, 2004), and J. E. Taylor, *Jesus and Brian: Exploring the Historical Jesus and His Times Via Monty Python's Life of Brian* (London: Bloomsbury/T&T Clark, 2015).

14. Issue 12, no. 1 of *Dead Sea Discoveries* (2005), edited by M. L. Grossman and C. M. Murphy, was devoted to the topic of the Dead Sea Scrolls and the media (itself the proceedings of a special session at the 2002 SBL in Toronto). Essays looked at print media alongside documentaries. See also J. Aston and J. Walliss, eds, *Small Screen Revelations: Apocalypse in Contemporary Television*, The Bible in the Modern World (Sheffield: Sheffield Phoenix, 2013). There are also a number of reflections on specific documentaries, such as the one by G. Vermes noted above. Otherwise, most discussion seems to take place within blogs.

these are entirely dramatizations, they all employed historical consultants and biblical scholars in their productions, and at least make some claim to being a 'historically accurate' accounts of events.

Our second purpose is to encourage an informed viewing audience. In a visual age, biblical documentaries are commonly used as aids for teaching, both in schools and universities. Most of the documentaries mentioned in this book can be purchased relatively cheaply from Amazon or are available on YouTube at no cost and can easily be added to course websites and reading material. At a very straightforward level, these programmes allow students to see and appreciate first-century artefacts without visiting a museum, and bring the scenes to life through drama.[15] But documentaries are no more 'neutral' interpretations than books and articles; each is a creative piece with its own agenda and interests (whether these be financial, religious or political). Part of the rationale for this book is to enable people to become more aware as viewers, to appreciate the aims of documentary makers, and the constraints under which participating academics (and producers themselves) need to operate.

The third aim of the book is to offer some glimpses of what it is like for an academic to be part of a TV programme. Twenty years ago, an academic who strayed into TV might have expected a certain amount of condescension from his or her colleagues. Media work was seen as 'selling out', as 'popularizing' (always a bad thing), as forsaking the ivory tower and selling one's soul. There was an assumption that serious scholars couldn't possibly also be 'media dons' (the sneers directed by colleagues towards David Lodge's Ralph Messenger have more than a grain of truth).[16] There were probably a variety of reasons for this, not least of which was professional jealousy. Nowadays, however, times have changed considerably. The rise of blogs and podcasts mean that anyone with even a basic knowledge of IT can find a voice and a platform to be heard. In the UK, funding councils and the regular academic census known (currently) as the Research Excellence Framework all ask not simply for cutting-edge scholarship, but also for evidence of academic

15. Dan W. Clanton Jr and Mark Roncace devote a chapter to 'Television Dramas and Documentaries', in *Teaching the Bible Through Popular Culture and the Arts*, ed. Mark Roncace and Patrick Gray (Atlanta: SBL, 2007), 353–5, though they briefly mention only three.

16. The same point is made by J. H. Mahan, 'The Dead Sea Scrolls in Popular Culture: I Can Give You No Idea of Their Content', *Dead Sea Discoveries* 15 (2005): 87–94, here 90. Curiously, radio seems to be rather more respectable; few scholars, however much they fear 'selling out', would miss an opportunity to take part in Melvyn Bragg's highly acclaimed *In Our Time* (BBC Radio 4).

'impact'. A new generation of academics is suddenly interested not only in publishing work but in getting it 'out there', disseminating their ideas to as wide an audience as possible. Quite how biblical scholars are to go about enthusing the wider public with their research is still a matter of some debate. Simply appearing on a TV programme as a 'talking head' is unlikely to cause many ripples, though taking a leading role on a major production (either as presenter or consultant) may well offer some outlets. Many academics nowadays positively want to be on TV, and though some of the old wariness still remains amongst an older generation, the newer crop (brought up on *Big Brother*, *The X-Factor* and reality TV) are only too happy to be part of it all. If we are to have any influence on the media, however, we need to understand the dynamics of television production and the constraints and demands of popular culture. If we are to enter the fray, it is good to do so as well-informed as possible, and the following essays (particularly those in the earlier part of the book) are designed for anyone who wants to take up the challenge.

The book has an unashamedly British focus. This may strike some readers as odd, particularly given the increasingly international scope of most documentaries – many, for example, are co-produced by BBC/ Discovery, or Channel 5/National Geographic. However, it seemed to the editors (both of whom are British) that both the design and reception of TV documentaries tends to be geographically specific, at least more so than films (which largely do cross international boundaries without difficulty). Indeed, while many documentaries are co-produced, it is common for slightly different versions to go out in the UK and the US. British audiences tend to like a presenter, often a well-known person with some link to the subject matter. North Americans, in contrast, tend to prefer talking heads and a disembodied narrator. To give one example, the BBC's *Son of God* was presented in the UK by Jeremy Bowen (a well-known journalist of the middle-east), while the US (and world) version substituted Mr Bowen with a voice-over.[17] The credibility of a programme for the British audience lies with the expert presenter and/or the experts being interviewed; in the US, the authority lies with the broadcasting channel itself – Discovery, National Geographic and so on.[18] Furthermore,

17. Smaller differences include the length of the show: a programme destined to be aired by the BBC (which does not have advertisements) would be 59 minutes in length, while its US equivalent (leaving room for adverts) would be 45 minutes. Titles also often change: the documentary noted above, *Son of God*, was given the title *Jesus: The Complete Story* in the US.

18. I am indebted to Jean-Claude Bragard for much of the information in this paragraph; personal communication, 16 August 2015.

the dominance of the BBC within British broadcasting has led to very specific trends within religious programming; both the BBC charter and the Broadcasting Act 1990 (which covers independent TV channels) made religious programming a mandatory part of the output.[19] Much of what is said in this book will apply to documentaries in general (and two studies are devoted to small screen adaptations in the US), but we have preferred to keep the primary focus of the collection on the UK and to allow readers from other contexts to extrapolate whatever information seems appropriate to their own situation.

The essays in this collection are arranged in a specific order. In the earlier ones, a number of influential film makers and producers discuss the constraints both on TV producers and networks in terms of religious programming: what is the audience? How should the programme be pitched? And how have biblical programmes changed over the years? The decision both to include and to start with the film-makers is an important feature of this book. Disseminating biblical scholarship needs to start, not with academics and their theories, but with the current broadcasting landscape and the views of experienced TV controllers as to what the public want.

In the opening chapter, Richard Wallis sets the volume in context with an overview of religious broadcasting in the UK. He concentrates on the first five decades of the BBC and the transition from a radio-dominated to a television-dominated broadcasting era. Many of the developments which were to play out in the decades that followed, he argues can be traced back to the foundational cultural shifts of this period: the gradual erosion of the privileged relationship between the churches and broadcasters, the role of commercial pressure and the need to win ratings, the new generation of TV 'professionals' without theological training, and a new sense that 'impartiality' presumed a lack of religious commitment on the part of programme-makers.

In the following chapter, Jean-Claude Bragard draws on his own wide experience as a TV programme-maker to chart the changes in the Bible on TV since the 1970s. He notes the huge number of programmes made about the Bible (far greater than other comparable genre), but asks why, when there are more channels than ever, this has not led to a greater diversity of academic views being represented. While programmes from

19. For an analysis of late twentieth-century religious programming on independent channels, see B. Gunter and R. Viney, *Seeing Is Believing: Religion and Television in the 1990s*, Independent Television Commission/Television Research Monograph (London: John Libbey, 1994). For discussion of the BBC charter, see Richard Wallis's chapter below.

the 1980s and 1990s *did* reflect the thinking of biblical scholars, he suggests that those from roughly 2000 onwards have tended to reflect the thinking of others – the programme-makers themselves, mavericks or non-biblical scholars. The general rise in biblical illiteracy has also led to a return to simple story-telling in Bible programmes made for TV, with History's *The Bible* and BBC's *The Passion* as good examples of this latest phenomenon.

Taking a rather different approach from the rest of the volume, Chapter 3 is a transcript of an interview with award-winning producer of religious documentaries, Ray Bruce. The editors of the volume ask him how he got into television documentary production, about his work with the TV production company CTVC (for which he was Head of Production and Executive Producer) and about his passion for religious programming. We also take the opportunity to ask him about the practicalities of film production – the costs, fundraising, how to choose which broadcaster to go with, the different expectations between viewers in the UK and the US, what topics make a good biblical documentary, scheduling and how to cope with viewer reactions. We will hear what qualities make a good presenter or academic contributor, where he sees the future of biblical documentaries and his dream project.

David Batty rounds off these early essays with a reflection of his involvement in the Lumo Project, a five-year project instigated by film-maker Hannah Lender to turn each of the four gospels into a stand-alone feature film for cinema, TV or a range of electronic devices. What's distinctive about the approach is that the unedited biblical text forms the film's script, superimposed on the drama by well-known actors. David discusses a host of topics: from securing funding to finding the perfect cast; from recreating miracles to the challenges of shooting four versions of the same story; and ends with some insights into the less glamorous side of filming biblical dramas.

In the next group of essays, a number of academics who have acted as talking heads, historical consultants and presenters discuss their experiences of working on TV documentaries. To what extent were they involved in the process? Were their ideas valued? And what kind of audience response did they encounter? These contributions are of necessity rather anecdotal, but it is our hope that personal reflections will give a unique insight into the art of popularizing biblical scholarship.

In the first essay, Joan Taylor's wide experience of TV work, both in New Zealand and the UK, leads her to reflect on the particular challenges encountered by women in television, especially surrounding authority and gravitas. How can women present themselves as 'intellectual' and 'authoritative' without being annoying 'know-it-alls'? She offers some invaluable advice to scholars on the full range of TV work: how to respond to an initial contact from a production company, negotiating a fee, practical aspects of appearing on camera (from appearance to crafting the perfect 'sound bite'), and tips for working on location and consultancy.

Robert Beckford, who is both a distinguished academic and an acclaimed presenter of TV (and radio) documentaries, discusses in his chapter his motivations and aims as a TV presenter. He tells how, in his TV work, he has sought, on the one hand, to defy and oppose industry constraints – and contradictions – within which black TV presenters often work (using the critical framework of the politics of containment to describe these contradictions), and, on the other, to challenge common TV stereotypes of Black Christians and to offer, indeed to *embody*, an alternative Black Christian representation. Analysing press reviews of his TV documentaries, he considers how that representation has been received and perceived.

My own chapter reflects on my involvement with two very different TV programmes exploring Jesus' nativity. First is the BBC's *Virgin Mary* (2002), a highly controversial attempt to uncover the 'real' Mary behind the myths. I analyse the reaction to the documentary, asking what the response tells us about contemporary culture as much as the programme itself. Second, and in complete contrast, is the BBC's *The Nativity* (2010), for which I acted as historical consultant. While this miniseries rightly received wide critical acclaim, and can even be seen to be a continuation of the 'rewritten Bible' so common at the time of Jesus, the popularity of biblical dramas at the moment, I argue, may not be an entirely positive development from the point of view of the biblical scholar.

Eddie Adams' chapter looks at how the apostle Paul is dealt with in the series *David Suchet: In the Footsteps of St Paul*, for which he acted as academic consultant. He considers the series' approach to Paul as a travelogue in the mould of H. V. Morton's *In the Steps of St Paul* and as Suchet's pursuit of Paul's character, in which the presenter has an interest as an actor and also a Christian. Adams looks at how the New Testament sources for Paul are used in the series, and also at how the input of academics is deployed. Overall, he sees the production as an effective TV treatment of the apostle, which is largely down to Suchet's skill as a presenter and his passion for the subject.

Adams's chapter provides a good transition to the last few essays, in which a number of scholars assess the finished products. What do they tell us about modern receptions of the Bible? How useful are Bible documentaries in offering a lively way to convey biblical scholarship to the wider public, both religious and secular? And do they, in their turn, influence biblical scholars and set a new scholarly agenda?

In Chapter 9, Cherryl Hunt surveys a few examples of responses to productions based on biblical stories and characters from viewers who self-identify as Christians, or at least indicate that they make use of the Bible and are familiar with it. The survey draws mostly on online reviews and blogs for more recent presentations, and also on focus group materials for some earlier productions. She finds that, despite common perceptions that television productions do not entirely faithfully and adequately present the biblical texts they portray, many Bible-users nevertheless find watching dramatic presentations of parts of the Bible on the small screen to be a positive and often emotionally stimulating and/or thought-provoking experience.

As both a scientist and a biblical scholar, Mark Harris has a particular interest in documentaries portraying the miraculous events of the Exodus. After surveying 14 recent works, along with three focusing on the eruption of Thera, he notes that nearly all of them have a particular preoccupation with questions of historicity. Although these films often include interviews with biblical scholars, their cautions are invariably dismissed as unwarranted scepticism. In their place, the films turn to half-understood scientific explanations, presenting outdated theories as new proofs that the Exodus actually took place. Overall, he finds a conservative literalism in these films, in which the more pressing concerns of the biblical text are ignored.

Conservative Christians are also the target audience for the History Channel's dramatization, *The Bible* (2013). In Chapter 11, Meg Ramey looks at the producers' motives for making the ten-part miniseries and finds that, despite the plethora of historical consultants (and the title of the channel!), their primary concern was to be faithful to the biblical narrative. For producers Mark Burnett and Roma Downey, biblical history – with its miracles and outlandish events – is simply 'real' history. While Ramey is appreciative of the attention to the socio-political context in episodes portraying the New Testament, she finds a number of more disturbing trends: the 'Christianizing' of the Bible in which the Jewish Scriptures are seen to point to Jesus; a sanitizing of events coupled with a sensual and often problematic portrayal of women; an ambiguous portrait of a capricious God; and a pervasiveness of violence. What, she asks, does this tell us about our own society?

Finally, in Chapter 12, David Tollerton focuses on ABC's miniseries *Of Kings and Prophets* (2016) – a graphic retelling of the story of Saul and David – and asks why it failed so spectacularly (only two of the original eight episodes were shown). The miniseries had been expected to capitalize on the box office successes of the biblical films *Noah* and *Exodus* (both from 2014), and yet it did not. The reasons, David suggests, are specific to the small screen. First, the episodic nature of a TV series inevitably means that complicated ethical matters are left unresolved at the end of individual programmes, and film-makers require a determined and hardy returning audience (unlike in a cinema where the audience is largely captive until the end). Second, TV's heavy reliance on advertisers make it vulnerable to targeted lobbying, as was the case here. David's chapter reminds us that the Bible doesn't always sell, and that the success of a particular miniseries or documentary is dependent on a raft of social, cultural and artistic factors that aren't always easy to disentangle.

Chapter 1

GENESIS OF THE BIBLE DOCUMENTARY:
THE DEVELOPMENT OF RELIGIOUS BROADCASTING
IN THE UK

Richard Wallis

Television genres and sub-genres are rarely stable over time. The Bible
documentary is a form of factual programme-making that emerged recog-
nizably during the 1970s, reflecting broader stylistic trends in television.
Today more than ever, in a climate in which the stakes are high for the
winning and retention of audiences, television commissioning editors
are caught between a cultural aversion to risk-taking, and an ambition to
claim the next big 'genre-busting' hit. The consequence of these contradictory pressures is that programme genres are not so much invented
as developed through a process of cultivated adaptation and hybridity:
a tendency towards small iterative changes. To a significant extent, the
template for the modern 'authored' documentary remains the seminal
Civilisation (BBC, 1969): art historian Kenneth Clark's personal view of
the philosophy, art and architecture of the Western world. The remarkable
impact of this thirteen-part series is attributable, in part, to the erudition
and urbane authority of its on-screen presenter (Clark was knighted for
his achievements), and in part to its visual richness (being one of the first
such series to be filmed in colour) establishing the lavish travelogue style.
It was this approach that was repeated by *Civilisation*'s producer, Peter
Montagnon, in his subsequent thirteen-part series *The Long Search* (BBC,
1977), written by the scholar Ninian Smart, which examined the world's
major religions.

There are other reasons, however, why the documentary was embraced
as a vehicle for religious programmes during the 1970s, and its particular

history should be understood in the context of the evolution of religious broadcasting in the UK more generally. This chapter aims to provide this broader frame. The way in which religious broadcasting was established, and the way it subsequently evolved over its first five decades, is central to understanding how and why the Bible documentary emerged as it did, when it did. As will be seen, the transition from a radio-dominated, to a television-dominated, broadcasting era was marked by a number of important cultural shifts that had significant impact on religious broadcasting practice. It is against this background that the developments that follow (and that are discussed by others in this volume) may be understood. In particular focus here are: the way in which Bible-related themes came to be treated within the documentary genre; the controversies and tensions that have arisen, especially between broadcasters and the churches; and the changing role that advisors and 'experts' have played throughout.

Religion on 'the Wireless'

Religion has been part of broadcasting output in the UK since Christmas Eve 1922, when the Rector of Whitechapel delivered the first 'wireless' sermon. In his address, he wondered at the extraordinary technological development that had enabled him, in one moment, to speak to more people than the apostle Paul had done in his entire lifetime. Such technological developments had certainly been profound, but it would be a mistake to assume that it had been technology that had determined the way in which public service broadcasting developed, or that there was anything inevitable about the way in which religious programmes evolved with reference to it. The BBC Charter of 1927 – like the Television Act that was to follow twenty-seven years later – carried no mandatory requirement that religious content should to be produced. Yet religious programmes have played an important part in the story of UK broadcasting since its inception. The way in which this occurred, the forms that programmes took and the role that advisors and experts came to play is largely due to the distinctive and formative role played by the BBC's first Director-General, John Reith.

Reith was the son of a Presbyterian minister and viewed his position in terms of a 'calling'.[1] He was determined that the BBC should actively promote religion, and that this should be of the right kind. He held

---

1. Andrew Boyle discusses in some detail Reith's religious convictions in his biography *Only the Wind Will Listen: Reith of the BBC* (London: Hutchinson & Co., 1972).

strong personal Christian convictions while being generally opposed to narrow dogmatism. Reith wanted the BBC to represent a practical, non-denominational faith, broadly representative of what he thought of as the mainstream of historic Christianity.

As the Sunday evening address became a regular feature of BBC output, Reith established a 'Sunday Committee' to provide him with expertise and advice. This small hand-picked group of clerics was intended to be broadly representative of the Christian churches, but crucially, chosen by Reith and not their institutional constituencies. By July 1926 the group had become known as the Religious Advisory Committee, and later, as regional advisory committees were set up, it became the Central Religious Advisory Committee (CRAC). CRAC was to be the model for advisory committees on a number of subject areas during the early years of the BBC, and extended its influence still further with the establishment of ITV. Its central role in the evolution of religious broadcasting, the relationship between it and the religious institutions that it ostensibly 'represented' and its defence (and sometimes criticism) of broadcasting practices are an essential part of this story.

CRAC's early role was primarily to offer advice to the BBC on Sunday speakers. It also provided a line of resistance to sustained criticism of the BBC's approach to religion, including from many within the churches, some of whom believed that the medium and the message were simply incompatible. In 1923, for example, the Chapter of Westminster rejected the request to broadcast the marriage service of the Duke of York (soon to be King George VI) on the grounds that men in public houses might be listening with their hats on.[2] Three years later, the magazine *Life of Faith*, published a series of letters debating the question of whether or not the very medium was the work of the devil. One contributor demanded: 'Are we not told to avoid even the appearance of evil? "Come out from among them and be ye separate". "Touch not the unclean thing". Are not the world's pleasures, the wireless, cinema, etc. unclean today?'[3] At a purely pragmatic level, there were widespread concerns that the broadcasting of church services might result in a fall in church attendance. At the same time, organizations like the British Humanist Association, the Rationalists and Fabian Society objected to the primacy of place being given to the Christian religion, whilst groups like the Christian Scientists and the Seventh Day Adventists were angered at having been excluded by what the BBC had decided constituted 'mainstream'.

2. K. M. Wolfe, *Churches and the BBC 1922–1956* (London: SPCK, 1984), 79.
3. *Life of Faith*, 11 August 1926.

Against this criticism, Reith enlisted allies from those who shared his own vision for 'BBC religion': a version of Christianity best illustrated by his recruitment of Dick Sheppard, vicar of St. Martin-in-the-Fields. Sheppard was initially drafted in to join the Sunday Committee, but subsequently became a major contributor to the BBC's output, with broadcasts from St Martin's becoming a staple part of the BBC's output (continuing to the present). Sheppard's 'diffused rather than sectional Christianity'[4] was what Reith identified as the middle ground of Christian consensus, and justified in terms of the BBC's public service duties:

> In a national service to which nothing that pertains to the life of men is foreign, it was natural that from the beginning religion should find its place in British Broadcasting. It could not be otherwise. Even if the programmes aimed only at providing education and recreation, religion could not be denied a place; but when those who were responsible for Broadcasting set before themselves the object of raising the national standard of values and of a constructive idealism, it was obvious that the religious service should be one of the regular programme features.[5]

What was obvious to Reith was not obvious to everyone, yet Reith pursued his vision with energy. Reith wanted more than just church services and epilogues. The first religious 'talks' series was *God and the World Through Christian Eyes* (BBC, 1933). Across two 12-part series', eminent academics and theologians addressed themselves to a range of subjects broadly grouped around the themes of 'God', 'Christ', 'Man and His World' and 'Christianity'. In the first series, J. Y. Simpson, Professor in Natural Science at New College Edinburgh, spoke on Science and the Idea of God; Maude Royden, the theologian and suffragist, spoke on God and the World of Art; and the New Testament scholar, C. H. Dodd, spoke on 'Christ Crucified'. Much effort was concentrated in trying to find the most engaging and convincing speakers to communicate Christian ideas. Being an ardent Sabbatarian, such programmes – and only such programmes – dominated Sunday broadcasting, although nothing was broadcast during the normal hours of church services. Early religious broadcasting on 'the wireless', therefore, consisted of a limited Sunday listening diet of mainly church services, sacred music, talks and (sometimes more ambitious) religious educational content aimed at children.

4. Wolfe, *Churches*, 8.
5. *BBC Handbook, 1928* (London; BBC, 1928), 131.

The War Years and After

Reith departed the BBC in 1938. The war years that followed constituted the period that most solidly established the Corporation's reputation as an institution of national and cultural importance. As well as being a reassuring source of information and entertainment, it also became an instrument of national unity as it developed more of a mass audience appeal. The changes that resulted from the BBC's role of keeping the nation cheerful were evidenced in all departments, including new opportunities for religious broadcasting. The accessible combination of fireside chat, theology and Christian apologetics made the wartime talks of contributors like C. S. Lewis enormously popular.[6]

One of the most ambitious projects during this period was *The Man Born to Be King*.[7] James Welch, Director of Religious Broadcasting, commissioned the popular crime writer, Dorothy L. Sayers, to write a dramatization of the life of Christ for the Sunday Children's Hour. Sayers, who had also written works of theological scholarship,[8] agreed, on the condition that the character of Jesus should be portrayed with the same degree of realism as other characters, and not 'lost in a kind … of Apollinarian mist'.[9] The result provoked a good deal of controversy. Many objected to the very idea of a Bible dramatization. The Lord's Day Observance Society asked the BBC to 'refrain from staging on the wireless this revolting imitation of the voice of our Divine Saviour and Redeemer'.[10] The campaign prompted over two thousand letters of complaint prior to the broadcast, although the subsequent reception of the programmes was mostly favourable. The (eventually acknowledged) success of the series signified that religious broadcasting did not have to be limited to devotional talks and church services.

The BBC television service pioneered from 1936, but closed at the beginning of the war, was re-opened when hostilities ended. Initially television was treated as radio with pictures. The first televised religious programme was a service of consecration of a war memorial chapel at

6. Lewis's talks were adapted and published as *Mere Christianity* (New York: Macmillan, 1952).

7. Dorothy L. Sayers, *The Man Born to Be King: A Play-Cycle on the Life of Christ*, BBC, 1941–42.

8. Dorothy L. Sayers, *The Mind of the Maker* (London: Methuen, 1941) was published the same year.

9. Cited in Wolfe, *Churches*, 219.

10. H. H. Martin of The Council of the Lords' Day Observance Society, Letter to the BBC, 12 December 1941; BBC Archives, cited in Wolfe, *Churches*, 227.

Biggin Hill, transmitted on 15 September 1946, but only an enthusiastic minority had the equipment to view it. It was not until the Coronation of 1953 that general public interest in television was really awakened, although the thought of television cameras violating the 'rightful intimacy'[11] of the ceremony was too much for some. Fears were expressed particularly about intrusion into the sacred environment east of the church screen. After some considerable negotiation and compromise, permission to televise was granted, and the effect of the broadcast on the general public was significant, as for the first time a television audience exceeded a radio audience. The new age of television had dawned.

The Aims of Religious Broadcasting

Throughout the war years, CRAC's definition of the aims of religious broadcasting remained true to Reith's original vision 'to make Britain a more Christian country'.[12] In a report prepared for CRAC in October 1948 'four distinguishable aspects of this aim' were set out:

1. To maintain standards of truth, justice and honesty in private and public life.
2. To explain what the Christian faith is, to remove misunderstanding of it and to demonstrate its relevance today.
3. To lead 'non-churchgoers' to see that any really 'Christian' commitment involves active membership of an actual church congregation and to give 'churchgoers' a wider vision of what church membership involves.
4. To provide opportunities for that challenge to personal faith in Jesus Christ as Saviour and Lord which is the heart of 'conversion'.[13]

Reith's original view that the Corporation's entire output should be based upon 'the stated and official religion of the country'[14] positioned religious broadcasting as the Corporation's missionary arm. No programmes had been allowed to present attacks or undermine this position. Despite the

11. Wolfe, *Churches*, 498.

12. 'Broadcasting and Religion', in *BBC Handbook 1928* (London: BBC, 1928), 131–3.

13. Confidential paper prepared for CRAC in October 1948 by Frances House. BBC Archives.

14. J. C. W. Reith, *Broadcast over Britain* (London: Hodder & Stoughton, 1924), 192.

ban on controversy having been lifted the year before, in 1948 the then
Director-General, William Haley, stated:

> There are many demands of impartiality laid upon the Corporation but this
> is not one of them. We are citizens of a Christian country, and the BBC –
> an institution set up by the State – bases its policy upon a positive attitude
> towards Christian values. It seeks to safeguard those values and to foster
> acceptance of them. *The whole preponderant weight of its programmes is
> directed to this end.*[15]

Nevertheless, the world was changing. Ever since *God and the World
Through Christian Eyes*, there had been pressure from both within the
Corporation and elsewhere to allow a certain amount of dialogue between
Christians and non-believers. In 1949 Lord Beveridge (the principal archi-
tect of the welfare state) was asked to undertake a broadcasting review,
primarily to examine the BBC's position of monopoly. The Report's
discussion of religious broadcasting is of particular interest in that it
distinguishes between *two* responsibilities of the BBC: first, the 'highest
duty' of the Corporation to make an 'impartial search for truth'; and
second, those duties of an institution 'set up by the State in a Christian
country': 'The two considerations are reconciled in practice by having
both controversial broadcasting and religious broadcasting as distinct
activities of the BBC'.[16] This distinction of activities, the Report observed,
took place through the functions of the Talks Department and the Religious Department respectively. The clear implication here is that the
Religious Department has a duty to propagate the Christian faith, while
the Talks Department has the 'higher' duty to seek after 'truth' impartially,
although this should be done 'in close consultation' with the Religious
Department. We see here, then, the advancement of a gradual process
in which a religious paradigm shifts from being the basis of general
broadcasting policy, to becoming the basis of the broadcasting policy of
the Religious Department alone. Beveridge's response to complaints of
exclusion from non-religious groups like the Ethical Union was to recom-
mend that they be allotted time by the Talks Department. The Report also
suggested that the Governors should consider a 'Hyde Park of the air'
to allow other minorities to put over their views. A statement published
in the *Radio Times* summarized the change as allowing broadcasting to

15. William Haley, 'Moral Values in Broadcasting', address to the British Council
of Churches, 1948 (emphasis original).

16. *Report of the Broadcasting Committee 1949* [The Beveridge Report],
Command Paper 8116 (London: HMSO, 1951), 63.

'move within the climate of public opinion'.[17] The profound importance of this distinction was not felt for some time. It was, however, a shift that was to have significant repercussions over the following years.

Religious Broadcasting in Competition

The decision to allow 'some element of competition'[18] in television was made in 1952. The BBC would maintain its monopoly of radio broadcasting only. BBC television was to be subject to commercial competition. Reith's now famous outburst in the House of Lords demonstrates the strength of feeling that there was on the subject:

> A principle absolutely fundamental and cherished is scheduled to be scuttled ... Somebody ... introduced Christianity and printing and the uses of electricity. And somebody introduced smallpox, bubonic plague and the Black Death. Somebody is minded now to introduce sponsored broadcasting into this country.[19]

Despite many objections, the Television Act of 1954 established an Independent Television Authority (ITA) to govern the newly emerging independent television companies, of which there were initially four: Associated-Rediffusion; Associated Television; Granada; and the Kemsley-Winnick Group.

The first religious programme on ITV was an Epilogue (Associated-Rediffusion) broadcast on the first day of transmission, 22 September 1955. A broadcast service took place in November (ATV). The first religious discussion programme, *About Religion* (ATV), followed later, although religious broadcasting on both BBC television and ITV was initially fairly limited. This, however, changed significantly when ITV took the decision to begin broadcasting within the dead seventy-minute break in transmission on a Sunday evening between 6.15pm and 7.25pm (assumed to be the normal hours of church worship). Restrictions on broadcasting hours imposed by the Postmaster-General had enforced this 'closed period'. Ironically, however, because religious broadcasting was exempt from the rules of broadcasting hours, it was this very time that was adopted for the broadcast of religious programmes. Eventually, by agreement between the BBC and the ITA, religious programmes were

17. BBC *Radio Times*, 15 March 1947.
18. *White Paper on Broadcasting Policy*. Command Paper 5550 (London: HMSO, 1952).
19. Lord Reith's speech to the House of Lords, 22 May 1952, Hansard Col. 1297.

transmitted simultaneously within this period ('back-to-back'). The result was that religious television broadcasting suddenly increased dramatically to take full advantage of the additional time.

Church services continued to be broadcast on television in much the same way as had been done on radio (although the operation was far more costly). After some initial caution from the churches, they were eventually welcomed, and considered to be a way of 'opening-up' the rituals and practices of the churches to those who, for various reasons, would not go to church themselves. Audiences were presumed to be religiously sympathetic, if not actively committed (typically thought of as the would-be churchgoer who was sick or housebound). It was an approach that remained largely unchanged up to the 1990s (albeit with some occasional experimentation with studio-based alternatives, mainly by the BBC). ITV's long-running *Morning Worship* (ITV) – the 'citadel' of its output[20] – was transmitted live each Sunday from a different location, and contained no narrative comment or interruption. The presiding minister might welcome viewers as fellow participators in worship, with the service conducted as if it were an ordinary local church gathering.

The 1954 Television Act, like the BBC Charter, lays no mandatory requirement on independent television companies to produce religious programmes. The ITA was to ensure that programmes 'contain a suitable proportion of matter calculated to appeal to the tastes and outlook of persons served by the station' and, as far as possible, ensure that 'the programmes maintain a proper balance in subject matter and general standard of quality'. Beyond this the Act only required that when religious programmes were produced, they be made in consultation with a religious advisory panel 'representative of the main streams of religious thought'.[21] Not surprisingly, therefore, it was to the already established Central Religious Advisory Committee (CRAC) that the ITA turned.

By the time that CRAC became the advisory body for the ITA, its task had become considerably broader than simply advising the BBC on Sunday speakers. It now advised on the whole gamut of religious broadcasting on both BBC radio and television. It had also developed to include prominent clergy and lay people of all denominations that were in membership of the British Council of Churches and Roman Catholic Church. It was in this way that the problem of what constituted 'main streams of religious thought' was justified (although the group was later widened to include representation of the Jewish faith, and eventually

20. As described in E. Croston, ed., *IBA Yearbook: Television & Radio* (London: Independent Broadcasting Authority, 1983).

21. Section eight of the *Television Act 1954* (London: HMSO, 1954), Chapter 55.

other religious traditions). The BBC and ITA made appointments to CRAC jointly, 'in consultation with the churches'.[22] The definition of 'consultation' in this respect was ambiguous. There were no clear terms of reference and such decisions tended to be left to the 'better judgement' of the department heads at the BBC and ITA respectively. Consequently, the extent to which CRAC could be seen as truly 'representative' was often brought into question.[23] CRAC was thought to be well positioned to advise the new ITA as it did the BBC, on general matters of broadcasting policy, but not to offer advice on practical day-to-day programme planning. Consequently it was decided that in addition to CRAC a small Panel of Religious Advisors should be set up which would meet monthly for the ITV companies.

By the late 1950s, the growing ITV network was flourishing. With the UK transmission of popular American comedy like *I Love Lucy* (CBS, 1951–57), and crime dramas like *Dragnet* (NBC, 1951–59), audiences grew rapidly. Hughie Green's *Double Your Money* (Associated-Rediffusion, 1955–64) and other quiz and money games were also introduced. From 1957 onwards profits increased to such a degree that Roy Thomson of Scottish Television was prompted to make his famous analogy of an ITV license being like a license to print money. By the end of the decade ITV was watched by more than 70 per cent of the audience who had a choice.[24]

'Authentic' Religious Programmes

If the 1950s had been the decade of ITV, the 1960s were to see a renewed sense of confidence on the part of the BBC under Director-General Hugh Greene. The Corporation was granted a second channel in 1964 (BBC2). Greene wanted to lose the Corporation's 'auntie' image, and to reflect something of the spirit of the sixties. New series like *Z Cars* (BBC, 1962–78) about tough and cynical police in a working-class northern town, and the satirical *That Was The Week That Was* (BBC, 1962–63) were so far removed from what had come to be expected of the BBC that many people took exception. *That Was the Week That Was* in particular pushed at the boundaries of what was acceptable for public taste, with almost no area of public life spared from its savage wit, religion included.

22. *Report of the Committee on the Future of Broadcasting* (Annan Committee). Command Paper 6753 (London: HMSO, 1977).

23. A matter debated by the General Synod of the Church of England, in *Broadcasting, Society and the Church* (London: Church Information Office, 1973), 63–4.

24. A. Davis, *Television: The First Forty Years* (London: Severn House, 1976), 18.

During the early days of television, religious broadcasters had experimented with different programme styles and formats. *Jesus of Nazareth* (BBC, 1956) was an early attempt to use drama[25] to achieve for religious television what Dorothy L. Sayers's series had achieved for radio. Without the formidable personality of Sayers to drive it forward, the project became ensnared in a tortuous consultative operation, which nearly sunk the project entirely (involving representatives from the Ministry of Education, University departments, as well as clergy). Nevertheless, despite the difficulties, and the inevitable misgivings in advance of the broadcast, the eight-part series was enthusiastically received, and went on to win a BAFTA. Personalities like Malcolm Muggeridge and Donald Soper had also become well known for their appearances in religious discussion programmes and television 'panels'. The straight-to-camera religious talk was now well established in the form of the nightly epilogue, and a variety of different treatments were used in televising church worship. Despite these developments there remained concerns that television was fundamentally ill equipped to deal with religion; that it was an inherently more trivializing medium than radio; and that increasing the quantity of programmes should be a concern secondary to increasing their quality.

By the early 1960s, the full effect of competition was beginning to be felt. There was a concerted effort to make the devotional programme more accessible and entertaining. *Songs of Praise* (BBC, 1960–ongoing) featured popular hymns sung in churches, but without the accompanying rituals or sermons (interviews were included in later years). This music-based formula was pushed still further in the direction of mass audience appeal.

The closest that religious television in the UK has come to a light entertainment format was *Stars on Sunday* (Yorkshire Television, 1969–79). The show was conceived by Yorkshire Television's Head of Children's Programmes, Jess Yates, noted for the success of his *Junior Showtime* (Yorkshire Television, 1969–74). Yates saw the Sunday evening 'closed period' as a perfect opportunity to find a populist show that 'over 65s could call their own' by harnessing it to popular religious sentiment:

> Religion comes into it because we felt that the period devoted to religious-type programmes was the only really suitable time for a series of this kind. In any case, the majority of the people for whom we were catering sought warmth, comfort and peace from religion.[26]

25. A major Italian co-production of the same name was aired on ITV some 21 years later: F. Zefferelli's *Jesus of Nazareth* (ITV, 1977).

26. *Stars on Sunday*, programme from the Futurist Theatre, Scarborough, 1972, 3.

The new show was launched as a 13-part series in Autumn 1969. Yorkshire television's design department provided an ornate country house set (30ft high pillars, ornamental lake, waterfalls and ever-blooming rose garden) in which celebrities appeared singing popular sacred songs and hymns, or reading passages from the Bible. In addition to these well-known 'stars', Yates also used the programme as a showcase for up-and-coming talent (similar to the approach he had taken with *Junior Showtime*). The show had a degree of glitziness previously unknown to religious broadcasting in the UK, which attracted large audiences and repelled critics in equal measure. Reviewing for *The Sunday Observer*, Clive James described one episode of the show as:

> ... self-serving sentimental goo, a substance which spreads like a steaming fen in the diabolical *Stars on Sunday*. Jess Yates was on particularly winning form last week, telling us to ring somebody up – anybody – and thank them, not omitting a quick call to God to thank him too ... T.S. Elliot once pointed out, unarguably, that the *New English Bible* had been compiled by people who didn't even know they were atheists. The same applies in full measure to *Stars on Sunday*, in which all the faith is blasphemy and every piety is an insult.[27]

Despite the hostility, within its first year *Stars on Sunday* attracted over 250,000 letters of gratitude and requests for prayers, hymns and Bible readings. Within two years it was attracting a regular viewing audience of 15 million, sometimes growing to 17 million, making it the first religious programme to enter the viewing charts.[28]

The tension between adopting a populist approach to reaching a mass audience on the one hand, and producing what would be acceptable religious content on the other – a conflict between medium and message – soon became a significant problem. The show was demonstrably popular, yet the ITA was reprimanding Yorkshire Television for failing to provide authentic religious content within the closed period. Yates turned to the Evangelical cleric, Brandon Jackson (an ITV Advisor),[29] for scripts that would provide the programme with the religious authenticity being demanded. Jackson took the offer as an evangelistic opportunity, and set about attempting to use the format to blend what he saw as the value of folk religion and popular sentimentality on the one hand, with orthodox

27. Clive James, 'O Lord, Preserve Us', *The Sunday Observer*, 19 May 1974.
28. Figures cited in the Scarborough theatre programme.
29. ITV Advisor, Jackson, was vicar of St. Peter's, Shipley, and later became Dean of Lincoln Cathedral, where he was caught up in other controversies.

theological and biblical reflection on the other. Throughout, Jackson fiercely defended the programme against its critics within the Church of England, convinced that, through its broad appeal, it could achieve a great deal for religion:

> It appealed to those people whom the church fails to touch. It was doing something that the churches were not able to do, not because the churches don't try, but because the church has still not come to terms with modern methods of communication […]. At this time it was doing what I think was an awful lot of good and making the churches, on the whole, very very cross.

Nevertheless, Jackson felt himself to be in a continual state of tension between message and medium:

> It was a battle that I never really won. I wanted to make it an authentic Christian religious progamme, but the image or picture is stronger than the spoken word. The image can very often negate the spoken word, and the lavish 'country house'-style and the gorgeous dresses of these girls (often very low cut and looking very sensuous) didn't always comply with the sort of message that one was trying to put across.[30]

The fashioning of Yates into what James had unkindly dubbed 'the Deity's private secretary'[31] was to trigger the demise of Yates's career. Jackson's words, as spoken by Yates, proved to be a toxic mix when revelations about the presenter's private life surfaced in July 1974. Appetite for highly populist formats for religious programmes waned, and it was to the documentary that attention then turned.

The Rise of the Documentary

In the same year as Montagnon's epic series *The Long Search* (BBC, 1977), the BBC also broadcast, *Who was Jesus?* (BBC, 1977), presented by the Cambridge philosopher, Don Cupitt (at the time attracting widespread controversy for his contribution to the symposium *The Myth of God Incarnate*); and a major series called *BC: The Archaeology of Bible Lands* (BBC, 1977), in which presenter Magnus Magnusson travelled through Palestine and Syria examining the Bible through archaeology, from pre-history to the fall of Jerusalem in 70 CE (courting controversy

---

30. Very Rev. Brandon Jackson, Provost of Bradford; interview with the author, 25 October 1985.
31. James, 'O Lord'.

by what many considered to be a selective and partial account). On ITV, Bamber Gascoigne's *The Christians* (Granada Television, 1977) was a similarly styled thirteen-part series on the history of Christianity. It was also the year in which the BBC launched their new religious documentary series *Everyman* (BBC, 1977–2005). These were all programmes *about* religion, as distinct from *religious* programmes in the sense that would have been understood by an earlier generation of programme-makers.

This emergence of the religious-themed documentary must be seen in relation to a new kind of programme-maker that was emerging in television at this time. Wherever there is industrialization or the kind of expansion that broadcasting had undergone since 1954, division of labour and new types of specialism emerge. Occupations that grow out of such specialism are defined and justified in terms of 'an ordered distribution of work which carries with it some moral responsibilities, in return for which [workers] acquire moral legitimation for the part they play in the social drama of work'.[32] In the early days of television, programme-makers had inevitably been drawn from elsewhere, often for their specialized knowledge of a particular discipline (religious broadcasting departments being headed by clerics, for example). During the sixties, however, a new generation of programme-makers began to emerge whose specialized area of knowledge was of the medium itself. Colin Morris describes them as the Young Turks: a cultural elite, mainly from the middle-classes and moulded by public school and Oxbridge:

> Having been trained to use film or video, operate in studios or outside broadcast units, many Young Turks can move effortlessly from science to music and arts, from current affairs to sport. Some inevitably stay put in one department and in this sense specialise, but more give a fair impression of being modern Renaissance men and women – immensely versatile in their interests and knowledge.[33]

In his study of the BBC, Tom Burns discusses how widely the term 'professional' was being used during the time of his first study in 1963, and how its use increased over the following decade:

> There were times when it seemed that the word was being credited among programme staff with an almost talismanic quality, representing some absolute principle by which to judge people and achievement. Ten years

---

32. T. Burns, *The BBC: Public Institution and Private World* (London: Macmillan, 1977), 131.

33. Colin Morris, *God-in-a-Box: Christian Strategy in the Television* (London: Hodder & Stoughton, 1984), 51.

later the word seemed to occur even more frequently, to have acquired a
wider and more potent range of meanings and connotations, and to be used
throughout all reaches of the Corporation. Among senior management in
charge of television and radio it had assumed the character of some ultimate
rationale …[34]

Burns found that this 'cult of professionalism' had slowly superseded
the notion of public service as the principal rationale for evaluating
programmes:

> … the transition of broadcasting from an occupation dominated by the ethos
> of public service, in which the central concern is with quality in terms of
> the public good, and of public betterment, to one dominated by the ethos of
> professionalism, in which the central concern is with quality of performance
> in terms of standards of appraisal by fellow professionals; in brief, a shift
> from treating broadcasting as a means to treating broadcasting as an end.[35]

This change would inevitably have repercussions for religious broadcasting. Whereas in the past, programme-makers were presumed to
possess an understanding of religion and an empathy with religious
practice, this new professionalism was more commonly characterized by
scepticism about religion, and distance from religious practice.

The first significant effect of these young professionals upon religious
programmes was felt in 1975 with the appointment of Peter Armstrong
to replace the Revd. J. G. Day as Head of Religious Programmes at BBC
Television. Armstrong was young and he was not a cleric. He disliked
what he perceived as being a 'closed period mentality' within religious
broadcasting at the time: 'It felt like a piece of propaganda by the Christian
lobby; something like a party political broadcast … In other words, the
Church would always win the argument.'[36] His aim was to develop a
strand of programming that would both physically move out of the traditional 'closed period', and would look at religious issues in the same way
as *Horizon* (BBC, from 1964) would cover science and philosophy, or
Panorama (BBC, from 1953) would examine current affairs:

> We wanted to try and find a programme that would quite consciously work
> from the normal assumptions, and the best assumptions that we thought to
> take were the Current Affairs ones … And we'd say to the viewer, 'we're
> going into this question in a completely open-minded way'. It may be that

34. Burns, *The BBC*, 123.
35. Ibid., 125.
36. Peter Armstrong; interview with the author, 11 July 1985.

it would come out as an attack on the Church, or support for the Church, or it may be on a secular issue which the Church doesn't think is important and ordinary people do ... We tried to create a format that would be clearly honest reporting for the general audience.

This move made room within the department for more Young Turks:

We had young television professionals, not clerics. On the whole the producers of the 1950s and '60s were retrained clergy, whereas I preferred to take young television professionals who were interested in religion and who would learn more about that – if they didn't know it – rather than trying to learn television technique.

Recalling his time as a young researcher in the religious programmes department in the late 1970s, Mark Thompson (later to become Director-General of the BBC) recalled that 'most editions of *Everyman* were only "religious" in the broadest possible sense': 'Even among religious programme-makers ... there was a real anxiety about whether religion as a thing in itself was a topic of any real interest. And outside the specialist departments, religion was marginal at best'.[37] Thompson suggests that the prevailing background assumptions ('so widespread – both within and beyond the media – as to be normative') were:

... that familiar post-Enlightenment claim that the rationalist arguments against belief in God are so persuasive that they spell the inevitable long-term decline of organised religion. Progress brings education and knowledge, and education and knowledge inexorably undermine belief.

Everyman was launched in the schedules on Sunday at the later time of 10.30 pm. The risky decision to break out of what had become 'the God slot' prompted much debate within CRAC as to the wisdom of such a move. For the first five years after restrictions on broadcasting hours had been officially lifted (in 1972), the seventy-minute period of back-to-back broadcasting with ITV on a Sunday evening had remained in place by mutual agreement. Placing a religious programme outside of this period might be an indication of BBC confidence in *Everyman*, but the consequent reduction of the closed period could end up being more broadly detrimental in the longer term. *The Economist* predicted:

37. Mark Thompson, 'Faith and the Media', Speech given at Cardinal Cormac Murphy O'Connor Lecture 2008 series; Faith and Life in Britain Today, Westminster, London. Thursday 10 April 2008, http://www.bbc.co.uk/pressoffice/speeches/stories/thompson_faith.shtml.

... there may be some grumbling from the ranks of the more conservative churchmen – and laymen – who may see the halving of the God slot as the thin end of the wedge and the beginning of the end of religion on the air – despite the BBC's assurances.[38]

Robert Runcie, then Bishop of St. Albans and chair of CRAC, however, enthusiastically supported Armstrong's decision. It was Runcie's conviction that religious broadcasting generally should be encouraged to 'stand on its own feet' and compete for viewing time. As a result the decision was taken to reduce the agreed period of back-to-back broadcasting with ITV to thirty-five minutes, and allow the remaining time to float between 4.00 pm and 10.45 pm. For the time being, ITV would continue to occupy the full 70 minutes with religious programmes. *The Daily Telegraph* asserted that 'the claustrophobia of the old closed period has at last gone for good',[39] but *The Guardian* suggested that CRAC may have been 'bought off' by 'BBC progressives'.[40] It was a debate that was to blow up again six years later.

Significantly, the first *Everyman* programme, *Inspiration Incorporated* (10 April 1977), was a cautionary tale of US-style unregulated religious broadcasting: a sceptical appraisal of the work of controversial 'televangelist' Bob Schuyler, noted for his weekly *Hour of Power* broadcast from his Crystal Cathedral in Orange Grove, California. *Everyman* was questioning, interrogative and explicitly not the mouthpiece of religious orthodoxy. The second programme, *The Lord's My Shepherd and He Knows I'm Gay* (17 April 1977) profiled the recently founded (and at the time, controversial) Gay Christian Movement. Programmes were committed only to the 'normal assumptions of television', and presented by 'religious sceptic' Peter France, in the style of other mainstream documentary strands, indistinguishable but for a focus on religious or moral themes.

Everyman became the longest-running religious documentary series ever produced for UK television, and signified a major shift in approach that was reflected in many shorter-lived series, including Joan Bakewell's *Heart of the Matter* (BBC, 1987–2000), and *Credo* (London Weekend Television, 1978–1986). Reverend John Lang, the BBC's overall Head of Religious Broadcasting, described the changes in terms of 'strong plants'

38. 'On Its own Feet', *The Economist* 258, 13 March 1976, 29.
39. Peter Knight, 'Giving More Scope to Religion', *Daily Telegraph*, 29 August 1977, 5.
40. Baden Hickman, 'God Slot for the Chop', *The Guardian*, 1 March 1976, 17.

that at last could be 'put out into the garden',[41] exemplifying a prevailing optimism that religion was 'coming out of the ghetto'.

Changing Objectives and the Demise of the 'God Slot'

By the publication of a further Government-commissioned Report on the Future of Broadcasting (The Annan Report) in 1977, the aims of religious broadcasting were felt to be in need of 'revision and reinterpretation'. Annan's report devoted a total of nine pages (Chapter 20), to the subject of religion, beginning with the observation that whilst church attendance had declined, there remained a considerable interest in religion, and people were still asking questions about eternity. There had been a proportional decrease in the amount of time devoted to religion and a significant reduction in the time devoted to religion within the traditional 'closed period'. However, the Report observed that 'the best sermons are not necessarily the longest' and no recommendation was made that the time devoted to religion should be increased. The concern of the Committee, it said, was over the quality of those programmes that were produced.

An important aspect of this section of the Report is its discussion of the submission it had received from CRAC, in which the advisory body had reflected on its own position, and offered a revised set of guidelines for the aims of religious broadcasting. For the Pilkington Report fifteen years earlier, CRAC had defined religious broadcasting as having three objectives:

> The first was to reflect the worship, thought and action of those churches which represent the mainstream of the Christian tradition in this country. The second was to stress what was most relevant in the Christian faith for the modern world. The third was to try to reach those outside the churches or only loosely attached to them.[42]

The 'revision and reinterpretation' of these objectives became:

(i) To seek to reflect the worship, thought and action of the principal religious traditions represented in Britain, recognizing that those traditions are mainly, though not exclusively, Christian.

41. *Daily Telegraph*, 29 August 1977, 5.
42. *Report of the Committee on the Future of Broadcasting* (Annan Committee). Command Paper 6753 (London: HMSO, 1977).

(ii) To seek to present to viewers and listeners those beliefs, ideas, issues and experiences in the contemporary world which are evidently related to a religious interpretation or dimension of life.

(iii) To seek also to meet the religious interests, concerns and needs of those on the fringe of, or outside the organized life of the Churches.[43]

Although Annan comments that this was 'less of a change than at first sight appears', in reality it was an important shift on two counts: first, the term 'religion' had broadened from meaning exclusively Christian; second, while broadcasting was to cater for the 'needs' of people outside the churches, it was not to proselytize.

ITV's initial response to *Everyman*'s place in the schedule was to continue with its own religious programmes across the seventy-minute God slot as before. By 1983, however, *Credo*, the principle occupant of the 6.00 pm slot, was losing a considerable percentage of its viewing audience to the BBC's travel and light-entertainment programmes. Consequently, in August 1983, *Credo* was rescheduled to the Sunday 'graveyard' slot of 2.00 pm. This time, the move was strongly resisted. *The Times* leader column rebuked the Independent Broadcasting Authority (IBA)[44] for having thrown an important debate – that of the place of religion on television – 'into the brutal cockpit of the ratings battle': 'It is not easy to regard the Authority's decision as having enhanced the quality of British television, or as having properly protected the public interest, which they exist to do'.[45] The article went on to then admonish the BBC retrospectively for its 'aggressively competitive' scheduling against ITV: 'They are both slaves ... to the doctrine that ratings are the all-important test of public wants and needs, and that what really matters is to drive the figures upwards at all costs'.

The accusations and justifications ran on, as evidenced in a series of exchanges in *The Times*. Colin Morris, then Head of Religious Broadcasting for BBC Television, pointed out that in the case of *Everyman*, the move had been to reach a larger, not a smaller audience. John Whitney, Director General of the IBA, justified *Credo*'s move on the basis of it being impossible for a self-financing service to 'overlook the realities of its commercial situation'.[46] Angus Wright, Head of Religious

43. Annan Report, 319.
44. The responsibilities of the ITA were expanded to include commercial radio in the Sound Broadcasting Act of 1972, and the Authority was renamed accordingly.
45. *The Times*, 18 August 1983, 9.
46. *The Times*, 23 August 1983, 9.

Programmes for Television South, countered this by pointing to recent figures indicating huge increases in ITV revenue and audience figures, referring to the cheaper studio-based format that *Credo* had adopted as a 'progressive rundown in resources and production values of the principal occupants of the 6.00 pm Sunday slot' – just another symptom of ITV's 'bad scheduling'.[47] Paul Neuburg, the Editor of London Weekend Television's *Credo*, refuted this, blaming 'the demise of the back-to-back arrangement for religious programmes between ITV and BBC'.[48]

The end of the seventy-minute closed period and the ensuing debate both in 1977, and then again in 1983, highlighted a growing unease among many people that religion was being 'pushed out' of the schedule. Despite its earlier support of the BBC, the move of ITV's *Credo* to the early afternoon was strongly resisted by CRAC. Donald Reeve, a serving member of CRAC for nine years, reflected this tension:

> The Mafia of professional religious broadcasters and media bureaucrats have the idea firmly installed in memoranda and in their heads that religion is a minority interest like potholing. That is why the Independent Broadcasting Authority has decided to switch ITV's main religious programmes on Sunday from 6.00 pm to 2.00 pm. The Central Religious Advisory Committee is dismayed. The decision could mark the beginning of the end for religious programmes on television ...[49]

A view that was becoming increasingly discernible within the churches by the 1980s was that religious broadcasting was 'under attack' and CRAC could do little about it.

The most significant outcome of The Annan Report was the proposal it made for what was to become Channel 4. Although the Report's particular vision for the channel was not implemented in full, it nevertheless set in motion a plan for a fourth channel that was to be funded by advertising, have a public service remit and cater for minority groups and interests. It is important to note just what the prospect of a fourth Channel represented for many within the churches at this moment. As has already been suggested, by the late 1970s there was an escalating sense of lost ground. The privilege and protection that religious broadcasting had enjoyed up to and through the war years – initially unappreciated, and subsequently, largely taken for granted – could no longer be presumed. Commercial pressures, as illustrated by the demise of the God slot, and new notions of what constituted

47. *The Times*, 22 August 1983, 11.
48. *The Times*, 30 August 1983, 11.
49. 'The Big Why?', *The Universe*, 19 August 1983, 6.

'professionalism' (and 'impartiality') seemed to be evidence of a powerful secularizing process at work. Religious broadcasting was felt by many to be moribund. These factors, together with the widespread take-up of the VHS, and the possibilities that seemed to be on the horizon with the arrival of cable and satellite broadcasting, all suggested a very uncertain future. There was a consequent growing interest in (as well as widespread alarm about) religious groups accessing airtime more directly, and US-style religious programmes now seemed like a distinct possibility.[50] The idea of Channel 4 as a *publisher*-broadcaster, challenging the old duopoly by commissioning content from a broader pool of programme-makers, but with a public service remit to cater for minority groups, seemed to promise much. A number of independent religious groups set about organizing themselves to take programme proposals to the new channel, including the mainstream denominations who collectively initiated the British Churches Committee for Channel 4 (BCCC4).[51]

These great expectations for what the new channel might offer religious broadcasting, against the background of a growing sense of disaffection about the direction of travel of the religious output of both the BBC and ITV, go some way towards explaining the enormous disappointment that was to follow. Channel 4's first Commissioning Editor for Religion was John Ranelagh, a self-described 'enthusiastic agnostic'.[52] Ranelagh had no interest in CRAC and the existing advisory structure, believing that professional programme-makers would seek out advice appropriate to the needs of their projects. During his first year at the channel he rejected *all* of the programme ideas that had been submitted to him by the BCCC4 (as well as those from other independent religious groups), and instead, turned to one of the big beasts of ITV, London Weekend Television, for his first major commission. *Jesus: The Evidence* (London Weekend Television for Channel 4, 1984) was a highly tendentious Easter documentary series that set itself up as revealing an explosive debate (illustrated by an exploding image of Jesus) which, it claimed, had been 'simmering quietly for the last two centuries'.[53] The furore that surrounded the series (orchestrated principally by the evangelical magazine, *Buzz*) represents a high water

50. Manchester-based Good News Television, for example, approached US televangelist, Jim Bakker, and produced a UK pilot version of his talk show, *The PTL Club*, which was then offered to (but rejected by) Channel 4.

51. Rt. Rev. Stewart Cross, Bishop of Blackburn, a proposal for the 'British Churches Committee for Channel Four' (London: unpublished, 1982).

52. John Ranelagh; interview with author, April 1985.

53. Julian Norridge, 'Jesus: The Evidence', *What's New at LWT* 13, April 1984, 4–5.

mark in a rising sense of disentitlement on the part of the churches. It became emblematic of the cultural dissonance that by now was felt to exist between the religious and the broadcasting institutions.[54] It was Clifford Longley, the Religious Affairs Correspondent for *The Times*, who accurately noted that Channel 4 was 'not so much the last of the main public service channels to arrive, as the first swallow heralding the broadcasting pluralism of cable and satellite'.[55] This was a reality that few in the churches had properly understood.

Conclusion

This chapter has aimed to provide a context for the Bible documentary by setting its emergence within the broader frame of religious programme -making from its earliest days. To help make sense of subsequent trends discussed by others in this volume (including the approaches taken by programme-makers, the role of advisors and the attitude of the churches), it has been important to note several significant changes that occurred over the period discussed here. At its birth, religious broadcasting in the UK was privileged and protected to a degree that, even given the less secu-larised society of the time, was far from inevitable, and was ultimately unsustainable. The primary objective of religious broadcasting from the beginning was unashamedly evangelistic, and this was positioned as entirely compatible with the BBC's public service remit and educational agenda, based on the justification that, historically, British society was Christian. Accordingly, those involved in religious broadcasting were generally expected to have been theologically trained, and have an under-standing of, and empathy with, religious practice – indeed, many were clerics. However, from the war years onwards, this position began to alter. Key features of these changes included: a shifting idea of what the objec-tives of religious broadcasting ought to be; growing commercial pressure and the need to attract bigger audiences, particularly on television; and the rise of a new generation of programme-makers, who crucially, were neither theologically trained (rather, they were television *professionals*) nor did they have much affinity with, or understanding of, religious practice. A consequent shift away from older notions of what was meant by public service, and the way in which television professionalism came

54. For a full account, see Richard Wallis, 'Channel 4 and the Declining Influence of Organised Religion on UK Television: The Case of Jesus: The Evidence', *Historical Journal of Film Radio and TV* 16 (2016): 668–88.

55. Clifford Longley, 'Sceptics Discount Vital Evidence', *The Times*, 9 April 1984, 14.

to be defined, made orthodox and exegetical approaches to religious programmes seem anachronistic. Indeed, it came to be accepted that 'impartiality' ought to presume a religious *non*-commitment on the part of programme-makers (a view that would have been anathema to Reith). Throughout this period, television was trying, and struggling, to find sufficiently popular formats and styles that were thought to be commensurate with religious content, particularly when attempting to reach wider audiences (as illustrated by the problematic nature of *Stars on Sunday*). This tension between medium and message has continued to be a challenge for programme-makers, and this is illustrated by a tendency towards the tendentious in factual and documentary religious programmes (albeit a feature that is by no means unique to religious programmes). By the 1970s, the questioning, interrogating and sceptical approach to which the documentary genre lent itself seemed to be better suited to the new generation of programme-makers who were also progressively distancing themselves from traditional structures of advice (CRAC and the ITV advisors increasingly considered to be less than impartial, and outdated). Instead, they relied principally on the perennial skills of the television researcher: personal networks of contacts, publishers and individual academics and experts brought in only on a programme-by-programme basis. Collectively, these changes resulted in an escalating sense of disentitlement on the part of the Christian churches, which had been slow to welcome or appreciate their initial advantages, and were then slow to understand their altering circumstances, generally lacking the initiative, the coordination or the strategies to be able to engage with changing times.

There is one further observation that should be made as a concluding point. The twenty-first century has brought with it a realisation that the seemingly inexorable march of Western secularisation has faltered. Over a period that has been characterised by globalisation, migration and increasingly complex connections between nations and cultures, religion has resurfaced as a major social, political and cultural force. 'God is Back!'[56] and on the whole, has caught traditional media organisations by surprise. Media professionals, in general, have found themselves to be particularly ill-equipped to engage with a religious landscape that has so long been presumed to be on its way to irrelevance (illustrated by the failure of most media organisations to stem the persistent deprioritising of religious expertise, for example[57]).

56. The title of a book by Adrian Wooldridge and John Micklethwait, published in 2010.
57. This is a problem highlighted in the Open University's recent report *Religion, Security and Global Uncertainties* (2015).

A review undertaken by the BBC in 2017[58] resulted in the publication of an ambitious plan within the Corporation to address a growing anxiety about what Adam Dinham has described as the 'lamentable quality of conversation about religion just when we need it most'.[59] The BBC's review pledges to 'raise our game across all output', including: increased specialist expertise with the appointment of a new Religious Affairs Team and Religion Editor in News; new investment in 'landmark' programmes; more diversity; more cross-genre religious commissioning; a concerted attempt to reach a younger audience; and improved religious literacy training for its staff. At the time of writing, it is still too early to know whether or not this development has, indeed, 'reset' the BBC's approach to religious broadcasting. The review states that the Corporation will 'continue to develop Faith Films on TV – outstanding single documen-taries that explore issues of faith within all the major religions in the UK'.[60] That the Bible documentary has a role to play in providing such insight into religious ideas and practices, and helping audiences to make sense of them in public discourse, is self-evidently vital at a moment when religion is touching our lives in previously unimagined ways.

58. BBC (2017) *Religion & Ethics Review*. December 2017. Internal report, http://www.bbc.co.uk/corporate2/insidethebbc/howwework/reports/religion_and_ethics_2017.

59. Professor Adam Dinham in EHRC Dialogues for the Equality and Human Rights Commission (EHRC) and the Government Equalities Office, http://www.religiousliteracy.org/ehrc-dialogues.

60. BBC *Religion & Ethics Review* (2017), 14.

Chapter 2

THE BIBLE ACCORDING TO TV

Jean-Claude Bragard

Joe Zias, archaeologist and former Curator of Archaeology and Anthropology for the Israeli Institute of Antiquities, used his blog in a campaign to halt what he regarded as irresponsible TV programmes about the Bible. Talking about one particular fight in 2011 to get a deal cancelled, he urged his followers to remember that 'the public paid for our education and we owe them something in return'.[1] With this cry from the heart, Zias put his finger on a sea change in the way the Bible was shown on TV. In the 1980s and 1990s, TV shows about the Bible reflected the points of view of the academy. The BBC's *Who Was Jesus?*[2] was presented by an Oxford scholar – Don Cupitt – and it took a then fashionable humanist view of Jesus. *Jesus the Evidence*[3] on Channel 4 featured dozens of eminent New Testament scholars and told the story of a hundred years of study of the historical Jesus. It mirrored the mainstream highly minimalist views of the Rudolf Bultmann School. And Channel 4's *Testament*,[4] presented by Egyptologist John Romer, told the story of how interpretations of the Bible had evolved over the centuries.

These were hugely popular TV series, attaining good audience ratings. However, in the last decade, TV shows about the Bible began to reflect a very different constituency. What the Academy was now debating about the Bible was rarely getting a look in. Instead we watched shows that

1. Joe Zias, http://www.joezias.com, 23 August 2011.
2. First aired on BBC One, 14 April 1977.
3. First aired on Channel 4, 8 April 1984.
4. First aired Channel 4, 1988.

mirrored the agendas of programme-makers. At one end of the spectrum of this recent trend were shows that told the basic stories of the Bible – such as History Channel's *The Bible*.[5] Whilst such series did employ academic consultants, they did not in the main reflect discussions or trends in biblical scholarship. Their aim was to inform audiences increasingly ignorant of the Bible. At the other end of this spectrum were shows with little if any connection to issues explored by the Academy. Often they consisted of investigations by intrepid explorers, historical detectives and academics from non-biblical specialisms who went in search of secrets and mysteries in the Bible. It could be the quest for Noah's Ark, the Ark of the Covenant, the parting of the Red Sea, the romantic relationship between Jesus and Mary Magdalene, the tomb of Jesus or whether Jesus died in India. Their aim was to entertain audiences with sensational stories from the Bible. By and large it is these latter shows that Joe Zias was castigating.

Why has the Bible on TV changed so profoundly in the last thirty to forty years? Why, in an age when there are more channels than ever on television, is there not a *greater* diversity of views from the Academy on the box? That's the question – and paradox – of this chapter. To answer it I will survey TV shows made about the Bible over that period. In my thirty years making television programmes about Bible topics, I've often heard Christians or Bible scholars complain that television's coverage of the Bible is patchy at best. In fact, TV has been rather generous to the Bible. My estimate is that in the last four decades there have been at least 150 programmes about the Bible on English-speaking channels. That is five programmes a year, an average that other genres might well give their right arm for. It would be tedious to provide an exhaustive catalogue of the whole output, so my aim is limited to identifying the milestones, crossroads and trends that help explain how the Bible on TV has changed over the decades.

1970s: In the Beginning

Before the Bible on TV came the Bible on the Cinema. The sheer spectacle of the Bible stories was just what the silver screen craved, and Hollywood studios lost no time in ordering sword and sandals blockbusters. In the last hundred years studios in the US and Europe have made nearly two hundred films about the Bible, the first as early as 1906.[6]

---

5. History Channel, 2013.
6. http://en.wikipedia.org/wiki/List_of_films_based_on_the_Bible.

It took television a little longer to realize the Bible's potential. In 1974, film producer Lew Grade made *Moses the Lawgiver* for television,[7] quickly followed in 1977 by ITV's *Jesus of Nazareth*, a miniseries directed by Franco Zeffirelli, starring Robert Powell as Jesus.[8] With a reported audience of 28 million in the UK and 90 million in the US, *Jesus of Nazareth* reached audiences that even the final of the football world cup could only dream of. The story goes that the film was the fruit of an exchange with Pope Paul VI, when Lew Grade was received at the Vatican. The Pope congratulated Grade on the making of *Moses the Lawgiver* and suggested that his next film might be about the life of Jesus.[9]

Jesus of Nazareth is a neat example of the Bible on TV reflecting the point of view of faith – well almost. Robert Powell's portrayal of Jesus matched popular devotional images of Jesus in Western art – a view that TV would not challenge for at least another quarter of a century. Even so, *Jesus of Nazareth* was not as faithful to the Bible as it appeared. For dramatic reasons, the screenwriter merged or created scenes that were not in the New Testament. Unwittingly, some amounted to significant revisions of convention, as in the portrayal of Judas Iscariot, not as the betrayer of Jesus (Jn 12:6 and Lk. 22:5), but as a well-intentioned man. It would be years before TV viewers would hear *scholars* make the same claim.[10]

Nonetheless, for the first time, and not for the last, TV executives were taken by surprise – they woke up the day after transmission to find that a series about Jesus had been a massive ratings hit. 21 million viewers[11] – just over 37% of Britain's population – had sat down to watch the miniseries, almost certainly because its format brought to a Christian audience the dramatic intensity of Jesus's mission, an audience that was not only familiar with, but that also believed in the basic story. The producers knew which buttons to press – and also which ones to leave well alone. For whilst Hollywood was quite happy to bring to life the spectacular nature miracles of the Bible, TV was rather timid, preferring to stick to the miracles where Jesus healed the sick or cast out demons. So *Jesus of Nazareth* pointedly left out the water into wine at the wedding

7. First aired ITV, March 1976.

8. First aired ITV, 3 April 1977.

9. Ben Falk and Quentin Falk, *Television's Strangest Moments: Extraordinary but True Tales from the History of Television* (Stuttgart: Franz Steiner, 2005), 131–2.

10. William Klassen in *Son of God*, BBC One, 1 April 2001; also *Gospel of Judas*, National Geographic Channel, 9 April 2006.

11. Sergio Angelini, 'Jesus of Nazareth (1977)', *BFI Screenonline*, http://www.screenonline.org.uk/tv/id/1137783/.

of Cana, the stilling of the storm and the Transfiguration. Maybe the producers felt that the extravagant supernaturalism of these miracles would sit uneasily with a modern audience, even a Christian one. After all, society in the 1970s was becoming more secular, and maybe the producers were anxious not to push their luck. The strategy clearly worked. But even as ITV was basking in the warm glow of rave reviews, over at the BBC a chill wind was blowing. It came from a sea change that would transform the way the Bible was portrayed on the box for decades to come.

1980s: Minimalism

The study of the historical Jesus began in earnest in the nineteenth century. Although most New Testament scholars were Christians, by the early twentieth century many of them were thoroughly sceptical of the orthodox view of Jesus proclaimed by the Bible and the Churches. However, it was a long time before the public got to hear about any of it. In 1977 the BBC aired *Who Was Jesus?* – a two-hour investigation into the historical Jesus by Don Cupitt, Dean of Emmanuel College, Cambridge, and one of the original media dons.[12] Although Cupitt was a Christian – and a priest – his series questioned traditional Christian views about the divinity of Jesus. It was potentially revolutionary stuff, and yet it barely caused a ripple of protest amongst the faithful. No doubt this was partly because it was so reasonably presented. But perhaps more influential was the fact that the series was framed as Cupitt's very personal perspective on Jesus, so viewers could either take it or leave it.

Seven years later, in 1984, Channel 4 returned to the same territory with its series *Jesus the Evidence*.[13] This time the gloves were off. The self-styled iconoclastic series bluntly and unapologetically reflected what the Academy thought about Jesus, regardless of the discomfort caused to viewers.

Jesus the Evidence was a three-part series made by London Weekend Television[14] for the new kid on the block, Channel 4. Although the channel's brief was to be countercultural, it did not anticipate the amount of noise, controversy, lobbying, acres of print and Christian outrage the series generated.[15] There was a call to advertisers to boycott

12. BBC 2, 4 April 1977.
13. Channel 4, 8 April 1984.
14. At the time LWT owned the ITV franchise for the London region from Friday to Sunday evenings.
15. 'Editorial', *Church Times*, 6 April 1984; 'Jesus on Trial', *The Universe*, 6 April 1984; 'Outrage at TV Series', *Methodist Recorder*, 12 April 1984.

the series from the editor of the *Christian Herald*,[16] and an appeal by Simon Coombs, the then Conservative MP for Swindon, to Channel 4's Controller Paul Bonner to postpone the series.[17] The production team was summoned to appear on Channel 4's *Right to Reply* programme, *Private Eye* mocked the series in its inimitable way,[18] whilst the *Catholic Herald* ran a front page article in which Father Nicholas Murphy fulminated against the series as 'a load of drivel' and even offered the suggestion that 'The researcher ought to be shot'.[19] As Geza Vermes was to write years later, Father Murphy's comment was hardly a very Christian proposition.[20] In any event, they were headlines today's programme-makers can only dream of. So what was all the fuss about?

The idea behind the series was the brainchild of John Birt, then the Controller of programmes at LWT. He had read a review of a recently published book, *The Gnostic Gospels* by Elaine Pagels. The book argued that there were other gospels about Jesus proclaiming a different perspective to the one taught in the Bible and by the Churches. John Birt thought this would be just up Channel 4's street.

Thirty years ago, the steers of a TV Controller were far more advisory than they are today. Instead of making a programme exclusively about the Gnostic Gospels, the production team decided to get up to speed on the state of academic opinion about the historical Jesus. What they discovered surprised them. Many New Testament scholars seemed to be saying that there was far less that could be known with certainty about Jesus than either the Bible or the Churches pretended. The year was 1983, and the field of New Testament Studies was dominated by the legacy of the Bultmann school, which in essence maintained that – other than the existence of Jesus, his death by crucifixion and his Kingdom of God sayings – very little could be known for certain about Jesus.

The kind of programme eventually made proved to be a watershed in shows about the Bible on TV. Instead of reflecting one presenter-scholar's perspective, it featured more than a dozen Biblical scholars. And instead of presenting the fashionable minimalist views of the Academy as given, it put them in context, telling the history of the quest for the historical

16. Colin Reeves, 'A Call to Boycott Distasteful TV', *Campaign*, 18 May 1984.

17. 'Vain Bid to Postpone TV Series', *Church Times*, 13 April 1984.

18. *Private Eye*, 18 April 1984.

19. *Catholic Herald*, 6 April 1984.

20. Geza Vermes, 'A Television Documentary on Christ and the British Press: Channel 4's *Jesus the Evidence*', in *Searching for the Real Jesus* (London: SCM, 2009), 63–70, here 65.

Jesus. Accordingly, Episode 1 began with Luther, and continued with the views of Friedrich Strauss, William Wrede, Karl Ludwig Schmidt, Albert Schweitzer and Rudolph Bultmann. It covered form criticism, redaction criticism and historical criticism. The approach of the programme was to peel away at the layers of mythologizing that had built up around the historical Jesus. It featured leading scholars from Bultmann's University of Marburg such as W. G. Kummel. By the time the episode reached the theories of Bultmann, the episode gave TV audiences the impression that Christian Biblical scholars had destroyed the traditional image of Jesus.

This was all controversial enough for a TV programme about Jesus. But *Jesus the Evidence* went even further. It ended the first episode with the theory of a professor of German at London University called George Wells. Unlike the majority of New Testament scholars, Wells was neither Christian nor Jewish, nor indeed even a Biblical scholar. But he had entered the fray with several scholarly books arguing that Jesus had not existed.[21] Whilst experts were invited to criticize George Wells, the first programme nevertheless ended with a bleak challenge: was there anything about the historical Jesus of tradition that could be ever recovered?

The answer was provided in episode two with the views of three academics whom the production team believed reflected a spectrum of contemporary perspectives. On the more traditional wing of this spectrum was the theory of Anthony Harvey, Canon of Westminster Abbey, who argued that there was convincing evidence that Jesus was seen in his time as the Messiah.[22] In the centre of the spectrum was Geza Vermes, Professor of Jewish Studies at Oxford, who had argued in his seminal work *Jesus the Jew* that the most one could say with confidence about Jesus was that he was a Galilean Jew who went around the countryside preaching, casting out of demons and healing – one in a long line of itinerant Jewish holy men who performed similar roles in Palestine at that time.[23] And at the other extreme was the maverick theory of Morton Smith, Professor of Religion at Columbia University, who argued that Jesus should best be seen as a 'magician' in the style of holy men and shamans from other religions.[24]

21. G. A. Wells, *The Jesus of the Early Christians* (London: Pemberton, 1971); *Did Jesus Exist?* (London: Prometheus, 1975); *The Historical Evidence for Jesus* (Buffalo: Prometheus, 1982).

22. Anthony Harvey, *Jesus and the Constraints of History*, Bampton Lectures 1980 (Philadelphia: Westminster, 1982).

23. Geza Vermes, *Jesus the Jew* (London: Collins, 1973).

24. Morton Smith, *Jesus the Magician* (New York: Harper & Row, 1978).

The third episode concentrated on what happened after the death of Jesus. Its main witness was the professor of New Testament studies at Harvard University, Helmut Koester, a student of Bultmann. Koester argued that the resurrection stories were the product of mythologizing by later Christians. Only then did the programme begin to address the subject which had originally inspired the series, the Gnostic Gospels. With contributors such as the eminent Dutch expert Gilles Quispel, the programme maintained that early Christianity developed not along one single strand as tradition maintained, but along several strands, including Pauline Christianity, Jewish Christianity and Gnostic Christianity.

Jesus the Evidence was undoubtedly the most minimalist series ever made about the historical Jesus. To make sure the revelations were accessible to a wide audience the series deployed shock cinematic techniques, such as dramatized reconstructions of the Council of Nicea and slow-motion exploding statues of Jesus. LWT was under no illusion that *Jesus the Evidence* would be controversial. It had enlisted religious advisors from the Church of England, the Catholic Church, the Methodist Church as well as eminent New Testament scholars to approve the scripts for accuracy. But their only significant criticism was to tone down the sensationalist style of commentary, so LWT and Channel 4 felt they had a winner in their hands. What could possibly go wrong? Once again, broadcasters failed to anticipate the impact the Bible on TV can have.

A few weeks before transmission a script of the series was obtained by Steve Goddard, editor of *Buzz* magazine, at the time an independent publication for Evangelical Christians. Goddard had been approached at Greenbelt in 1983 by a member of the crew filming *Jesus the Evidence* who was feeling uneasy about the content of the TV series.[25] Goddard was shown the first script and, clearly scenting a story, requested an interview with LWT's production team for his magazine. LWT could see the potential for extra publicity and allowed Goddard to see the first two episodes, which Goddard recorded on a pocket dictaphone, had transcribed and then sent round for comment to forty theologians and Church leaders. After consultation with Clive Calver, Director of the Evangelical Alliance, a full campaign was mounted demanding more balance to the content.[26] In particular, LWT was accused of ignoring the evidence from conservative

25. Steve Goddard, Personal Communication.

26. Richard Wallis, 'Channel 4 and the Declining Influence of Organised Religion on UK Television: The Case of *Jesus: The Evidence*', *Historical Journal of Film Radio and TV* 36 (2016): 668–88.

scholars.[27] The production office felt the brunt of the campaign, receiving two thousand postcards from Evangelical Christians, some quoting lines from the Bible such as 'The wages of sin is death' and 'Repent'. On the day of transmission on Easter Sunday 1984, ITN news reported on the controversy aroused by *Jesus the Evidence*, thereby generating yet further publicity for the series due to begin immediately after the news.

The first episode achieved an audience rating of 1.85 million viewers[28] – a success for a young broadcaster like Channel 4, airing at 10 pm, in a genre like religion. TV reviewers had a field day satirizing the sensationalist approach of the series. Bernard Levin of *The Times* bemoaned its 'unbelievable awfulness',[29] whilst Auberon Waugh damned it as 'sweetly babyish'.[30] But as the series director pointed out in a letter to *The Times*, he made 'no apology for using every available device, clichéd or otherwise ... to bring out into the open this division between clerical and lay beliefs'.[31] *Jesus the Evidence* proved the old adage – producers are damned with ridicule if they do sensationalize the subject, and damned with obscurity if they don't. As we shall see, time and again, TV shows about the Bible that aspired to make a big impact would be impaled on the horns of this dilemma.

The early reaction to the series might have given the impression that the series had spectacularly missed the mark. But as the dust settled, respected voices did raise their heads above the parapet and gave the series a more measured assessment. *The Sunday Times'* religious correspondent called it 'a decent popular statement of the present state of New Statement scholarship',[32] whilst *The Listener* remarked that 'It was hard to see how anyone but the most fanatical literalist could have been offended by a scrupulously phrased, lucid and quite fascinating script, in which 100 years of biblical scholarship was summarized, leaving one hungry for more'.[33] In the *Financial Times*, its TV reviewer described the hostility towards *Jesus the Evidence* as reeking of the same intolerance as the Inquisition.[34] As Geza Vermes observed many years later, in the

---

27. Steve Goddard, 'Jesus – The Evidence', *Buzz*, April 1984.

28. 'TV Top Ten', *Broadcast*, 13 April 1984.

29. Bernard Levin, 'No, Jesus Will Survive even Jesting Jeremy', *The Times*, 13 April 1984.

30. Auberon Waugh, 'Summa Pilgerica', *The Spectator*, 14 April 1984, 6.

31. David W. Rolfe, Letters to *The Times*, 26 April 1984.

32. John Whale, *The Sunday Times*, 8 April 2014.

33. *The Listener*, 12 April 1984

34. Chris Dunkley, 'Some Fresh Air at Last on Channel Four', *Financial Times*, 25 April 1984.

aftermath of all the furore the religious press came to accept that they had overreacted to the series. Even the *Catholic Herald* struck a more serious tone.[35]

It is rare for the reverberations of a TV series to last long. But *Jesus the Evidence* left its mark in ways it had not anticipated. A week after the end of the series, LWT's religious weekly magazine series *Credo* interviewed the Bishop of Durham, David Jenkins, a biblical scholar in his own right.[36] *Credo* put to him some of the questions raised by *Jesus the Evidence*. Did *he* as a leading Christian figure in the Church believe in the miracles, in the Virgin Birth and in the Resurrection? The Bishop of Durham must have felt on safe ground because he answered candidly but in scholarly language that he did not believe in the literal truth of the supernatural stories in the gospels.

> The virgin birth, I'm pretty clear, is a story told after the event in order to express and symbolize a faith that this Jesus was a unique event from God, you see, so it's different from the other miracles in my view and I mean, if I might be allowed to say so, I wouldn't put it past God to arrange a virgin birth if he wanted but I very much doubt if he would, because it seems contrary to the way in which he deals with persons and brings his wonders out of natural personal relationships.[37]

Like London Weekend Television and Channel 4, David Jenkins had underestimated the impact of what he was saying. He later reflected in an interview with the Observer:

> I was on the programme, so I understood, because I was known to be a theologian familiar with, and sympathetic to, modern critical ways of thinking who, none the less, combined this with a commitment to orthodox Christian faith, built round a traditional understanding of God as the Holy Trinity and Jesus Christ as the man who was God. As the critical position I was stating has been in wide circulation for something up to one hundred years and reflects questions which have been discussed for over two hundred years, and as the form of my Christian faith is, probably, unusually traditional and orthodox among scholars and intellectuals, it never occurred to me that anyone would be interested in my answer, let alone excited by it.[38]

35. Vermes, 'A Television Documentary', 65.
36. *Credo*, LWT, 29 April 1984.
37. David Jenkins, *Credo*, LWT, 29 April 1984.
38. Ted Harrison, *The Durham Phenomenon: What Does Today's Most Controversial Bishop Really Believe?* (London: Darton, Longman & Todd, 1985), 11.

How wrong he was. *Credo* was not a programme watched by large audiences and the explosive content of the interview could easily have been lost in the Bishop's careful vocabulary. But the Bishop's academic words were helpfully translated into a press release that Fleet Street could digest. The following day the front pages of the papers announced that a leading Church of England Bishop did not believe in the Virgin Birth or the Resurrection stories.[39] The story ran for days.

For all the justifiable criticisms of *Jesus the Evidence*, the series was a milestone in religious broadcasting. It revealed a disconnect between what the public on the one hand believed about Jesus and what scholarship and even some in the Church on the other hand believed about Jesus. Today we might be tempted to say that *Jesus the Evidence* was ahead of public opinion. The irony of course is that it was actually behind academic opinion in New Testament studies. For, as we shall see, conservative scholars had already begun laying the groundwork for a major reappraisal of the quest for the historical Jesus. And *Jesus the Evidence*, it appears, played a role in that too. Professor James Dunn, a New Testament scholar from Durham University, said he was inspired by *Jesus the Evidence* to find better ways of defending the Jesus of tradition.[40] The result was his seminal book *The Oral Gospel Tradition* that explored the role of oral tradition in passing down accurate information about the historical Jesus.

Jesus the Evidence was – in the television industry jargon – a 'category killer'. No broadcaster commissioned any major TV programmes about Jesus for at least another decade. Channel 4 did air in 1987 a four-part series about the *Gnostics* made by Border TV that examined gnostic beliefs in detail,[41] a bold and brave attempt to flesh out some of the interest generated by Elaine Pagels's book. But the broadcaster's more notable contribution to the Bible on TV was a series about the Old Testament. If the New Testament was ripe for debunking, surely the grand old stories of Noah, Moses and Joshua were sitting ducks? Channel 4 commissioned Antelope Films to make a seven-part series about the Old Testament.[42] Fronted by Egyptologist John Romer, it aired in 1988, but unlike the heady sensationalism of *Jesus the Evidence*, *Testament* was an example of a well-crafted and measured approach to the Bible on TV. Instead of trying to shock its audience, it quietly acknowledged the lack

39. Terry Chinery, 'The Doubting Bishop', *Daily Mail*, 30 April 1984.

40. James D. G. Dunn, *The Oral Gospel Tradition* (Grand Rapids: Eerdmans, 2013).

41. Mark Goodacre, ntweblog.blogspot.co.uk, 26 October 2009.

42. *Testament*, Channel 4, 1988.

of archaeological evidence for most of the stories in the Old Testament, but it used what circumstantial evidence existed and the symbolism of the stories to skilfully weave a history of both Israel and the roots of Western civilization.

1990s: Creativity

Testament brought one phase of the Bible on TV to a close. TV genres go through fashions, and unless there is something new to say, or at least a new way of saying the old, TV will happily let go of a subject, even for a decade. But something must have happened in the intervening period because in 1996 the Bible exploded again on TV. The first to hit the screens was a single film made by CTVC in collaboration with BBC's Religion department for its ethics strand *Heart of the Matter.* It is little remembered now, but at the time it exploded like a small hand grenade on Easter Sunday.[43] With the benefit of hindsight, in TV terms the film wasn't a grenade but a ticking time bomb.

Heart of the Matter ran an Easter special called 'The Body in Question', in which theologians Gerd Lüdemann, Michael Goulder and Tom Wright discussed the meaning of the resurrection of Jesus. The programme made the front page of the *Sunday Times* on the morning of the broadcast with the headline 'The Tomb that Dare Not Speak Its Name'.[44] The controversy was sparked off by the production team's ingenious idea to base the discussion on the hypothetical discovery of the bones of Jesus. 'What would Christian theology make of the resurrection if the bones of Jesus were actually found?' In order to make the show more interesting, the team travelled to Israel to film some actual bones from first-century ossuaries in the basement of the Department of Antiquities in Jerusalem. To add to the intrigue, the team asked the Keeper of the Ossuaries Directory if they could film an ossuary with the name of Jesus on it. The Keeper replied that there are 71 such ossuaries – it was a common name at the time. So to narrow it down further they inquired if there was an inscription for 'Jesus son of Joseph'? Again, there were many, Joseph was the most common name after Simon. Pressing their luck the team wondered if there was an ossuary with the name of Mary? Of course, Mary – or Miriam – was the most common female name at the time. And so the team was eventually taken to a warehouse in Rommema where they were directed to a shelf containing a cache of ossuaries found in 1980 in the East Talpiot district of Jerusalem. They filmed an ossuary

---

43. *Heart of the Matter*, BBC 1, 31 March 1996
44. 'The Tomb that Dare Not Speak Its Name', *Sunday Times*, 31 March 1996.

with the names Jesus son of Joseph and Mary inscribed, as well as other ossuaries with familiar names from the gospels, such as Judas, Martha and Joses.[45]

There was a suggestion that the *Sunday Times* article was an April Fool's joke when in fact it was publicity for the broadcast. The programme-makers, the experts on the panel and all manner of authorities dismissed the discovery as a coincidence – the names were very common and the ossuary could have belonged to any man called Jesus. The *Sunday Times*, however, saw it differently and could not resist asking whether in fact the body of Jesus had been found? The story came and went but it would undergo its own special resurrection ten years later when it was picked up again by the Discovery Channel with a TV special on 'the discovery of the tomb of Jesus'.[46] That is when the time bomb exploded, but more on that later.

Elsewhere BBC TV producers were busy plotting an imaginative major new series on Jesus. The challenge at the time was how to revisit the subject without rehearsing the minimalist conclusions of the Bultmann School. One solution was *Lives of Jesus*, a four-part series presented by the BBC's India correspondent Mark Tully, and made by the BBC's Religion Department. It aired through November and December 1996.[47] The distinctive feature of *Lives of Jesus* in the context of the Bible on TV is the inventive way it too reflected the state of academic opinion about Jesus. Its title said it all – the series did not pretend to be a definitive perspective about Jesus but a definitive reflection of the then *diversity* of academic opinion about Jesus.

One episode, *Jesus the Jew*, spoke to the ongoing hold of Geza Vermes's theory, already adumbrated in *Jesus the Evidence*, that Jesus was best seen as an itinerant holy man. Another episode, *Jesus the Son of God*, reflected the traditional Christian view of Jesus as a divine saviour. This episode made the inspired decision to travel to India to film Sai Baba, the Indian guru and spiritual leader. Sai Baba was worshipped by his followers as a miracle worker, a saviour and a reincarnation of an earlier saint, and so provided a helpful parallel to understand how Jesus came to be worshipped as God incarnate. The episode *Jesus the Rebel* reflected a view that had been fashionable within and outside academic

45. See the excellent summary of the background to the BBC show by Laurence Gardner, 'The Jesus Ossuary: A Report Concerning the Discovery Channel Documentary *The Lost Tomb of Jesus*, http://www.bibliotecapleyades.net/biblianazar/ esp_biblianazar_36.htm, March 2007.
46. The Lost Tomb of Jesus, *Discovery Channel*, 4 March 2007.
47. *Lives of Jesus*, BBC 1, 24 November 1996.

circles since the 1960s, namely that Jesus was best seen as a revolutionary Che Guevara figure fighting the occupying Roman forces and the corrupt religious authorities.

Finally, the episode *Jesus the Cynic* reflected the views of the *Jesus Seminar*, a group of about 150 critical scholars and laymen who were continuing to look at the historical Jesus through the sceptical spectacles of Rudolf Bultmann. The group presented Jesus as a wandering Jewish wise man influenced by the Greek Cynics, a healer who used parables and sayings to preach liberation from injustice. Like its predecessors at Tübingen University, the members of the seminar did not regard the miracles or the resurrection as authentic stories; it also gave equal weight to non-canonical sources such as the *Gospel of Thomas*. Famously, the group voted with coloured beads to decide which actions and sayings of Jesus were authentic.

Lives of Jesus is unique in the history of the Bible on TV in at least one respect. It is the only postmodernist television series about Jesus ever. It rightly won the top prize in the UK's Sandford St Martin Religious Awards.[48] It was a brave decision to reflect a plurality of theories about the historical Jesus rather than just one. Today that would be inconceivable – television demands a particular point of view, a very clear argument, and the more provocative the better. *Lives of Jesus* may have deprived viewers of easy conclusions, but it would have offered plenty of food for thought.

But perhaps the most original example of the Bible on TV in the late '90s came from an animated series for children called *StoryKeepers* that aired on ITV in 1997.[49] Acknowledging the Academy's consensus that the only thing one could be sure of was that stories about Jesus were circulating orally for decades after his death, *StoryKeepers* made a virtue of this handicap. The series told the stories of Jesus *through* the very stories of the people who were telling the stories!

The idea was the brainchild of Brian Brown, a lecturer in the sociology of education at Oxford Polytechnic and an advisor on religious and children's TV programmes. Brown was looking for a way to entice children into reading the stories of Jesus, but he was conscious not only of the prevailing minimalism, but also of a warning in 1996 by Alan Dale in *New World* that telling those stories directly was a waste of time.[50] The hero – Jesus – was an adult, not as easy for a child to engage with as if the leading character was a teenager.

---

48. Sandford St Martin Awards, Lambeth Palace, 1998.
49. *StoryKeepers*, ITV, February 1997.
50. Alan T. Dale, *New World* (Oxford: Oxford University Press, 1974).

Brown's colleague Professor James Dunn (then Lightfoot Professor of Divinity at Durham University) had recommended a recent novel written by the German theologian Gerd Theissen, *The Shadow of the Galilean – The Quest for the Historical Jesus in Narrative Form*. Theissen's hero is not Jesus but a fictional character who meets people who themselves have met and been impressed by Jesus. To add spice to the story, the Romans arrest the fictional character for sedition.

Theissen's approach inspired Brown to bypass the whole debate about the historicity of Jesus. *StoryKeepers* would tell the story of Christian teenagers living under persecution in Rome, thirty years after the death of Jesus. The teenagers were part of a community of early Christians who were prepared to die for their faith. Their adventures included eluding Roman soldiers on their way to an underground meeting house to hear the apostle Peter tell stories about Jesus. According to Brown, the formula would engage children with fictional characters they could relate to, and it would introduce the stories of Jesus through the adventures of teenage heroes.

> It was fortunate that this situation, the historical context in which the gospel stories were kept alive, lent itself easily and without strain to adventure, excitement, intrigue, threat, danger, escape and resolution – all the ingredients of a Hollywood movie, the television soap opera, the thriller which are the genres most appealing to audiences, particularly young audiences. But the justification was academic not artistic or creative. It came from study of what Biblical scholars were saying, not what Hollywood studio bosses were demanding.[51]

The commissioning process speaks volumes about the role of chance. Brown tells how he met a new ITV commissioner on the very day that a report from the Independent Television Authority landed on the commissioner's desk, urging the broadcaster to improve its religious programming.[52] On the spot Brown was commissioned to make a 13-part series for Sunday mornings on ITV. The series was a great success, with ratings at least a third higher than the Disney offering in the previous slot. The *Methodist Recorder* was hugely impressed, praising it as 'Simply the best religious programmes for children yet made'.[53] It was repeated numerous times on ITV and sold to 104 territories. Following the success

---

51. Brian Brown, *The Bible Is for All* (unpub. mss), 172.
52. Brian Brown, personal communication.
53. David Bridges, *Methodist Recorder*, 18 June 1998.

of *StoryKeepers*, Brown secured another major production for children based on stories from the Jewish Bible and the New Testament. The 39-part epic, *Friends and Heroes*, was screened by the BBC in 2006.[54]

In their own ways, *StoryKeepers* and *Lives of Jesus* were faithful to trends in the Academy. If there was little that could be known for certain about the historical Jesus, then the oral history approach of *StoryKeepers* was the only one consistent with minimalism. For its part, *Lives of Jesus* reflected the spectrum of views about the historical Jesus, acknowledging the co-existence of sceptical approaches within scholarship alongside more traditional approaches.

1996 and 1997 were good years for the Bible on TV, but in terms of TV exposure even better ones were just round the corner. In the 1990s conservative scholars had begun seriously to challenge the Academy's minimalist view of the historical Jesus. Normally audiences would have had to wait another ten years before enjoying another television series about Jesus. But within three years of *Lives of Jesus*, the BBC commissioned a series that would make even more noise than *Jesus the Evidence*. *Son of God* would become one of the most successful programmes about religion ever, breaking the record for television ratings, and making the front pages of newspapers in Britain and around the world. Arguably, it was the beginning of a golden decade for the Bible on TV.

2001: A Watershed

Son of God was a three part series made by the BBC's Religion Department for the BBC and Discovery Channel.[55] It aired in the lead up to Easter 2001 and it became a television landmark in terms of the way the Bible and even archaeology and history more generally were put on the box. It was also a watershed in that at a stroke it overturned the minimalism of the previous two decades, at least in the minds of TV audiences.

Son of God was commissioned because a new technology – computer generated images or CGI – allowed the story of Jesus to be told in a new way. CGI had been used to great effect by BBC Religion in a ten-part series about ancient cultures called *Ancient Voices*.[56] CGI was used to recreate the temples of past civilizations, so why not apply the same technique to the Temple of Jerusalem?

54. Brian Brown, *Methodist Recorder*, 6 April 2006.
55. *Son of God*, BBC 1, 1 April 2001 (shown as *Jesus: the Complete Story* on Discovery Channel, 15 April 2001).
56. 'Ancient Voices', BBC 2, 1998–99.

The problem was that CGI was expensive, but the BBC could see that CGI was the future. In production at the time was a series that would rely exclusively on CGI, *Walking with Dinosaurs*,[57] so the BBC was prepared to break its record for the funding of a television programme about religion. Still, it was clear that BBC money alone would not be enough to fund *Son of God*, so like *Walking with Dinosaurs*, it had to rely on a new way of funding television programmes – coproduction. A key partner was Discovery Channel. The year before, in 1998, Discovery had commissioned from BBC Religion a fifty-minute special, *Who Was Moses?*[58] It was Discovery's first fully funded commission from the BBC. The program only aired on the Discovery Channel, but it was so successful the channel had no hesitation in co-funding *Son of God*. But even financial support from two major broadcasters was not enough to meet the ambitions of the *Son of God* brief. In addition to CGI, *Son of God* would feature dramatized reconstructions and extensive filming around the world: more co-producers were needed. France 2 agreed to join the venture, but the real knight in shining armour was Jerusalem Productions, a media production company set up in 1990 to improve understanding of the Christian faith. Jerusalem Productions would play a vital role in putting the Bible on TV over the next 15 years. It generously filled the funding gap and *Son of God* was green lit.

Son of God's budget was no guarantee that the series would deliver the impact it did. After all, the only novelty the pitch to the Channel Controller promised was the use of CGI to reconstruct the world in which Jesus lived. But content is always king, and on the face of it there seemed to be little new to say about the historical Jesus. By a twist of fate, *Son of God* brought together programme-makers from *Jesus the Evidence* and *Lives of Jesus*. Together they alighted on Tom Wright's seminal book *Jesus and the Victory of God*.[59] It appeared to the production team that Tom Wright had single-handedly overturned a sceptical consensus that had endured for a hundred years. The Bultmann approach to the historical Jesus said that the Gospel writers had invented much of what was written in the New Testament about Jesus. The evangelists were smart editors – they found in the Old Testament prophecies about the coming of the Messiah, and then invented deeds and sayings for Jesus that fulfilled those prophecies. So, for example, Jesus did not really enter Jerusalem on a donkey. That was an Old Testament prophecy about how

57. *Walking with Dinosaurs*, BBC 1, 4 October 1999.
58. *Who Was Moses?* Discovery Channel, 1998.
59. Tom Wright, *Jesus and the Victory of God* (London: SPCK, 1996).

the Messiah would enter Jerusalem, so the Gospel writers applied it retro-spectively to Jesus. According to the Bultmann approach, no one had any idea what the historical Jesus did – his deeds could barely be discerned through the layers of mythologizing.

Tom Wright in effect turned Bultmann's argument on its head: if the evangelists were so smart at making up stories that fulfilled Old Testament prophecies, why couldn't Jesus do the same? Why not give Jesus the credit for weaving a narrative that he was the saviour of Israel, that he was deliberately fulfilling the prophecies? If one assumes that Jesus was as steeped in the Scriptures as the evangelists were, then it was simpler to suppose that it was Jesus himself who decided to enter Jeru-salem on a donkey, precisely because he knew such a symbolic action would conform to public expectations about how the Messiah would enter the holy city.[60]

To the production team, Tom Wright's breakthrough appeared to banish any residual minimalist or post-modernist doubts. Indeed, it encouraged the production to approach the quest for the historical Jesus in a cautiously maximalist way. Archaeological finds from the previous fifty years were re-assessed and used to recreate the daily life of Jesus, including the type of place Jesus would have been born in, his childhood, the games he might have played, village life in Nazareth and Capernaum, how and where the disciples sat at the Last Supper, exactly how Jesus would have been crucified and so on. It all amounted to a catalogue of new revelations about Jesus – new at least to television viewers who had relied on *Jesus the Evidence* and *Lives of Jesus* for their image of Jesus.

But it was the approach adopted to tell the story of Jesus that ultimately made *Son of God* a hit. The first idea was to assign a secular journalist – the BBC's Middle East correspondent Jeremy Bowen – to front the series. Feedback from viewers confirmed that this decision had a positive effect on audiences: it attracted secular viewers who were reassured that this would not be a confessional programme, but it also reassured Christians who appreciated the BBC assigning a high-profile prime time name to present a religious series. The involvement of Jeremy Bowen also allowed the production team to exploit his knowledge of current affairs in the region. A scene about the circumstances of the birth of Jesus was filmed in a cave where modern Palestinian refugees lived, in conditions not unlike those in the first century CE; Jeremy Bowen had previously filed a report about their plight. He also used his knowledge

60. Ibid., 422.

of honour killings in modern Palestine to shed light on what it would have meant for Mary to conceive without having been betrothed to Joseph.

A second novelty was the combined use of drama and CGI. Today, dramatized reconstructions are the stock-in-trade of historical programmes, but at the turn of the century they were rare in the factual genre. More significant still was the use of computer graphics to recreate the environment in which Jesus lived – Herod's port of Caesarea, Bethlehem, Nazareth, Sepphoris, Jerusalem, the Temple and Golgotha were all recreated in CGI, with buildings emerging dramatically from the soil. It was the first time a factual series had made systematic use of computer graphic images to reconstruct villages, towns and cities. The approach was so successful it would be copied time and again over the next decade by other TV genres. CGI reconstructions of ancient sites are now even part of the stock-in-trade of the Academy with interactive recreations of the Giza plateau[61] and the Holy Land.

Engaging as all these techniques were, the most eye-catching idea in *Son of God* was the attempt to reconstruct the real face of Jesus. Of course, there was no skull of Jesus with which to recreate it, but the production team consulted with Israeli physical anthropologists to attempt an approximation. The known images of Jesus were discarded as unreliable. The frescoes in the Roman catacombs were idealized portraits in the Hellenistic style. As for the earliest icons of Jesus, they were dated to the fifth and sixth centuries. Moreover, experts considered that the long, thin shape of the face in the icons reflected the shape of faces typical of the eastern Mediterranean, whereas skulls from first-century Palestine were thought to be rounder and more robust. In order to achieve a nearer approximation of Jesus, experts chose that of an adult male found in a first-century burial in Jerusalem. A cast was made and sent to forensic experts at Manchester University who reconstructed the face of the first-century adult male.

Son of God's production values convinced the then controller of BBC 1 that it should lead the channel's 2001 Spring launch: '*Son of God* sums up my BBC 1' she said to the press.[62] But it was the new face of Jesus which gave the series a degree of publicity that has rarely been matched

61. E.g., 'Bringing the Giza Pyramids to Life', Digital Arts and Humanities, Harvard University, http://www.darthcrimson.org/bringing-the-giza-pyramids-to-life/); 'The Qumran Visualization Project', UCLA, www.virtualqumran.com.
62. Lorraine Heggessey, *Daily Telegraph*, 27 March 2001.

by TV programmes since. However, as *Jesus the Evidence* had shown, the more noise and ratings a TV show about the Bible generates the more sniping it draws from the TV critics, and so it proved with *Son of God* too. The *Mirror's* Victor Lewis-Smith thought the face of Jesus recon- struction was 'an April Fool's joke',[63] whilst *Mail* TV critic Nigel Andrew decried the 'wham-bam, special effects-laden style, which doesn't really fit the subject of the life of Jesus'.[64] But programme-makers will have regarded that a fair price to pay for the publicity gained. The series made the coveted cover of the *Radio Times* and the front pages of most newspapers. It made the cover of magazines around the world, including, bizarrely, the American engineering publication *Popular Mechanics*.[65] Radio and TV programmes debated the face of Jesus – even overseas. In Uruguay, a panel of Christian priests from different denominations discussed the BBC's reconstruction of the face of Jesus. The Anglican priest welcomed it as a realistic interpretation; the Methodist represent- ative said that it did not matter what Jesus looked like – *faith* in Christ is what mattered. The only real note of dissent came from the Catholic spokesman who insisted that Jesus could not possibly have looked like the BBC face – 'It was too ugly'!

As Bible on TV, *Son of God* was significant because, as Tom Wright said at the time, it put Christianity on the map in a way no other series about Jesus had – drawing large numbers of Christian and non-Christian viewers alike. The first episode was viewed by an average of 6 million viewers.[66] The Discovery version – called *Jesus: the Complete Story* – was viewed by 12 million, and it was repeated for years. Jerusalem Productions sold the series to over one hundred countries.

2000s: A Golden Age?

Son of God also left a profound legacy on television programming about Jesus and the Bible more generally. Suddenly – or rather once again – a new generation of secular commissioners and studio executives discov- ered that the Bible was 'sexy'. In 2004 Tom Wright was back on TV screens with *The Resurrection*,[67] this time on Channel 4 in a one- hour documentary made by Blakeway Productions in association with

---

63. Victor Lewis-Smith, 'Skulduggery!', *Daily Mirror*, 31 March 2001, 6.
64. Nigel Andrew, 'Pick of the Day', *Daily Mail*, 31 March 2001, 40.
65. December 2002.
66. '6 million witness Son of God', *Broadcast*, 2 April 2001.
67. 'Resurrection', Channel 4, 12 April 2004.

Jerusalem Productions. It was a unique opportunity for the then Bishop of Durham to present to a wider audience his arguments in favour of the physical resurrection of Jesus as outlined in his *The Resurrection of the Son of God.*[68]

The next 13 years was arguably a golden age for the Bible on TV, at least in terms of the sheer number and variety of documentaries, factual dramas and TV dramas ordered by broadcasters in the UK and the US. In budget terms, the high points of this period were two BBC drama series – *The Passion* and *The Nativity*, and a factual drama from the History Channel – *The Bible*. But in between these milestones dozens of factual singles and series were commissioned – Old Testament factual drama blockbusters, travelogues, sensational investigations, thoughtful historical analyses and even animated series. Even Hollywood got the bug with hits like Mel Gibson's *Passion of the Christ* in 2004 and Ridley Scott's *Noah* and *Exodus: Gods & Kings* in 2014. So what are the characteristics of this 'golden' phase of the Bible on TV? Why did broadcasters up their commissioning of shows about the Bible? What new formats were developed to portray the Bible on TV? And what was the relationship of such shows to the state of biblical scholarship?

The sheer *number* of TV shows about the Bible was a testament to a new-found confidence amongst broadcasters that the Bible could rate highly on the box, although as we shall see the Bible on TV still retained the power to surprise even the most seasoned broadcasters. As for the sheer *variety* of approaches to putting the Bible on TV, it was a testament to the confidence of producers in experimenting with different ways of telling biblical stories.

The floodgates were first opened in the wake of *Son of God*. In an unprecedented step, BBC, Discovery Channel and Jerusalem Productions came together to order a slate of new factual dramas about the Bible from BBC Religion – *The Virgin Mary*, *Moses & the Exodus*, *Noah & the Ark* and *St Paul*. The expectations were high: generous budgets were allocated for foreign filming, high profile presenters, drama reconstructions and CGI in order to deliver big audiences. But *Son of God* had shown that high production values alone would not guarantee high ratings. It would be vital that the programmes also have a strong editorial content, in other words that they say something new – at least to television audiences. The difficulty was that the conservative and maximalist reaction to minimalism experienced by New Testament

---

68. Tom Wright, *The Resurrection of the Son of God* (London: SPCK, 2003).

Studies had not taken place in Old Testament scholarship – and maybe it would never take place. Tom Wright and others had overturned two centuries of scepticism in the quest for the historical Jesus, but the majority of scholars still doubted that the spectacular stories of Moses and the Exodus, and of Noah and the Ark were at all historical. They even doubted that Moses and Noah were once real flesh and blood people.[69] This was a huge problem for television as it meant there would be very little to show on screen, and very little to engage big family audiences on BBC and Discovery Channel if this new slate of Biblical shows devoted itself to proving that the great stories of the Old Testament were myths. The challenge for producers was how to make a TV blockbuster out of these epic stories that was both factual and dramatic?

The solution – and one that did not necessarily please everyone in the Academy – came in response to a recurring criticism made by many conservative Christian viewers and opinion formers. Minimalist shows about the Bible seemed to rely largely on the authority of Biblical scholars who were sceptical of the Bible as history. As TV production teams were usually staffed by university graduates, and as factual programming in any genre on TV thrived on anything that challenged received wisdom, this reliance seemed perfectly natural to producers. But it was clear from the correspondence received by programme-makers that to some Christian faithful and clergy this reliance smacked of a liberal secular prejudice all too prevalent in the media. What about the Bible itself – and indeed the Church – as alternative sources of authority? What about the views of conservative Biblical scholars? It was pointed out that there were many academics outside the top European and American universities who upheld more traditional readings of the Bible. Some criticisms went yet further – what about the opinions of *non*-Biblical scholars – astronomers, geologists, oceanographers, volcanologists, biologists, historians, Egyptologists, psychiatrists and anthropologists – who had applied the insights of their respective professions to the study of the Bible? Why weren't any of their views ever taken into account?

Valid or not, it was a criticism that programme-makers had never quite engaged with. Perhaps it was time to take such views seriously? Maybe such criticisms could even help solve the challenge of turning the Old Testament's epics into blockbusters? In fact, the solution

    69. Donald B. Redford, *Egypt, Canaan, and Israel in Ancient Times* (Princeton, NJ: Princeton University Press, 1993); Israel Finkelstein and Amihai Mazar, *The Quest for the Historical Israel: Debating Archeology and the History of Early Israel*, ed. Brian B. Schmidt (Atlanta: Society of Biblical Literature, 2007).

adopted proved so successful in terms of television ratings that most broadcasters would take it up over the following decade. The formula was simple – begin the programme acknowledging the scepticism of the Academy towards the great Biblical epics, but then offer the promise of new findings in science and history that might just make the story credible. It was an approach first adopted in 1996 by the BBC's *Horizon* science strand with *Noah's Flood*,[70] a film featuring Bill Ryan and Walter Pitman's theory that the deluge was caused by a massive flood of the Black Sea. The formula was repeated by BBC Religion with *The Great Flood* in 1999,[71] with *Moses*[72] and again with *Noah's Ark* in 2005.[73] *Moses* examined evidence by Biblical experts James Hoffmeier and Hershel Shanks suggesting the presence of Hebrews in Egypt whilst earth science experts suggested natural causes for the Ten Plagues and the Parting of the Sea of Reeds. *Noah's Ark* rejected the scriptural interpretation of a universal flood, but it brought in climate and geology experts who favoured a regional flood. Combined with dramatizations and CGI, the formula delivered exactly what the broadcasters were hoping for: *Moses* was watched by 5.6 million viewers, *Noah's Ark* by 5 million.

Just like Hollywood studios, TV commissioners wanted more of what works. The maximalist formula quickly became the standard, copied repeatedly by broadcasters to this day. In 2003 Discovery Channel and the BBC aired *Bible Mysteries* from BBC Religion, a nine-part series exploring the evidence for Joseph, Joshua, David, Herod, Jesus, Mary Magdalene, the Disciples, Peter and Revelation.[74] Since then, National Geographic, Discovery, History, Smithsonian, ITV, Channel 4 and many European channels have all commissioned similar programmes or series with varying permutations of the words 'Bible', 'Mysteries', 'Evidence', 'Secrets', 'Code', 'Revealed', 'Real', 'Search' and so on.[75] The budgets are no longer as generous so the ratings are much lower, and the 'discoveries'

---

70. 'Noah's Flood', *Horizon*, BBC 2, 16 December 1996.
71. 'The Great Flood', BBC 2, January 1999.
72. 'Moses', BBC 1, 1 December 2002.
73. 'Noah's Ark', BBC 1, 21 March 2004.
74. 'Bible Mysteries', BBC 2, 15 February–24 April 2004.
75. E.g., *Mysteries of the Bible*, National Geographic Channel, 2006; *Ancient Evidence*, Discovery Channel 2004; *Joanna Lumley: The Search for Noah's Ark*, ITV, 23 December 2012; *Bible Secrets Revealed*, History Channel, 2013, *The Bible's Greatest Secrets*, American Heroes Channel, 2013; *The Real Noah's Ark: Secret History*, Channel 4, 14 September 2014.

are rarely new, but every year someone somewhere is making a maxi-malist documentary series on the Bible, with maverick scholars from the sciences or the fringes of Biblical scholarship taking centre stage, and mainstream Biblical scholars providing context and balance.

At the same time as fuelling several shows about the Bible, *Son of God* – or *Jesus: The Complete Story* as it was titled in the US – fed a demand for more sensational revelations about Jesus. American broad-casters led the way, surprising many in the industry who believed that US channels would only commission TV shows that would be reassuring to Christian audiences. But the reality is that American TV channels were compelled to attract audiences, and as the American population became more secular, it made commercial sense to make provocative programmes that would attract a younger, less traditional, demographic.

The first of these brash, noisy, controversial but hugely popular shows was Discovery Channel's 2004 documentary *James, Brother of Jesus*, made by Simcha Jacobivici of Associated Producers. The existence of the ossuary of James was announced on 21 October 2002 in Washington, DC at a press conference jointly arranged by the Discovery Channel and the Biblical Archaeology Society. If authentic, the discovery was potentially significant and sensational. Significant because it counted as evidence for the existence of Jesus, and sensational because it challenged Catholic dogma that Jesus was an only child. What actually happened was that the discovery was embroiled in a protracted debate over its authenticity. The Israeli Antiquities Authority claimed that the inscription was forged at a much later date; then, in December 2004, the owner of the ossuary, antiq-uities dealer Oded Golan, was charged with forty-four counts of forgery, fraud and deception, including the forgery of the ossuary inscription. Eminent scholars testified for and against the authenticity of the ossuary. Seven years later, on 14 March 2012, Golan was acquitted of the forgery charges but convicted of illegal trading in antiquities. The judge said this acquittal 'does not mean that the inscription on the ossuary is authentic or that it was written 2,000 years ago'.[76]

Discovery Channel's appetite for more sensational revelations about Jesus showed no signs of abating. In 2005 it aired *The Real Family of Jesus*, a two-hour factual drama made by BBC Religion.[77] Featuring leading American and British scholars such as James Tabor, Robert Eisen-mann, Mark Goodacre and James Charlesworth, it challenged Catholic teaching and popular perceptions about Jesus. It revealed for the first time

76. *The Times of Israel*, 14 March 2012.
77. *The Real Family of Jesus*, Discovery Channel, 27 March 2005.

on TV the extent of Jesus' family and their role in Jesus' mission. This special was not shown in the UK, but the theme was picked up again in 2006 in *The Secret Family of Jesus*, a one-hour programme made by CTVC for Channel 4 and presented by theologian Dr Robert Beckford.[78]

Back in the US, Discovery Channel was still hungry for noisy discoveries related to the Bible. In 2007 it aired the factual drama *The Lost Tomb of Jesus*, made by James Cameron and Simcha Jacobovici of Associated Producers.[79] The film marked a return to the 1996 BBC investigation into the ossuaries found in the Talpiot Tomb in Jerusalem in 1980. With information that was not available in 1996 and new interpretations of some of the ossuaries, the film claimed to have found the family tomb of Jesus. It also argued that the James ossuary was the 'missing link' from the tomb. When the Talpiot Tomb was first discovered, ten ossuaries were found, but one had since gone missing. Jacobovici believed the James Ossuary could be the tenth from Talpiot.

To a lesser degree, a similar appetite for programmes that shocked or at least surprised Christian sensibilities continued on the other side of the Atlantic. In 2007 and 2008, Channel 4, a broadcaster with a brief to air iconoclastic content, showed *The Hidden Story of Jesus*, an investigation by Dr Robert Beckford into the parallels between Christianity and other religions, some of which predated it.[80] The implication was that Christianity was not as original or unique as the Christian tradition maintained. At Easter 2008, Channel 4 broadcast *The Secrets of the Twelve Disciples*,[81] in which the ubiquitous Dr Beckford explored secrets such as Thomas the Apostle's travels to India. Finally, that same year, Beckford's documentary *The Nativity Decoded* premiered on Channel 4, examining the traditions, history and meaning of the Nativity.[82]

This is not the place to pass judgement on *The Lost Tomb of Jesus*, save to say that it was a milestone in the evolution of the Bible on TV. It was the first Jesus documentary since *Jesus the Evidence* and *Son of God* to generate so much controversy. And it would not have come as a surprise that such a big sensationalist revelation about Jesus would generate welcome publicity for the broadcaster, whilst at the same time alienating the Academy. In *The Washington Post*, a Biblical archaeologist condemned the show as 'nonsense' and as 'hyped up ... intellectually

---

78. *The Secret Family of Jesus*, Channel 4, 25 December 2006.
79. *The Lost Tomb of Jesus*, Discovery Channel, 4 March 2007.
80. *The Hidden Story of Jesus*, Channel 4, 25 December 2007.
81. *The Secrets of the Twelve Disciples*, Channel 4, 23 March 2008.
82. *The Nativity Decoded*, Channel 4, 25 December 2008.

and scientifically dishonest'.[83] But as the dust settled, and not for the first time, the controversy was eventually appropriated by the Academy with a symposium and publications,[84] effectively vindicating the TV producers who for a decade had persisted with the story of the Talpiot Tomb.

The Lost Tomb of Jesus is also important because it helps answer the question posed at the beginning of this chapter, namely: Why has the Bible on TV changed from shows that reflect the thinking of the Academy to shows that reflect the interests of television? Before the 1980s programme-makers would not have had the temerity to broadcast content that challenged traditional beliefs. Then, for the next twenty years, programme-makers were more than happy to challenge tradition provided they had the support of leading biblical scholars. But from the 2000s onwards programme-makers became bolder, happier to challenge both tradition *and* the academy, provided they had the support of *some* scholars. It no longer mattered if they were in the minority within biblical scholarship, or even if their expertise lay in fields other than the Bible. The Academy spotted this trend and was not best pleased. Duke University's Eric M. Meyers expressed the frustration of many biblical scholars when he pointed to the widening disconnect between how the media portrays biblical history and what biblical scholars and archaeologists actually say about the Bible. The consequences, he added, are serious: 'Until TV journalism, as well as major magazines and newspapers in print and online, catch up with the field and turn to real experts for advice, the larger public is destined to remain ill-informed'.[85]

Joe Zias, former Curator of Archaeology and Anthropology for the Israel Antiquities Authority, was equally frustrated, arguing that it was the duty of scholars to do what they could to stop sensational broadcasts. In 2011, he blogged about another documentary being prepared about the 'Jesus tomb':

> Case in point is the $ign of the Profit, book/film by $imcha and Tabor from UNC- Charlotte. We've been fighting it day after day, week after week, inc letters to the univ., the publisher, National Geographic, TV and the BBC.

83. *The Washington Post*, 28 February 2007.

84. 'Third Princeton Theological Seminary Symposium on Jewish Views of the Afterlife and Burial Practices in Second Temple Judaism: Evaluating the Talpiot Tomb in Context', Jerusalem, 2008; James H. Charlesworth, ed., *The Tomb of Jesus and His Family? Exploring Ancient Jewish Tombs Near Jerusalem's Walls* (Grand Rapids: Eerdmans, 2013).

85. Eric M. Meyers, 'The Chasm Between the Media and Biblical Archaeological Scholarship', *Biblical Archaeology Review* 40 (2014): 26–7.

After weeks of fighting this, National Geographic cancelled the deal and it looks as if they are back to square one. You win a few and lose a few, but remember the public paid for our education and we owe them something in return.[86]

Joe Zias and his colleagues may have won that skirmish, but not necessarily the battle. The producers found another broadcaster to air their programme. The bigger question was – and remains – who will win the 'war'? The hunger for sensational and shocking revelations surely will only intensify. Many Internet articles about Biblical matters already dispense with scholarly references. And so-called Biblio-bloggers pontificate about any and every biblical subject under the sun. One can't help wondering if TV producers will join this trend and eventually dispense with scholars altogether too?

I headlined this section the 'golden age of the Bible on TV'. In an age when public service broadcasters were required less and less to air programmes about religion, it was perhaps a small miracle that so many shows about the Bible were made for the box. As we have seen, the Academy could be forgiven for taking a less sanguine view. They saw billowing dark clouds of ignorance about the Bible at a time when perhaps rays of illuminating insights are what were needed. However, a survey of the Bible on TV shows that the outlook was not as gloomy for the Academy as it feared.

2006: A Silver Lining

There was a silver lining to the late 2000s in the shape of ample scope in the schedules for alternative takes on the Bible, including perspectives that were more aligned with biblical scholarship. There are only so many shows that mainstream public sector broadcasters can make either proving the spectacular stories of the Old Testament on the one hand or shocking Christians with revelations about Jesus on the other. From the middle to late 2000s a small but important trend of programmes about the Bible on TV emerged that tried more accurately to reflect the actual findings and research interests of the Academy.

The Gnostic Gospels were a case in point. Television had not discussed them since Channel 4's series in 1987, but it was obvious that more and more scholars were specializing in the cache of 'heretical' texts found in Nag Hammadi, in Upper Egypt, in 1948. In the middle of the 2000s two

---

86. Joe Zias, http://www.joezias.com, 23 August 2011.

programmes arrived in quick succession – *The Gospel of Judas*[87] and *Lost Gospels*[88] – which rigorously and dispassionately examined the texts outside the canon of the New Testament and the so-called 'heresies' of early Christianity.

National Geographic's *The Gospel of Judas* aired with great fanfare in 2006, and justifiably so. After lengthy negotiations, National Geographic had secured exclusive rights to broadcast the story of the Gospel's discovery.[89] The codex was discovered in Egypt, then stolen and smuggled into Geneva where it was sold to Swiss antiquity traders for a sum rumoured to be between $3 million to $10 million. The National Geographic special centred on a panel of leading experts in early Christianity, including Bart Ehrman, Elaine Pagels and Craig Evans, which took viewers painstakingly through the story of the discovery and presented the scientific tests that authenticated the age of the gospel. They also suggested that the Gospel overturned the traditional understanding of Judas as the betrayer of Christ. The show appeared rigorous and measured, but the amount of publicity it generated was bound to draw some critical comment. April D. DeConick, a professor of biblical studies at Rice University, said that the National Geographic translation was critically faulty in many substantial respects, and that based on a corrected translation, Judas was actually a demon, truly betraying Jesus rather than following his orders.[90]

Lost Gospels, made by BBC Religion, and presented by the Reverend Pete Owen Jones, aired in 2007 on BBC 4. Featuring amongst other scholars Bart Ehrman, Stephen Emmel and Bernard Green, it revealed to TV audiences the diversity of alternative Christianities in the first few centuries of the faith. *Lost Gospels* devoted only a few minutes of airtime to the third-century Gospel of Judas because the main experts were contracted to talk exclusively on National Geographic's forthcoming *Gospel of Judas*. *Lost Gospels* was the first programme to present the specialized field of Patristics – the study of the early Christian writers – on TV, an effort that impressed the *Daily Telegraph* TV reviewer who praised it as 'one of the most interesting religious broadcasts in living memory'.[91] Its appeal no doubt also lay in the airtime devoted to the *Gospel of Mary*.

87. *The Gospel of Judas*, National Geographic, 9 April 2006.

88. *Lost Gospels*, BBC 4, 9 December 2008.

89. *The Lost Gospel of Judas*, National Geographic, 1996, http://www.nationalgeographic.com/lostgospel/index.html.

90. *The New York Times*, 1 December 2007.

91. Stephen Pile, 'The 16 Gospels that Were too Hot to Handle', *Daily Telegraph*, 15 December 2007.

BBC Religion's series *Bible Mysteries* in 2003 had already dedicated one episode to Mary Magdalene, but Dan Brown's *The Da Vinci Code* had promoted Mary Magdalene to the premier division of iconic biblical figures alongside Jesus, Moses and Noah. Over the next few years, broadcasters would find programmes about the 'truth about the repentant sinner' irresistible. In 2008 CTVC made *Secrets of the Cross: Mary Magdalene* for National Geographic.[92] Although few programmes have shed any new light on Mary Magdalene, broadcasters have returned time and again to the subject. In 2013 the BBC devoted its Good Friday slot to *The Mystery of Mary Magdalene*, a one-hour programme presented by Melvyn Bragg.[93]

Broadcasters returned again to the story of the 'alternative Gospels' in 2013 with *Bible Hunters*, a three-part series for the BBC and Smithsonian Channel made by CTVC.[94] In a refreshing approach to the subject, archaeologist-anthropologist Jeff Rose jumped on his vintage motorbike and retraced the journeys of nineteenth- and early twentieth-century British, German and American adventurers who travelled across Egypt in search of the earliest Christian texts. To their dismay, these intrepid Bible hunters discovered more than they had bargained for – different versions of the Bible and fragments of gospels that were not in the New Testament canon.

Lost Gospels, *The Gospel of Judas* and *Bible Hunters* offered an alternative perspective to the New Testament – the first in 23 years. TV viewers had to wait almost as long – 18 years – to watch an alternative take on the Old Testament. In 2006, PBS aired the miniseries *Walking the Bible*,[95] the first critical TV show about the Old Testament since Channel 4's *Testament* series in 1988. It received record ratings for the broadcaster and was viewed by 20 million people in its first month.[96] Its host was Bruce Feiler, a popular American writer and television personality who retraced iconic journeys of the Old Testament by Abraham, Joseph, Moses and Joshua. As he 'walks the Bible', Feiler finds that his journey is not quite what he anticipated. At every stage he is confronted with questions about the literal truth of the Bible – did Abraham really walk from Ur to Shechem in Canaan? Did the Israelites build the pyramids? What could have caused the ten plagues? Was it really the Red Sea that Moses crossed? As Feiler confronts these questions it dawns on him that

92. *Secrets of the Cross: The Mary Magdalene Conspiracy*, National Geographic Channel, 2008.

93. *The Mystery of Mary Magdalene*, BBC 1, 29 March 2013.

94. *Bible Hunters*, BBC 2, 13 February 2014.

95. *Walking the Bible*, PBS, 4 January 2006.

96. http://en.wikipedia.org/wiki/Bruce_Feiler.

its neither the location nor even the event that is important, but the fact that whatever was experienced was interpreted as an act of God. Feiler's material pilgrimage to the sites of the Bible metamorphosed into a spiritual pilgrimage into the meaning of the stories.

The PBS series was a high point in the history of the Bible on TV. It found in the idea of a pilgrimage by a TV personality an ingenious way of conveying the Academy's prevailing scepticism about familiar Old Testament stories. By turning the disappointment about historical and archaeological evidence into a personally uplifting spiritual experience, Feiler effectively defused any resistance Christian viewers might have harboured about the series. Oddly, *Walking the Bible* was never shown in the UK. Maybe commissioners felt they were already well served with homemade programmes about the Bible, perhaps reasoning that Bruce Feiler was unknown in Britain or that a travelogue would not rate highly. Travelogues boast spectacular landscapes and engaging presenters, but they can be short on revelation and sensation. They eschew the extremes of maximalism or minimalism, preferring to savour instead the journey, the historical context and the presenter's own responses to the story the Bible tells. Viewers in the UK had to wait six years before enjoying a travelogue in the style of Feiler's pilgrimage. In 2012, BBC aired the glossy travelogue *David Suchet: In the Footsteps of St Paul*[97] presented by the internationally acclaimed actor David Suchet. The series retraced Paul's missionary journeys, paying particular attention to everyday life details, such as Paul's tent making. As with Feiler's series on PBS, the appeal of the BBC series lay in Suchet's spiritual response to the journey. As a committed Christian, the experience became a personal pilgrimage in which he could articulate what the life and teachings of St Paul meant to him.

PBS's 2006 *Walking the Bible* was American TV's first foray into Old Testament minimalism. In the UK, Channel 4 had returned to one of the questions first raised in 1988 by John Romer in *Testament*. In 2004 Dr Robert Beckford hosted a one-off documentary called *Who Wrote the Bible?*[98] in which he challenged the long-standing belief of many Christians that the Bible is the literal word of God. But for a systematic presentation of Old Testament minimalism UK viewers had to wait until 2011 when BBC 2 aired *Bible's Buried Secrets*, a three-part series that took an unashamedly sceptical look at key iconic stories from the Old

---

97. *David Suchet: In the Footsteps of St Paul*, BBC 1, 23 December 2012.
98. *Who Wrote the Bible?*, Channel 4, 25 December 2004.

Testament.[99] Coincidentally, the NOVA strand from PBS had aired a similar series, with almost exactly the same title, three years earlier.[100] Both series were broadly in line with current thinking in Biblical scholarship, but their approaches could not have been more different.

NOVA'S two-part special – a Providence Pictures Production – questioned the historicity of Moses' Exodus, Joshua's Conquest of Canaan, Israelite monotheism and King David's empire. Explosive stuff. But, just as with *Walking the Bible*, PBS presented this minimalist perspective in the context of a journey – this time not the journey of a genial pilgrim like Bruce Feiler, but the journey of Biblical archaeologists eager to understand how the Old Testament and the Hebrew faith were formed. The revelations that there was no Exodus or that the Israelites were polytheists were dropped like small hand grenades, but they were contextualized as staging posts in the evolving narrative of how the Bible was formed, so their impact was instantly defused. It helped that the series boasted a truly stellar cast of scholars from American and Hebrew universities.

The BBC's *Bible's Buried Secrets* on the other hand did not pull its punches, questioning head-on the received wisdom about three iconic stories – King David and his empire, Israel's monotheism and the Garden of Eden. 'Did God have a Wife?' asked Francesca Stavrakopoulou, then a Senior Lecturer in the Hebrew Bible at Exeter University. 'Yes' she declared, underlining her case with layer upon layer of evidence. And no, David did not rule over a kingdom. It was the most minimalist series about the Bible on TV in 27 years, with newspapers carping that the BBC had 'hired an atheist' to front the series.[101] It was a cheap shot. Stavrakpoulou's impressive track record – a DPhil from Oxford University in Biblical Studies, a junior research fellowship at the same university, leading to a lectureship in Biblical Studies at Exeter University, spoke for itself. And like the PBS series, all her key arguments were supported on screen by other Biblical scholars. The series launched with 2 million viewers, proving that audiences were ready to watch sceptical perspectives on the Bible as long as programmes offered ground-breaking new content.

If there is a pattern to the history of the Bible on TV, it is the twin attractions of the forces of minimalism and maximalism. That is not surprising – the main interest generated by the Bible is whether its version

99. *Bible's Buried Secrets*, BBC 2, 15 March 2011.

100. *The Bible's Buried Secrets*, PBS, 18 November 2008.

101. 'BBC's face of religion is a self-proclaimed atheist who claims God had a wife and Eve suffered from sexism', *Daily Mail*, 9 March 2011.

of history, and its claims about God's interventions in the world, are true or not. The Bible matters to people of faith – they are interested in the authenticity of Scripture. The Bible also matters to people of no faith – they are interested in evidence that disproves the Scriptures. That seems to be the main axis around which the pendulum of TV programming about the Bible has swung. Factual television works best when it unsettles prevailing views. So, minimalist programmes on the one hand play on the assumptions of those who accept that the Bible is a fair representation of ancient history in the Holy Land. Maximalist programmes on the other hand play on prevailing assumptions that the Bible is bunk. And looking at the history of the Bible on TV over the last thirty years, the pendulum does seem to have swung metronomically from one extreme to the other.

But not all programmes about the Bible have fallen within these parameters. There have been strands of shows about the Bible that have revolved around a very different axis. These shows were not interested in whether the Bible was true or not; they focused instead on the meaning of the Bible – what it means to people in modern times, but also what it meant to people in Biblical times.

2006: It's Not All about the 'Truth'

One strand of such programmes focused on the legacy of the Bible. It could be a spiritual legacy – like *Walking the Bible* and *David Suchet: In the Footsteps of St Paul*, but it could also be a cultural, social and political legacy. Channel 4 was one of the first broadcasters to adopt this approach. In 2006, Dr Robert Beckford hosted *The Passion: Films, Faith and Fury*,[102] an exploration of the relationship between the Bible and Hollywood. Later in 2010 Channel 4 broadcast *The Bible: A History*,[103] a seven-part series made by Pioneer Productions. Instead of a single presenter, it had the original idea of featuring no fewer than seven presenters, one per episode, including author Howard Jacobson, the politician Ann Widdecombe, the ex-government minister Michael Portillo, former IRA supporter Gerry Adams, journalist Rageh Omaar and the historian and broadcaster Bethany Hughes. In each episode, the presenter made an impassioned argument for the effect of the Bible on a salient aspect of modern life. It could be as general as gender and creationism, or as specific as the conflicts in the Middle East and in Northern Ireland. Rageh Omaar, for example, travelled to Israel, the West Bank and Iraq to investigate the legacy of the story of

102. *The Passion: Films, Faith and Fury*, Channel 4, 15 April 2006.
103. *The Bible: A History*, Channel 4, 24 January 2010.

Abraham, and asked whether it was a source of great division or the key to peace and reconciliation. Bettany Hughes explored the feisty women figures of the Bible whilst Gerry Adams investigated the life and death of Jesus Christ, against the backdrop of Adam's own life and career at the heart of the Troubles in Northern Ireland.

The BBC's Religion department got in on the act in 2011 on the occasion of the 400th anniversary of the King James Bible, with a programme about the making of the famous seventeenth-century translation – *When God Spoke English*[104] – presented by historian Adam Nicolson, and with *The King James Bible: The Book that Changed the World*,[105] in which Melvyn Bragg traced the influence of the King James translation on language, literature, war, politics, democracy, the abolition of slavery and even science. In 2013 on BBC 2, Melvyn Bragg returned to the period with the widely acclaimed *William Tyndale: The Most Dangerous Man in Tudor England*.[106]

Also sitting outside the parameters of maximalism vs. minimalism was another strand of TV programmes about the meaning of the Bible that instead of looking forwards looked back at what the stories would have meant in Biblical times. An early and pioneering instance of this was Just Television and CTVC's *Dateline Bethlehem* – a series of six 15-minute programmes for ITV that aired in the run up to Christmas 1999.[107] The idea was to present the 2000-year-old story in the style of a TV news bulletin. The Three Kings were recast as a three-man delegation of foreign diplomats from Baghdad. The series was written and presented by journalist David Jessel, with ex-BBC newsreader Martyn Lewis as co-presenter. Simple, affordable and direct, it was as good an example of how the Bible can be put on TV in a manner that is both rigorous and engaging.

Perhaps the most ambitious series to tackle the meaning of the Bible was *Miracles of Jesus*,[108] a three-part series made by BBC Religion in 2006 for the BBC. The fact that it was presented by Muslim journalist Rageh Omaar was the least of its innovations. Its approach to the miracles

104. *When God Spoke English: The Making of the King James Bible*, BBC 4, 21 February 2011.

105. *The King James Bible: The Book that Changed the World*, BBC 2, 12 March 2011.

106. *William Tyndale: The Most Dangerous Man in Tudor England*, BBC 2, 6 June 2013.

107. *Dateline Bethlehem*, ITV, 22–28 December 1999.

108. *Miracles of Jesus*, BBC 1, 20 August 2006.

was a radical departure from the way TV had until then portrayed the life
of Jesus. As we have seen, by and large television had avoided dealing
with the miracles of Jesus. But had TV decided to address them, one can
be sure that the temptation would have been to ask whether the miracles
were true or not, and to explore rational ways of explaining away the
miracles. Instead, in a very deliberate rejection of the prevailing ration-
alism, *Miracles of Jesus* pointedly ignored the historicity of the miracles
and asked what the various miracle stories would have meant to the
people of first-century Palestine. For example, in the miracle where Jesus
raises the widow's son in Nain, the programme explained that in the first
century those who heard the story would have noted the similarities with
the Old Testament story of Elijah raising a widow's son in Nain. As Rageh
Omaar explained, people at the time would have asked themselves if Jesus
was Elijah returned? The story of Jesus' miracle of the loaves and fishes
would have been compared to Moses' miracles of the manna and the quail.
Again, it would have prompted the question: Was Jesus the new Moses?
Every miracle was put in the context of the period and first-century
people's knowledge of Scripture.

It was a mark of confidence by TV producers that *Miracles of Jesus*
never once addressed the question burning in the minds of many viewers.
Did the miracles really happen? With Discovery Channel and Jerusalem
Productions as co-producers, the series was able to create dramatized
scenes to flesh out the stories of the miracles, and to use computer graphic
images, special effects and time-slice technology to bring the moment of
each miracle to life. Nigel McCulloch, the then Bishop of Manchester,
said the award-winning series 'could become a bench-mark for good-
quality religion on television'.[109]

The most ambitious programme *theologically* speaking about the
meaning of the Bible came in 2010 on BBC's Good Friday slot with a
programme called *The Day Jesus Died*.[110] The title gave little away. It was
in fact a programme about the meaning of the Cross, in other words about
atonement theology, the first time the subject had been tackled by a TV
documentary. Historian and broadcaster Bettany Hughes chronicled the
history of the meaning of the Crucifixion over 2000 years, with contributions from no less than a bishop and three archbishops. It was one the most
overtly theological and academic programmes about the Bible ever shown
on TV. And yet it aired on BBC 1 to critical acclaim from both audiences
and scholars.

109. 'Religious TV Fights its Corner', *Church Times*, 2 November 2006.
110. *The Day Jesus Died*, BBC 1, 2 April 2010.

If earlier TV programmes about the historicity of the Bible stories were a response to the importance audiences attached to the *truth* of the Bible, what did the later appearance of TV programmes about the *meaning* of the Bible say about audiences? Probably that interest in historicity was gradually giving way to an interest in meaning. And that surely reflected wider changes in the role of faith in society. The West was becoming more secular, so the number of TV viewers who were believers was declining. The Bible was also ceasing to be as contested a space as it once had been, and Biblical literacy was weakening. As a result, viewers' interest in the Bible shifted – from the truth or otherwise of the Bible to its legacy and to what it was all about in the first place. Indeed, it is this wider shift to understanding what the Bible stories are about that surely explained the latest and most significant development in the story of the Bible on TV – the rise of full-scale dramas.

2009: Full-scale Drama

Between 2009 and 2014 viewers enjoyed several retellings of stories from the Bible as pure dramas, written and made by famous writers, directors and producers, and performed by leading actors. TV had not made dramas about the stories of the Bible for decades. So what possessed TV, in an increasingly secular age, to spend their precious budgets and limited slots on dramas about the Bible? Probably the very fact that as religion was being shunted out of the public arena, so audiences were no longer learning about the Bible at home, school or church. New generations were growing up ignorant of the Bible, so there was a new market that could be tapped into. Now, on the face of it all these dramas wanted to do is re-tell the Bible's great stories. They did not appear to be interested in any of the debates about the truth or the meaning of the Bible. However, as we shall see, most said a great deal about truth and meaning, but not in a way that TV audiences would necessarily have been aware of.

The first of these forays into Bible drama was BBC 3's *Manchester Passion*,[111] a live event that retold the story of the Passion for a contemporary audience. It featured a procession of the cross through Manchester city centre to a new soundtrack using the music of the cream of Manchester bands, including Oasis, The Smiths and Joy Division. Mixing passages from the Gospels with versions of classic Manchester songs, the BBC intended to present a version of the last days of Christ that would appeal to a modern audience. Although it was viewed by barely 300,000

111. *Manchester Passion*, BBC 3, 6 April 2007.

people, it drew a huge amount of publicity, and it must rank as one of the most inventive approaches to the story of Jesus' Passion – effectively a re-invention of the medieval mystery play for the twenty-first century. It also helped the BBC meets is public service obligations to engage with audiences in more direct ways. The format has never delivered big audiences, but it became a staple of the BBC's Christmas and Easter output for several years. In 2010 the BBC broadcast *The Liverpool Nativity*,[112] in 2012 *The Preston Passion*[113] and in 2014 *The Great North Passion*.[114]

Even more ambitious was the BBC's decision to devote prime time slots and glossy drama budgets to stories from the Bible. In 2008, the BBC broadcast the story of Jesus' last days in *The Passion* in four parts throughout Holy Week.[115] The significance of the BBC's drama was that it featured leading actors such as James Nesbitt and Penelope Wilton, and that it was written by Emmy Award winner Frank Deasy, produced by the award-winning producer of *Bleak House* Nigel Stafford-Clark, and directed by Michael Offer who made the drama thriller *The State Within*. The big names were a bold attempt to draw in large audiences with clever, surprising and contemporary writing and direction. An original device was to tell the story from three points of view – the religious authorities, the Romans and Jesus. For the first time, all the key characters in the story were intimately fleshed out.

The Passion rated extremely well for the BBC – 4.9 million watched the final episode, matching the ratings of other dramas.[116] Emboldened, the BBC asked writer Tony Jordan to write a script for a follow-up about *The Nativity*.[117] Jordan was asked how he would approach the subject, and he says that he came up with a 'ridiculous notion' of a story centred on the inn in Bethlehem, which he compared to the BBC 1980s sitcom 'Allo Allo!'[118] The four-part drama aired in the week before Christmas 2010. Again, it featured famous actors like Peter Capaldi and John Lynch, and it drew big audiences with the first episode watched by 5.21 million viewers.[119] Like *The Passion*, *The Nativity* was well received. Critics

112. *The Liverpool Nativity*, BBC 3, 16 December 2007.

113. *The Preston Passion*, BBC 1, 6 April 2012.

114. *The Great North Passion*, BBC 1, 18 April 2014.

115. *The Passion*, BBC 1, 16–23 March 2008.

116. John Plunkett, TV Ratings, *The Guardian*, 25 March 2008.

117. *The Nativity*, BBC 1, 20 December 2010.

118. Peter Stanford, 'Tony Jordan Interview: The Nativity Has Changed Me, and that's the Gospel Truth', *The Daily Telegraph*, 21 December 2010.

119. Paul Millar, TV News, *Digital Spy*, 21 December 2010.

admired the way both series emphasized the humanity of the leading characters Jesus, Mary and Joseph. In *The Guardian*, TV reviewer Sam Wollaston wrote 'What is nice about this new telling of an old story: it will resonate, and it's relevant. It's very human, too, because that's what it's about, the characters and what happens to them and between them, rather than the message. In short, it's not preachy, and that's a relief.'[120]

In the wider context of the history of the Bible on TV, both *The Passion* and *The Nativity* illuminate what it takes to make good TV out of the Bible that will be watched by millions. First, a programme needs writers, producers, directors and actors of the highest calibre. High production values are a quality everyone can endorse. The second quality, however, may stir ambivalent feelings in those Christians and scholars whose interest in the Bible goes beyond its stories. As Wollaston pointed out, the appeal of *The Nativity* lay in the telling of the story in a manner that resonated with audiences. By stressing the *humanity* of Jesus and Mary both dramas ensured that all audiences – of any faith and none – were drawn in. And who would not welcome that? But to Christians and Bible scholars the satisfaction of seeing the Bible on prime time TV would have been tempered by the expedient of removing from the stories the very qualities that made the Bible stories special in the first place – the miraculous role of angels, of the Holy Spirit and of God. The story of Jesus is not the 'greatest story ever told' on account of the *human*, down to earth adventures of its hero. There are plenty of other stories that would merit that accolade. The story of Jesus is 'great' because the supernatural intervenes in the human plane in such a special and remarkable manner. To dispense with the divine is to dilute the Bible's unique qualities. Its story becomes indeed 'just another human story'.

So, whilst Bible dramas proudly proclaim not to get involved in questions of truth or meaning, they are in fact profoundly engaged with them, and in ways that are perhaps more insidious than their factual counterparts. And that, of course, is a conscious decision by TV. When controllers and dramatists say they just want to tell a great story in a 'fresh and compelling way', that is a coded signal to writer and director to minimize references to divine agencies. The resulting drama may be more compelling *as drama*, but it cannot avoid making a very clear statement about truth and meaning. It is saying that only the *human* dimension of the heroes is worthy of dramatizing and, by implication, of value or even true. It is also saying that only the *modern* meaning – the 'contemporary

120. Sam Wollaston, 'TV Review: The Nativity', *The Guardian*, 21 December 2010.

resonance' – is worthy of expression. This may disappoint Christians and Bible scholars who understand that the intention of the Bible writers was not to compose literature. They may have used literary devices, but their intention was to redeem the world. Then again Christians and Bible scholars may judge that this is a price worth paying to get more people interested in exploring the Bible further. Tony Jordan says that when he started writing *The Nativity* he did not believe in the Nativity story, but that since writing *The Nativity*, his opinion changed. A neat illustration perhaps of some of Jesus' parables.

Drama's love affair with the biblical stories reached a climax in 2012 with *The Bible*, a ten-part television miniseries that aired on History Channel.[121] There had been a long drama series for TV about the Bible before – in 1993 a European consortium funded production of *The Bible*, a series of 21 films shot between 1994 and 2002 in Ouarzazate, in the southern Moroccan desert.[122] It starred Hollywood actors like Richard Harris and Barbara Hershey. Thanks to the dry weather, the sets for the series could be left standing and re-used year after year. Seven years later, when BBC Religion arrived in Ouarzazate to shoot *Virgin Mary*, *Moses*, *Noah* and *St Paul*, the sets were still standing and so they were adapted to the new requirements. Morocco once again became the location of choice for the History Channel's epic.

The 2012 series *The Bible* was produced by Roma Downey and Mark Burnett, best known for producing prime time hit reality shows. 13.1 million viewers saw the first episode of the miniseries, the largest cable television audience of the year.[123] Subsequent episodes drew on average more than 10 million viewers. The series used its budget of under $22 million on a combination of drama, narration and computer graphics. According to its producers, the stated aim of its over-arching narrative was to 'affect a new generation of viewers and draw them back to the Bible', to show them that 'God loves each one of us as if we were the only person in all the world to love'.[124] Downey and Burnett's epic could well end up being the most watched TV series about the Bible. Their

121. *The Bible*, History Channel, 3–31 March 2013.

122. *The Bible* was produced by Lux Vide, KirchMedia and Quinta in association with a variety of broadcasters and distributors including RAI, France 2, Antena 3, ARD, MTM, Czech TV, NCRV BSkyB and Beta.

123. James Hibberd, 'Mark Burnett's "The Bible" Begets Record Ratings', *Entertainment Weekly*, 4 March 2013.

124. Roma Downey and Mark Burnett, 'Making the Bible a Daunting, Deep Experience', *The Huffington Post*, 28 February 2013.

2. BRAGARD *The Bible According to TV*

distribution plans are to sell it all over the world, and where appropriate, to show it in churches and missions. 'More people will see this series than everything we ever made; together, combined. Billions of people will see this series. Billions.'[125]

The Bible miniseries was a milestone in the history of the Bible on TV. Like other landmarks in the genre, it surprised the TV industry. The 13 million rating for the first episode was the highest for a Bible programme on American cable TV, and one of the highest for the History Channel. It also dominated the broadcast trade press. The Bible's launch coincided with AMC's *Walking Dead*, which although hugely popular with more secular audiences, never quite matched the ratings of its religious rival. Of course, the two were only in competition in the eyes of the trade press who exclaimed astonishment every time an episode of *The Bible* outscored *Walking Dead*. Many welcomed the bravery of the broadcaster, whilst bemoaning divergences from the traditional text. These are inevitable in any attempt to condense the Bible. The series engaged numerous eminent academic consultants, including Craig Evans, Helen Bond, Paula Gooder and Mark Goodacre, as well as a wide range of pastors who approved the content.

In the UK, Channel 5 picked up the series where it aired in November and December 2013. It opened up with 1.3m – on the face of it a low rating for a terrestrial channel compared to a cable channel, but that was a very respectable audience for a minority broadcaster like Channel 5. It saw off competition in the slot from both BBC 2 and Channel 4. A measure of *The Bible*'s impact was that the curse of the 'noisy landmark' or glitzy special struck again, drawing both enviable publicity and stinging criticisms from TV reviewers in equal measure. The *Los Angeles Times* acknowledged the series was 'handsome and generally expensive', but *The Telegraph* dismissed it as 'utter tosh: tosh as television drama and tosh as a retelling of the Bible'.[126] But the Bible Society spoke for millions of Christians when it said it welcomed the broadcast of the series.[127] By the time the series is viewed by Christians all over the world, it will probably be Downey and Burnett who will be having the last laugh.

---

125. Ibid.

126. Jane Kellogg, 'History's "The Bible": What the Critics Are Saying', *Hollywood Reporter*, 3 March 2013; Christopher Howse, 'The Bible, Channel 5, Review', *Daily Telegraph*, 30 November 2013.

127. Matthew Van Duyvenbode, *Bible Society News*, 10 April 2013, http://www.biblesociety.org.uk/news/bible-society-welcomes-screening-of-the-bible-on-channel-5/.

The Bible is by no means the last example of the Bible on TV but it is a good place to bring this survey to a close. I started this chapter with a raft of Bible dramas – from *Moses the Lawgiver* to *Jesus of Nazareth*; I end it with another raft of Bible dramas – from *The Passion* to *The Bible*. So the Bible on TV appears to have come full circle. In a sense it has. After nearly forty years TV has returned to where it all began – the simple re-telling of Bible stories.

For a book that will be read mainly by those in or on the fringes of the Academy or the Faith, the main conclusion I draw from forty years of the Bible on TV is the way historic changes in the broadcasting landscape have shaped the relationship between the Bible in the Academy and the Bible on TV. Whereas in the 1980s and 1990s TV shows reflected the thinking of Biblical scholarship, in the 2000s and 2010s TV shows largely reflected the thinking of others, whether programme-makers, mavericks or non-biblical scholars. It was the proliferation of channels in the 2000s that triggered a shift in what type of shows about the Bible got made on television. One consequence of this change is that it does mean the public may well remain largely uninformed about what goes on in biblical studies, just as Eric Meyers has warned. Then again, we don't know what the future holds. There are big changes looming on the horizon – shifts in the broadcasting ecology, shifts in the role of public service broadcasting and shifts in the role of faith in civil society. Any one of these could have a huge impact on the Bible on TV – for better or worse – just as they have done in the past.

Chapter 3

INTERVIEW WITH RAY BRUCE

Edward Adams and Helen K. Bond

Internationally acclaimed and multi-award winning documentary producer Ray Bruce has a number of Bible documentaries to his credit,
including *John Meets Paul*, with John McCarthy (2001),[1] *David Suchet:
in the Footsteps of St Paul* (2011)[2] and *Countdown to Calvary* presented
by Hugh Bonneville (2018).[3] Formerly Head of Production and Executive
Producer for CTVC, he now has his own consultancy company. The editors of this volume managed to put a few questions to him …

How did you get into TV documentary production?
Ray Bruce: Having completed a degree at King's College London in
Theology and not feeling that ordination was for me, I chose instead to
teach Religious Education which was probably the biggest challenge
of my life, including my television career. But it was essentially from
an educational background that I got into TV documentary production,
developing first of all video material for religious education. The first TV
programme I did was on the Christian roots of Anti-Semitism. It was a
topic that I was really interested in, and I went to Channel 4 with it and
they said 'Go to this company, CTVC, and they might umbrella it', and
thus began my career in television documentaries. But it's important to

1. CTVC/ITV, produced by Geoff Dunlop.
2. CTVC/BBC/Athena Learning/Acorn Media Group, produced by Martin Kemp.
3. RTE/APT/ARTE/C4, directed by Gerry Hoban.

stress that I got into it from an educational background; all the documentaries that I've made over the last twenty-five to thirty years have been intended as educational resources.

When did you make the move into TV?
RB: It was in the mid- to late '80s, when religious broadcasting had a place in the television universe in a way that it doesn't now. At Channel 4 there was a commissioning editor for religion, and obviously at that time the BBC and ITV had a commitment to religious broadcasting.[4] Channel 4 was looking for topics that were edgy and controversial, and the whole issue of Christian Anti-Semitism going back to biblical times appealed to Bob Towler, commissioning editor at the time. That was the start. I worked on other projects for Channel 4 and then branched out into the other broadcasters in the UK and around the world.

Can you tell us about CTVC – what it does, and your association with it?
RB: I was full time as Executive Producer/Head of Programmes at CTVC for twenty-four years. CTVC essentially came out of the work of J. Arthur Rank. People don't realize that Rank was the father of the British Film Industry, and he was a profound Christian (Methodist) whose faith was very, very important to him. He was a great figure straddling the British film industry, involved in an extraordinary range of films working with likes of Laurence Olivier and David Lean, producing stand out classics of the British film history, right to the Carry On films. You'll see the gong appear and that's a J. Arthur Rank production. So CTVC is part of that. CTVC's remit is, wherever possible, to produce and develop those kinds of religious programmes, particularly dealing with the Christian story, that can appeal to a wide audience in much the same way that J. Arthur Rank's feature films did. So CTVC has a tremendous legacy linked to this incredible film maker.

Why have you devoted so much of your life to producing Bible-orientated programming?
RB: I'm passionate about biblical literacy, and that comes from my background in education. If you can keep sixteen year-old South-East Londoners, on a wet Friday afternoon, engaged with the story of the Passion through examining the Turin Shroud and have the students actually read the Bible to get the references, you've got to have

4. For an historical overview of this, see Richard Wallis's chapter in the present volume.

something going for you! Teaching school students was a good way into filmmaking. I just feel it's important that the Bible stories get out there, and I think television, the goggle box, is an important way of communicating them. I think that education is falling short if students are going through the system and they get to know nothing about the Bible. Biblical knowledge empowers their ability to understand the world. For this reason, I pay exactly the same attention to learning about other religions. In terms of understanding the world, one needs to get a sense of what religion is all about and the way in which it has informed our history and way of life.

How much does it actually cost to make a documentary, and how do you get the money?
RB: We're told that you can't serve God and Mammon, but in television broadcasting and programme-making, you can have a damn good try! I think there was a time when you could go to a UK broadcaster and if they were convinced that you had a good story to tell, they would pay for it, and that still holds true if there is a strong appetite for the project. So the whole budget could come from one source. Gradually, as religious programming became more marginalized it became more difficult to obtain that full upfront budget, so you had either to lower your expectations and ambition or look for co-production finance from other broadcasters. So essentially, you then had to work not only for a UK broadcaster, but for a Discovery Channel, a National Geographic Channel or an Australian channel. Obviously that brought its own set of challenges, in the sense of trying to satisfy a UK audience along with an American audience, along with an Australian audience. But it did mean that you got more money for your budget. Then you had to do distribution deals. You got some finance from a company representing your project worldwide who would sell your project to broadcasters. With the arrival of Netflix, Amazon and others, we have a radically changing TV landscape with new digital platforms and on-demand content. They have money to spend but it is becoming more competitive for producers. Incredible drama is being produced and we wait to see if documentaries with religious content will benefit. Budgets are tight. So there's no question now that any project that I'm involved in requires co-production funding because, basically, ambition is very, very high, and quality expectations are also very, very high. I think in this day and age, budgets can start around £80,000 but can get into the hundreds of thousands depending on scale, ambition and location requirements. But if you want to have that extra visual power through dramatic reconstruction, CGI and so on, the budget's going to be

higher. Yet, I think there's a lot to be said for simply having a presenter wandering through a biblical landscape. When you have someone like David Suchet or Hugh Bonneville, with their remarkable acting and presentation skills, people who can tell a good story, you don't need a cast of thousands or very expensive CGI. There is great power in simple story telling in an appropriate location. But certainly in the work that I am doing now, we're looking for as much money as we can get. You then have that incredible responsibility to satisfy a number of potential broadcast partners. A documentary about a biblical subject aimed first at a UK audience may have to undergo some revision if it's to be acceptable to an American audience.

Do you receive funding from other (non-broadcasting) sources?
RB: You have to be a bit careful about what I call third-party funding. It might seem very attractive when someone says, 'I'll give you a million dollars to do x, y and z', but then you have to consider what comes with that kind of money. Do the funders want to exert some kind of editorial control? To what extent, if you take the money, is there is an expectation that what this money represents is reflected in the programme? If one is dealing with money from, say, a more conservative Christian evangelical American source, then one has to be aware of what that particular group would want to see on screen. And as we know, that might not appeal to everybody.

To what extent are UK mainline broadcasters required to put on religious programming?
RB: It's part of the BBC's public broadcasting commitment to put on a certain amount of religious programming. But Channel 4, ITV or other broadcasters don't have to do it. So – quite rightly – we have to make good arguments as why they should be taking on this kind of programming.

How do you go about choosing an appropriate broadcaster for your material?
RB: You have to consider the tone of the programme and how it fits with a channel. The two series *David Suchet in the Footsteps of Saint Paul* and *David Suchet in the Footsteps of Saint Peter* worked well on BBC1, but they would not have been a good fit for Channel 4, which looks for more edgy and more counter-intuitive programmes. There are financial factors. Some channels pay more than others, and so you go to a channel that would perhaps give you a bit more money. Another factor is who is presenting it. If you have a presenter who is much loved on a particular channel, then obviously you would go to that channel saying 'I've got a

great Bible-based programme, and it just so happens that Person X, who's a great face on your channel, would present it'. International co-production, has its own set of challenges. A documentary using somebody famous in the UK might be fine for a UK producer, but there might be resistance to it in America. The American broadcaster might like the programme, but because the presenter is not as well known in the US, it might be difficult to get them on board. This is a big challenge these days since we now live in a co-production universe. You could get a celebrity who would cross all national boundaries in terms of profile and status, but your budget would be gone before you turn the cameras on. So, it's getting more and more difficult.

Can you say a bit more about the differences in the viewers in the US and the UK?
RB: As you know there is a strong Christian tradition in the US. When it comes to the programming of biblical material and stories, one has to be very, very sensitive to the fact that there is a large section of people who hold a particular view of the Bible, its integrity, its literal truth and so on (though there's a powerful anti-religion and anti-Bible force too). In the UK, there is conservative Christianity, but it doesn't have as big a voice as it does in America. Inevitably if you're looking for money from America for programmes about the Bible, you have to bear that in mind. It's a fine line maintaining the integrity of a programme and respecting the wishes of co-producers and broadcasters with different programming needs. Compromises have to be made.

What topics make for a good biblical documentary?
RB: A thumping good mystery! The Bible is full of great stories and thumping great mysteries. When archaeology is thrown in too, you've the potential for a really good programme. Some years back, I made a programme for ITV about the Shroud of Turin. It was at the time when there was a lot of interest in the Shroud. I was fortunate to be working with an archaeologist who had just uncovered a tomb in Akeldama in Jerusalem and, to his surprise and wonderment, inside there were the remains of a human body wrapped in a shroud. We had it carbon-dated, and it turned out to be from the first century! So, all of a sudden we had new material to work with, giving us a new angle on the mystery of the Turin Shroud. What was this shroud we discovered? How did it compare with the Shroud of Turin? So again, a good mystery makes for intriguing programming. I've been fortunate on two or three occasions to be around when a chance discovery is made that becomes part of the story and that gives you an edge on competitors.

Are programme ideas sometimes determined by popular trends?
RB: There are many days when I thank God for Dan Brown! Dan Brown
is probably more responsible than anyone else for contemporary popular
interest in Mary Magdalene, whether Jesus was married or not, the Council
of Nicaea and so on. I have produced three programmes about Mary
Magdalene all thanks to Dan Brown. When you get a blockbuster book
like *The Da Vinci Code*, you can be very clever and wrap a documentary
around it. So, you pick up those kinds of cultural signals that give you
an opportunity to explore a biblical story. But also, there are stories from
within the academic community that generate programme ideas. Someone
discovers a new Gospel that suggests that Judas didn't betray Jesus but
rather was Jesus' accomplice. Or a manuscript appears that suggests that
there was a Mrs Jesus. Obviously, as a television producer, you would be
stupid not to explore documentary possibilities around these topics.

Can you talk us through the process of making a programme?
RB: The first thing is the idea. The idea could be mine, or it could be an
eminent professor's, it could come from a newspaper article or anywhere
at all! Once you have an idea, you then need to develop a strong story.
Once you've done that, you have to write a proposal, within which you
state in two sentences why a viewer should want to watch this programme.
You also have to give some idea of what the programme might cost. Then
you take your proposal to a broadcaster. If you're sufficiently known to
a commissioning editor, you can do this in a short email, asking, 'Might
you be interested in this?' This can save an awful lot of time. If you
can convince a commissioning editor that you've got something worth
pursuing, they get back to you, saying, 'Yes, we're really interested in
that. Could we hear more?' Sometimes 'Could we hear more?' comes with
a bit of development money, which helps as you extend the proposal into
a treatment. This involves research and doing a proper costing. Ideally,
you'd want to make a three- or four-minute promotional tape, particularly with the presenter, that you can submit along with your treatment.
If the broadcaster decides to commission the programme, they will give
you production money. Inevitably it isn't enough, so then you have to
take your treatment to another broadcaster, in all probability in another
country, to see if you can get additional co-production money. Then of
course you've got to manage the expectations of different broadcasters,
as I mentioned earlier. And then you're into production. As executive
producer, which is the role that I've had over the years, you have to ensure
that you get the right team in place. Securing the right director – someone
who is familiar with the terrain or who has done a lot of similar work –
is especially important. And then you just run the production process,

ensuring all the way that the broadcaster/s supporting the project is/are informed about and happy with what you are doing. You should never, never surprise broadcasters. So, if you've convinced a broadcaster that the programme rests on a specific contribution from an eminent academic, and then all of a sudden that eminent professor is not available or pulls out because they don't like the director or the producer, you have a serious problem. You need to make the broadcaster aware of the situation right away. So, that roughly is the process. For an hour's programme or a series, production time can be between two and seven months.

Do you have an intended audience in view when you make a programme?
RB: Obviously, when you're dealing with biblical material you would hope that there is already a constituency – a Christian audience – that would be interested in what you might have to say about a biblical story. But I'd want as big an audience as I can gather. So I want to appeal to a broad constituency, not just people of faith. The trick is making it appeal to an audience who normally wouldn't give this kind of material the time of day. That's where having a good mystery helps. People always like a good mystery, especially when the mysteries are long ago and far away. But you have to make the 'long ago' and 'far away' as present to them as *Star Wars* is!

What do you want your programmes to achieve?
RB: On one level, my programmes are giving information – historical, archaeological, literary, cultural. But I don't just want my programmes to inform. I want them to empower viewers, so that they are better equipped to ask questions themselves about the subject. That's the educationalist in me! I want to help people to think more intelligently about the subject and to pose questions themselves in a way that they haven't done before.

How do you get big name presenters, like Hugh Bonneville and David Suchet, on board?
RB: You get them on board because people like to see them on telly! But the question you have to ask is whether you are just parachuting these people into a programme in order to sell it. That to me never works. There's got to be some kind of ownership on the part of the presenter in relation to the material they are presenting, or the story that they are telling. For example, not many people are aware that Hugh Bonneville studied Theology at Cambridge. He is fascinated by the Gospel story and how they came to be written. He is in demand as an actor not least because of the international popularity of Downton Abbey. In *Countdown to Calvary*, a documentary that pieces together the historical and political

events of Easter, Hugh could put his theological knowledge to creative use. He found this personally interesting. With David, he's a man of faith. He's also an actor with an interest in characters. The Bible is full of strong character stories, so he's engaged with it. Whatever their celebrity status, it's the presenters' attachment to the biblical subject matter that gives them the edge. The viewer then feels safer in holding out their hand and walking with them through the terrain; there's a feeling that they can see why that person wants to do this journey. That sense of ownership is crucial for the vitality of the story telling and for attracting an audience. But at the same time, I don't underestimate the appeal of celebrity!

What do you look for in your academic contributors?
RB: First, they must be an authority on the subject they are addressing. Second, they should have a presence on camera and an ease in speaking so that the audience can feel comfortable. They should be able to make their contribution accessible. They shouldn't mind explaining things in a way that people can understand. So I look for ease and efficiency, an ability to speak clearly and interestingly, and a sense of what the viewer might want to be told. An academic also needs to have a realistic awareness of how their contribution might be used in the programme. They do a two-hour interview on camera, but we might only use a three-minute or even two-minute section of that. It's also possible that in the end, for whatever reason, we might not use any of the interview at all.

Do you get much feedback from actual viewers? Do people write in to you and tell you what they think?
RB: Most of the feedback that I get is along the following lines: 'Dear Mr. Bruce, Thank you so much for the David Suchet programme. We think David Suchet is wonderful.' And that's obviously great. But I get another kind of feedback, from people who have a conservative view of the Bible and who feel that we've done a great disservice to the Bible by challenging its literal truth. Some of the letters I've had along this line have actually been quite nasty. I learned from very early on that if you start responding to people like that, it can go on and on and on. So, much as I would like to engage with them, it's really quite difficult. But it does make you realize that your programmes are going to be watched by people who hold the Bible very dear, and some of the issues you raise may be very upsetting for them. And it's a weighty responsibility. If you don't understand that, then you shouldn't be touching this area at all. I think you've just got to be aware that is the case and tread very, very carefully. It shouldn't stop you telling a good story provided there is integrity in what you do. There are some programmes that are just out to be sensational, and there are some

producers who want to play the sensational card just for the sake of being sensational. Now I want to be sensational too, but you need to temper that with a respect for the standing that the Bible has in the hearts and minds of millions of people in our culture. And that's why you want to do the thing in the first place.

Do you have any influence over the scheduling of your programmes? How do you achieve a prime-time slot?
RB: All that you can do is try and make a programme that you feel is worthy of a prime-time slot. But at the end of the day you're at the mercy of broadcasters' scheduling, and of course a lot of producers, not only those involved in the kind of programming that I like to do, have exactly the same problem. The programming that I do tends to be broadcast during Easter or Christmas, obviously important times and opportunities to tell the Bible stories. They do tend to appear in daytime rather than evenings, but I have to say that they still do very well in terms of viewing figures. The challenge is coming up with the programmes that can really break through and find a place at peak viewing times.

What happens to a programme or series after it has been broadcast?
RB: If a broadcaster commits itself to a programme, it can give that programme multiple showings over a period of time. That's useful to know. I must say that with the programmes that I've done, broadcasters do take up the option to repeat them. But that can be a negative thing if it means that rather than invest in new programmes, they just drag out stuff that they've already shown, particularly if it's related to Christmas or Easter. These festivals are evergreen, as are the stories attached to them. So if they have a programme that you made three years ago about Bethlehem and the Nativity, they'll just reuse that. It's a few more viewing figures, but sometimes it's just an excuse for not having the time, inclination or money to make original programming. I'm particularly keen on repurposing my material wherever possible. For example, I've just done a big Jesus project (the Lumo Project[5]) that I think could be a very good resource for teaching.

How do you keep up with the field?
RB: I keep up with websites, particularly those concerned with the history and archaeology of the Bible. I also read a lot of books, talk to a lot of people in the academic world and attend conferences. Keeping alert to

---

5. For more information, see David Batty's chapter in the present volume.

what's happening in the world of biblical scholarship is a way of perhaps getting the next big Bible documentary and possibly discovering in a car park in Jerusalem the bones of an important historical character!

What do you see as the future of biblical documentaries? Is there a future?
RB: In terms of biblical feature films, there is at the moment a burgeoning market, particularly in the US. In terms of TV documentaries, it's not going to be easy. The discovery of something that shakes the foundation of two thousand years of Christianity is obviously still going to be an important access point to a successful broadcast. But it seems to me that we increasingly need to cast biblically oriented topics within programming devoted to other disciplines – history, science, travel – especially if they have to do with manuscripts, locations and skeletons. We're back to bones again! It does seem to me that we have got to find subtle and diverse ways of getting this content out under other labels. This is not to con the viewer, but to bring out more clearly the historical or scientific dimensions of biblical stories and issues. So perhaps there is a way of refashioning biblical material within other programming genres.

As a freelance producer, is there a project you'd still like to do?
RB: I'm still preoccupied with the Jesus story and how we can explore that in new ways. I'm particularly keen to look at the trials and hearings of Jesus. Can we get a better understanding of why Jesus was crucified? It's all very well saying 'Well, he was a blasphemer', but I think we need to know more about the political context. That's not to say it hasn't been done before, but I think the more information we get, the better.

Chapter 4

THE STORY OF LUMO

David Batty

It all began with a phone call. In late 2008, I was producing a very pressured history series for Channel 4 with multiple celebrity presenters and film crews all over the world and as always never enough money to do what we really wanted to … when I heard some magic words being shouted at me across our chaotic office. 'There's a film producer who wants to talk to David'.

For battling producer/directors like me, the words 'film' and 'producer' in the same sentence are like manna from heaven; and all time stops. So I took the call. 'My name is Hannah Leader. I'm a film producer', she said. 'I'd like to film the Bible and I'd like you to do it'. 'Errr, which bits do you want me to film?', I asked, trying to buy time while I very quickly had to decide whether this was a crank call or not. 'All of it', said Hannah. Gulp. 'We can start with the Four Gospels'. And so began what was later called The Lumo Project ('Lumo' is close to the Latin word for Light but also apparently means 'charm' in Finnish!), an ambitious project to turn the four Gospels – Matthew, Mark, Luke and John – into four stand-alone feature films that could be viewed in the cinema, on TV, on iPads, smart-phones and all the other devices people use to access media these days. It was to take up almost six years of my life and still occupies a good part of my time today as we continue to post produce the films and create more and more language versions.

Lumo is the brainchild of the brilliant Hannah Leader. No crank she. Far from it. As I quickly discovered she's an extremely talented and experienced film producer with a host of major credits to her name (including *Gosford Park, Lucky Number Slevin,* and *Five Children and It*). She is also a practicing Christian and one day when she was trying to prepare some visual material for a Sunday School class she had an epiphany. She wanted her children to experience the Bible for real. All the filmed material she found was so bad and old fashioned and inappropriate that it convinced her to use her professional skills to create better material. Why didn't she film the Bible with all the resources, skills and people she might use for any other commissioned film script? So she called me!

Our first problem, as with any independent production, was money: how to finance the filming of four feature films – and they would be long feature films. If you read the four Gospels out loud and then leave appropriate pauses for dramatic effect, Mark comes in at about two hours whereas John is two hours 40 mins, Luke three hours and 20 mins and Matthew (perhaps surprisingly) the longest at almost four hours. That is roughly 12 hours of finished film, which is an awful lot to shoot and to finance. Just to put that in perspective, that is very close to the length of Peter Jackson's Hobbit trilogy whose budget was almost half a billion dollars. Ours, while still very generous, was slightly less at just $5 million. Even with this relatively modest figure, Hannah had a major battle to finance the project. In the end a wealthy American Christian family – the Greens of Hobby-Lobby fame – came to our rescue and funded the entire project; and most wonderfully they have by and large left us to get on with it, trusting our creative vision.

Lots of people often ask, Why bother? You have the book already, why not just read it and enjoy it like that. My answer is simple. The earliest versions of the gospels – Mark, Matthew and Luke – were thought to have been first written down in the mid- to late first century and John in the late first century or early second century. If you look beyond that, they were all originally oral gospels, spoken or rather probably performed before live audiences and passed down by word of mouth. That was their original purpose – as performances, not just to be read but experienced in the raw. So in a way a film is just helping us return to one of the ways the gospels were first encountered by people almost 2000 years ago but using the latest digital technology.

Hannah's original creative brief to me was very simple. 'Make it real', she said. So I did. The basic idea of the project was to dramatize the four gospels using the original 2000-year-old texts as our script. Unedited. Word for word. The end product would be a complete dramatized film, but with the biblical text read out by a famous voice – we have already used people like David Harewood (he was the head of the CIA in the hit

TV series *Homeland*), Richard E. Grant (of recent *Downton Abbey* fame), Brian Cox (*Bourne Ultimatum* and *X-Men*), the amazing Derek Jacobi, Rupert Penry-Jones (*Silk*, *Whitechapel* and *Spooks*) and the ubiquitous Tim Pigott-Smith.

Beyond that we wanted to transport our audience back 2000 years and immerse them in the world of first-century Palestine so that they felt they were one of Jesus's disciples, or a member of the crowd as he performed his famous ministry. As far as possible we wanted the films to feel like unfolding real-life fly-on-the-wall documentaries. Our first decision was where to film it. Of course, the obvious place would be modern-day Israel/Palestine itself, although most films are rarely filmed in the locations they are set for all sorts of practical reasons – cost, access, climate and politics. I have filmed many times in Israel/Palestine and while I love the region and its people, it is not the easiest of places to film because of its politics. Trouble can break out in an instant with violent riots and road closures. In addition most of the key locations are now 'spoilt' with modern intrusions – tarmac roads, electricity pylons and a particularly large wall. So unfortunately Israel/Palestine was out. Then there is Tunisia – very similar landscape, a small film industry and a tradition of biblical films being shot there, probably most famously Monty Python's *Life of Brian*. And in fact it was for that reason that I decided against it. Although I loved that film, I did not want ours to be compared to it in any way, for obvious reasons. And finally there was Morocco. Again very similar landscape, a sophisticated local film industry and a long tradition of filming biblical and other Hollywood epics, including *Lawrence of Arabia*, *Kingdom of Heaven*, *Troy* and *Alexander*.

The centre of Morocco's film industry lies in the middle of the desert about three very bumpy, scary hours in a car from Marrakesh over the Atlas Mountains. The small town of Ouarzazate – or, as the Americans rather arrogantly like to call it, 'where is that?' – is North Africa's equivalent of Hollywood, and hundreds of big American names have filmed there. On the outskirts of town, there is a hotel attached to one of the big studios that has a wallchart with all of the films, along with their stars and directors, that have been shot in Ouarzazate over the years, providing a chance to get your name among the roll of honour. The list includes: Michael Douglas and Kathleen Turner in *The Jewel of the Nile*, Timothy Dalton as James Bond in *The Living Daylights*, Halle Berry, Jean-Claud Van Damme, Russell Crowe, Richard Harris, Orlando Bloom, Martin Scorsese … and David Betty – my one big chance of glory and they spelt my name incorrectly!

Ourazazate is full of elaborate movie sets that have been built and added to over the years for the various productions and then just left in the sand – as land is so cheap there. So you, or rather we, could simply turn up years later and rent them for our production. For example there were three different sets for ancient Jewish Jerusalem, including the huge one built by Ridley Scott for *Kingdom of Heaven* and recently re-used for both HBO's *Game of Thrones* and the BBC's *Atlantis* series, plus also sets for Bethlehem, Nazareth and Capernaum. And if the sets weren't right you could rent whole ancient villages by the day. They are all built of stone and mud and basic thatch, just like they would have been in first-century Palestine, and the locals were generally very happy to temporarily move out … for the right price, of course. The surrounding landscape was also perfect with sheep-filled rolling hills, small fields and plenty of date palms; there was even a lake for the Galilee scenes. Morocco also has a large pool of professional film-making and acting talent that we could draw on. So it was perfect for us.

My background is as a documentary film-maker. I cut my teeth working on a Channel 4 series in the 1980s and early '90s called *Cutting Edge* where we made fly-on-the-wall films about ordinary people in extraordinary situations. My approach to filming the gospels wasn't much different, except that this was a film about extraordinary people in ordinary situations. So what I tried to do is to place the audience in amongst the action as if they were a member of the crowd, or a disciple or a close onlooker, and treat it like an unfolding documentary.

Another key factor that helped us to decide on Morocco was teeth … I knew we would need to use a lot of extras for all the street scenes in Jerusalem, shots of Jesus preaching to crowds, and classic scenes such as the feeding of the 5000 and the Sermon on the Mount. Morocco has lots of willing extras and they have loads of experience and most importantly – if you are trying to create the look of first-century Jewish peasants – they largely have rotten teeth. So they immediately look the part without the need for much elaborate make up.

That brings up another question I am often asked – if you filmed in Morocco, how did you cast everyone, Jesus, the disciples, the Pharisees and all the other hundreds of characters? The answer is that everyone – bar Jesus – was cast in Morocco, so is Moroccan and Muslim. We just could not afford to cast everyone in the UK and fly them in every time we needed to film a new scene. And in any case, in my personal view that is wrong – and something that is frequently wrong with other films made about the Bible or Jesus. First-century Palestine was not full of fair-skinned, blue-eyed Europeans … but olive-skinned Jews. And if you look at most Moroccans they bear a very close resemblance to what most historians now believe Jesus and his followers and the people of first-century Palestine probably looked like. The only exception to this was the part of Jesus himself. I did try to find someone in Morocco, but no one really fitted the bill. I also realized that as Jesus was so obviously crucial to the story, I would need to have perfect communication with him in terms of being able to direct and advise him about his performance. My French is pretty schoolboy and my Arabic is nil so it seemed wise that of all our actors, Jesus at least should be British. The person we chose is actually of half-Tamil origin – the brilliant Selva Rasalingham. And, as you will see, language differences were actually an advantage.

There have, of course, been hundreds of screen Jesuses over the years and I looked at as many as I could in order to try and get the right look and feel for our Jesus. In 1961, Jeffrey Hunter played him in *King of Kings* as a strawberry-blond blue-eyed Californian teenager. In 1965, Max von Sydow in *The Greatest Story Ever Told* was a Germanic accented European – and rather boring – Jesus. In 1973, Ted Neeley gave us the rock star Jesus in the musical *Jesus Christ Superstar*. In 1977, Robert Powell was – for me – too ethereal, humourless and had very creepy eyes in his *Jesus of Nazareth*. In the *Jesus Project* (1979) it was the turn of the overly caucasian Brian Deacon. In 1988, a young Willem Dafoe starred in the controversial *The Last Temptation of Christ*, a bold attempt to give a more human, morally conflicted Jesus that seemed totally to ignore his divine nature. In the 1999 miniseries 'Jesus', the lead was played by the ridiculously blow-dried Jeremy Sisto.[1] More recently, in 2004, Jim Caviziel could only scream in agony as he played the tortured Jesus in Mel Gibson's *The Passion of the Christ*. And then, finally, in 2013, we had Diego Morgado in the blockbuster *The Bible* TV miniseries, in which we return to classic Hollywood, all dreamy and model looks. For me, the one Jesus missing from this long list was the first-century Jesus, so with Selva signed up I felt we had a chance to do something different and to try and turn the clock back to a more authentic historical Jesus.

Our casting process was very interesting. As I have already said, I was looking for a more authentic first-century Jesus, so no blond blue-eyed caucasians. Selva's part-Tamil background gives him dark hair and olive coloured skin. It means he is often – somewhat frustratingly and waste-fully I feel- cast as the 'baddie' in British dramas, frequently playing terrorists and suicide bombers. Beyond look, I also wanted a Jesus with real presence so that every time he walked onto set you would immediately know who he was. Selva is a brilliant screen actor, with a keen awareness of the camera and how to act to it. He's also a big man and stood head

---

1. On this, see http://www.imdb.com/title/tt0199232/?ref_=nm_flmg_act_66.

and shoulders above the rest of our cast. Also interestingly – and I have to admit that it was chance not design – he stood out because he was the only non-Moroccan in our cast. As a result everyone – especially cast and extras – treated him slightly differently, with a mixture of respect and slight unease as if they were not quite sure what he might do next, and the lack of a shared language exacerbated all of this – which is exactly how I imagined Jesus would have been treated 2000 years ago. Everything I have read about the period told me that Jesus was different. He did things differently. He spoke in parables. He confronted the unconfrontable. He healed people and performed many miracles; so he must have been a slightly frightening and unsettling person to be around.

Selva also very cleverly provided a solution to another big problem we had – language. Although there was no scripted dialogue as such we still had to allow the actors to speak to each other, to act out the various scenes as they happened and to use a language to do this. We knew that it could not be any identifiable modern language, as that would break the spell we were trying to cast. It was also too complicated to have everyone learn the actual language Jesus used – Aramaic – so in the end we created our own. It has Aramaic sounding phrases in it, and wherever actual Aramaic words occurred in the Bible – such as on the cross where Jesus says *Eloi, Eloi lama sabachthani* (My God, My God, why have you forsaken me?) – Selva actually speaks these words. But the rest of the time it is completely made up. What is slightly ironic and amusing is that we've had many theological and historical experts check the film for us for authenticity and many of them, at the first viewing, think he is actually speaking Aramaic, which is of course just what I hoped. Selva was brilliant at doing this. He would take a speech in English, learn it and then transform it into his language and then perform it. And his real skill would show when I asked him to repeat a scene for a different angle or a change of camera lens and he would say the exact same made-up phrases. Word for word. That meant when we came to edit it we were able to sync his made-up language with the English voice-over.

Final proof of his skill – if it be needed – came at the party to celebrate the end of the shoot where we were all presented with mock-up Oscars from Hannah for our five years of hard work, and so of course we each had to make an acceptance speech. When Selva stepped up to the microphone he did a five minute speech, complete with all the appropriate 'thank yous' and emotional dedications in pure Jesus gobbledygook ... and we all knew exactly what he was saying. It was extremely funny.

As I have said, one of our key aims was historical accuracy. It was a very difficult aim – and I am sure we will have made some mistakes for which I apologise! – but we tried to be as accurate as we could in creating a first-century world. We were lucky enough to have access to the world of biblical scholarship either through contacts I had made via the many documentaries I have directed over the years or via our historical consultant Ray Bruce's fabulous contacts, particularly in the archaeological community. I also read very widely, and some of the most helpful books include Ed Adams's fantastic *Parallel Lives of Jesus: A Narrative-Critical Guide to the Four Gospels*, which helped me navigate the differences and similarities between the four gospels (and, crucially, the reasons for them), and gave me my filming mantra – 'four gospels, four writers, one life', along with the idea that you could have four different perspectives on a single life[2]. Helen Bond's *The Historical Jesus* in the 'Guides for the Perplexed' series – which I certainly was at times! – was also hugely helpful,[3] as were her wonderfully detailed and comprehensive studies on Pilate and Caiaphas (*Pontius Pilate in History and Interpretation* and *Caiaphas: Friend of Rome and Judge of Jesus?*)[4]. I have always enjoyed Geza Vermes's writings and in particular his thought-provoking *The Changing Faces of Jesus* for the wide variety of portrayals of Jesus both within the Bible and outside.[5] I also liked Bruce Chilton's *Rabbi Jesus*, which reads more like a novel and helped transport me back;[6] Burton L. Mack's *The Lost Gospel*, as an introduction to the Q debate, the origins of the gospels and their oral roots;[7] E. P. Sanders's *The Historical Figure of Jesus* and Ben Witherington's *The Jesus Quest* provide two differing views on the historical Jesus;[8] and Joan Taylor's brilliant – and wonderfully readable – biography of John the Baptist for all the detail of John's life, his battle with the authorities and the sheer

2. Edward Adams, *Parallel Lives of Jesus: A Narrative-Critical Guide to the Four Gospels* (London: SPCK, 2011).

3. Helen K. Bond, *The Historical Jesus: A Guide for the Perplexed* (London: Bloomsbury, 2012).

4. Helen K. Bond, *Pontius Pilate in History and Interpretation* (Cambridge: Cambridge University Press, 1998), and *Caiaphas: Friend of Rome and Judge of Jesus?* (Louisville, KY: Westminster John Knox, 2004).

5. Geza Vermes, *The Changing Faces of Jesus*, new edn (London: Penguin, 2001).

6. Bruce Chilton, *Rabbi Jesus: An Intimate Biography* (New York: Doubleday, 2000).

7. Burton L. Mack, *The Lost Gospel: The Book of Q and Christian Origins* (New York: Harper Collins, 1993).

8. E. P. Sanders, *The Historical Figure of Jesus* (London: Penguin, 1993); Ben Witherington, *The Jesus Quest: The Third Search for the Jew of Nazareth* (Carlisle: Paternoster, 1995).

detail of life in first-century Palestine;[9] John J. Rousseau and Rami
Arav's *Jesus and his World* was also great to dip into for archaeological
details to help us construct our scenes and sets.[10] Constant companions
which I frequently consulted were *Harper's Encylcopedia of Bible Life*
by Madeleine and Lane Miller and *Eerdman's Commentary on the Bible*
by James D. G Dunn and John W. Rogerson[11]. I also always of course
carried on set a copy of the script with me: the NIV version of the Bible
(the NIV was the first version we produced, although ultimately we will
produce it in other versions too). I have been lucky enough to work on
many Jesus documentaries which involved filming in Israel and Palestine
and there is no real substitute for experiencing the actual locations and
talking to people on the ground involved in the continuing research into
the archaeology of the Jesus story. In particular I have worked a lot with
Shimon Gibson (*Final Days of Jesus* and *The Cave of John the Baptist*),[12]
who is based in Jerusalem and is always at the cutting edge of research
there and finding new and amazing locations connected to the Jesus story.
I will never forget walking – very gingerly – through an old minefield
led by Shimon as he took us to the location of Aenon on the old Israeli/
Jordan border.

Four Stories, One Life

One question I am frequently asked is, How do you film the four stories?
They are all about basically the same thing – the life of Jesus – so do you
combine them all together into one story, that is, unify them into a single
narrative, or do you film them completely separately? For me the answer
is that they are the same story only told slightly differently, from four
different perspectives, four different angles if you like. They generally
have the same basic ingredients about the birth, life, death and resurrection of Jesus – with some crucial exceptions of course – albeit shuffled
and re-ordered according to the point of view of the four storytellers. I

9. Joan E. Taylor, *The Immerser: John the Baptist within Second Temple Judaism*
(Grand Rapids: Eerdmans, 1997).

10. John J. Rousseau and Rami Arav, *Jesus and his World: An Archaeological and
Cultural Dictionary* (Minneapolis: Fortress, 1995).

11. Madeleine S. Miller and J. Lane Miller, *Harper's Encyclopedia of the Bible*,
2nd rev. edn (Auckland: Castle Books, 2004); James D. G Dunn and John W.
Rogerson, *Eerdman's Commentary on the Bible* (Grand Rapids: Eerdmans, 2003).

12. Shimon Gibson, *The Final Days of Jesus: The Archaeological Evidence* (New
York: Harper Collins, 2009) and *The Cave of John the Baptist* (London: Arrow, 2004).

always think of it as four writers, four narratives ... but one life. So we filmed one story but ensured that wherever there was a different interpretation of a particular event we reflected this in our coverage by slightly altering the camera angle or the way we edited the story.

Each narrative shares a common story but is told in a unique fashion. Each writer has a different take on the key moments in Jesus' life, producing clear differences in emphasis and tone that contribute to four distinct views of one life. So each of our films has a distinct difference in tone, storytelling and look. In Mark, we see the action-packed, fast-paced story of a miracle worker, crucified for his beliefs. In Matthew, we follow an Old Testament prophet who teaches in riddles and parables as he fulfils the ancient prophecies and brings salvation to his people. In Luke, we feature the story of a first-century Gandhi, out to bring peace and healing to the world as he journeys to his eventual doom in Jerusalem. And finally in John we find the most profound and complex character-study of Jesus as he battles with the forces of evil out to deny him his rightful crown.

Of all the Gospels, it is John's that for me stands out as the most modern filmic version of Jesus' life. It was the most exciting and enjoyable to turn into a film in which Jesus's character, his life story, his battle with the forces of evil and eventual 'triumph' unfolds in a very dramatic and filmic fashion. It is a very intimate Gospel, and by that I feel that you are always 'inside' Jesus's head as his story unfolds.

There are lots of problems in filming the Gospels as we did. For a start, we couldn't change the basic script. As I said at the beginning, the intention was to film it word-for-word so I couldn't alter or omit any of those words. But also there are very few stage directions as to where, when and how things actually happened. Take a scene like Jn 3:1-21 where a Pharisee, Nicodemus, meets Jesus and questions his teaching. It is a classic episode where Jesus encounters one of his 'enemies' who violently oppose his ministry and eventually conspire to have him arrested and executed. All we know is that the meeting took place at night and that probably only Jesus and Nicodemus were present as no one else is mentioned in the text. But that's it. So when we sat down and discussed how we might film it we firstly looked at what had just happened in the previous scene – Jesus had gone to Jerusalem at the Passover, the busiest time of the Jewish year, when everyone is in Jerusalem and had walked into the temple, the centre of Jewish life, and caused a huge ruckus by turning over the tables of the money changers, a direct challenge to the authority of the Jewish leaders and making him a marked man. So it seemed possible that he might be hiding out, lying low for a while until tempers calmed down. This is why we set it inside, and also why there is a clear sense of tension between him and Nicodemus. We choreographed a scene in which two potential enemies circle round each other as they try to find out what makes the other tick. Then we tried to imagine what might have gone on when they met: what would first-century Jews have done in such situations? First and foremost you would always offer a stranger water to wash with. Jews were very strict on this ritual cleansing with its overtones of hospitality. And similarly it would be normal to offer a guest something to drink and eat. So with these extra elements we now had a visual story to integrate into the spoken script. And of course water, wine and breaking bread are hugely symbolic in a Christian context. We hoped that all this would combine to make the episode come to life in a new way, and bring a new perspective on the written word.

Another example also comes from the Gospel of John. In 6:25-59, we have one of the famous 'I am' sayings in which Jesus utters the immortal line, 'I am the bread of life'. Again the text is quite sparing as to its stage directions. At the start of the extract, it says that people find Jesus on the other side of the lake, and at the end it states 'he said this while teaching in the synagogue in Capernaum', but it is not clear how much of the previous speech was said in the synagogue or even what happens between the lake and the synagogue. So again we decided to do something slightly different. If you look at what has just come before – the feeding of the 5000 where Jesus performs a miracle to feed the huge crowd following him – and then read the following nine verses, you get a sense that Jesus is becoming increasingly frustrated at people's repeated inability to understand the real point about the bread. They cannot see that it is not just a case of him performing a miracle to produce food every time people are physically hungry, but rather that the bread has a higher symbolic spiritual significance as the spiritual nourishment that people will get by following him. This is the reason why he calls himself 'the bread of life'. So I decided to film the text in a less passive way (as in more traditional interpretations) and allow Jesus some human emotion, some frustration and even anger at people's continued blindness to his real message. So we created a sort of bread riot in which Jesus flings loaves of bread at his followers in an effort to make them realise the true sense of his message. We then calmed the situation down again by having him meet a beggar in the midst of all the chaos and have him – who normally goes hungry and thirsty – be the only one who really listens and understands Jesus. Again I hope it makes for a powerful moment and a chance to look at the text in a slightly different way.

Another example comes in the Mk 3:20-34, an episode often titled 'Jesus Accused by His Family and by Teachers of the Law'. Again the only 'stage directions' we are given are that Jesus entered a house and that a crowd gathered. But a little later in the text it says that the teachers of Law say 'By the prince of demons he is driving out demons!'. So to illustrate this I had Jesus in the courtyard of a house, rather than inside the house, and had him healing a demon-possessed man, that is, 'driving out a demon', with the teachers of the Law watching and complaining from the side lines. All in all, this makes for a more dynamic sequence – I hope – rather than just having Jesus and the teachers in another stand up confrontation.

As a film-maker, I am clearly making a statement as to my personal interpretation of Jesus as a character and how I feel he comes across to me in the text. Not for me the Jesus who is always standing in front of a crowd preaching. I have always felt that was too passive and uninspiring, and that whilst he did often preach in this traditional fashion, he also taught 'on the move' as he travelled through the markets and meeting places of Galilee and Judaea. For me, he was never the distant figure of authority preaching from on high, but would always prefer to get in amongst the people to touch them, hear them, feel their problems literally at first hand, and then to heal them. So when we filmed the Sermon on the Mount, for example, we might have started with Jesus preaching from a rock, but he soon dived into the multitude; and then I believe the text takes on a whole new dynamic.

I also have a personal theory about the parables and other elements of Jesus' more symbolic teaching. First-century Palestine was an agricultural society with the large majority of people living in small villages and surviving off the land in some form or other. Cities like Jerusalem, although very significant, were small in number and were places the majority only visited occasionally. Jesus's teaching – especially the parables – are full of references to this simple rural lifestyle and the characters that peopled it. Having gone through the process of trying to imagine the Gospels and how to film them as realistically as possible, I am absolutely convinced that Jesus got his inspiration from the people he met in the villages and towns and on the roads he walked, and that he then used these people to illustrate his teachings. So, where we could, we would try and show this by having Jesus walk through – for example – a crowded market square and see a woman buying something with a coin, only to cut to the parable of the lost coin, in which she plays the starring role. For me this was also part of the power behind Jesus's teaching for the people at the time –

and possibly why 2000 years later we still struggle to understand all its subtleties – in that he was drawing on real-life first-century episodes to illustrate his words.

This brings me onto another major point which Selva and I were constantly debating and refining: the real character of Jesus and the conflict within him of his divine and human natures. Whatever one's personal beliefs, there seems little doubt that someone called Jesus lived in Galilee and Judaea 2000 years ago. Whether you believe he was the Messiah and the Son of God, he was almost certainly a flesh and blood man, with parents and brothers and sisters. And so I – we – strongly believed that he had emotions, that he could be happy, sad, excited, tired, calm and angry, and all the others too. So we tried to build these types of human emotional reactions into our story, not to downplay or deny his divine nature but to complement it and make Jesus the extraordinarily complicated character he clearly was. Ours is definitely not a laid-back, ethereal Jesus of Robert Powell, but I hope he is closer to the real first-century Palestinian Jesus.

These films were shot over a five-year period. This was not completely out of choice, although we always knew it would take a long time and multiple trips back to Morocco, but we ran out of money on several occasions so filming had to be suspended while the finances were sorted out. The four films eventually took a hundred filming days to complete, and the main cast was well over 50 actors along with in excess of 2000 extras used over that five-year period. The long schedule brought its own set of problems, not least the fluctuating length of people's hair and beards; but then I guess Jesus's life and ministry spanned several years, and he and his disciples did not have the luxury of regular visits to the barbers.

Despite most people's illusions about the glamorous world of film-making, Lumo was at times a real ordeal. It was incredibly hot in Morocco, upwards of 40 degrees Celsius every day, often more than that, and when you are in confined spaces with lights and cameras all belting out heat it was frequently almost unbearable. Our days were often very long: up before the sun and finishing when it set – which in Morocco could mean 14 hours straight. We also faced the problem of extreme dust, a nightmare for camera equipment and humans alike. The slightest wind would blow up a sand storm that would cover all of us and all of the equipment, too, and get inside everything, including your throat and nose, which could be very unpleasant. We drank huge amounts of water – and I mean *huge*. My Director of Photography, cameraman Ben, used to take the bottle tops of each bottle of water and put them in his pocket so he could keep a tab on how much he drank. One day he counted 24, which is 12 litres of water in 12 hours, four times the normal amount.

Other problems included regular bouts of food poisoning, packs of feral dogs that stalked around our locations (as wherever there are film crews there is always a great deal of food) and flash floods that swept away some of our sets. It doesn't rain very often in Ouarzazate, but when it does it is biblical in its intensity. We also once faced a mutiny from a local village that entailed a large group of young men waving flags marching into the middle of our set – in this instance a wooden foot bridge over a river – sitting down and refusing to move until someone paid them some money. What had happened was that, although we had negotiated access to the owners of this bridge via the headman of the local village, he had rather 'absent mindedly' (or so he told us) forgotten to pay everyone off. The mutinous crowd were threatening to lynch him, but our very smiley handsome location manager – who all the British women on set promptly nicknamed George Clooney – stepped in and smoothed tempers, paid some more money and filming was allowed to continue.

By the end we had a large and extremely professional Moroccan production crew, all of whom were far more experienced than us (having worked on numerous large-scale Hollywood productions), lorded over by our wonderful Moroccan line producer, Hamid Herraf. But it wasn't always so. In the very early days, before we had become Moroccan veterans, we had a very different local producer who turned out to be a fraud and a gangster, intent only on fleecing us of as much money as possible. One day he brought the entire film shoot to a halt, forcing all the Moroccan crew and cast to go on strike (against their better judgment as we later found out), claiming that we owed him money (we didn't). When he was finally rumbled and summarily sacked by Hannah, for some reason he blamed me. A few days later, when I was walking outside our hotel, he spotted me and proceeded to try and run me over in his large 4 × 4. Luckily I was carrying a heavy tripod and managed to swipe his car door with it and avert a nasty 'accident'. He was reported to the Moroccan Film Minister and I am glad to say his licence to produce was revoked.

There were other more 'normal' film crew accidents. On the first shoot, on one of our days off, the twelve disciples were all mucking about round the hotel pool when Judas was 'accidentally' – some might think 'deliberately' – knocked over and broke his ankle. So for the last three days of that shoot whenever Judas was needed on set he had to be parked at the back of the group of disciples propped up by Thomas and Matthew!

A frequent shout on any interior set was 'more smoke, more smoke' … the theory being that smoke adds atmosphere to any set by diffusing the light. Normally in the UK you would have a special smoke machine that is (a) very safe, (b) non-toxic and (c) works all the time. But being Morocco they just either burnt incense or had real smoky fires. Both do the same job, but with added risk and unpleasantness for the cast and crew. So one day as we were filming the final part of the Last Supper, I yelled as always 'more smoke, more smoke' and indeed more smoke appeared, so much so that we had to run outside as we realized the set was actually on fire. Everyone got out safely and then the studio fire brigade arrived with a ca. 1930s fire engine complete with brass bell, wooden ladder and leaky canvas hose. It looked like a prop for a film, and probably was. The fire was luckily relatively small and was eventually put out with the crew's drinking water.

One trip we had our cameras impounded as the second unit camera man forgot his paperwork, but being Morocco as long as you knew the right people – and we did by this stage – we could get it out of customs after only a couple of days' delay. A few days later the same crew member broke the camera truck's front axle on a bumpy track, but again Morocco came to the rescue and all the camera gear was transferred to a huge cattle truck and filming continued.

Another day it got so hot on one set that we literally cooked the camera by burning out its electrics, which blew and stopped working. It was actually when we were filming the Nicodemus scene I mentioned earlier. These cameras cost upwards of £50,000 each. Luckily we always had two of them with us in case of accidents and we were near the end of that shoot, so at least no real damage was done to the schedule.

All the storm scenes (walking on water and calming the storm) were shot on the southern Moroccan coast as our Lake Galilee was too placid. This involved moving our entire crew (upwards of a hundred people) one hundred miles south to a beach near Agadir by truck and car, the only time we really left Ouarzazate. It meant these – although quite short – were easily the most expensive scenes to shoot; but they had to be done. They were also shot at night, which adds to the complications and the dangers. Just as we were finishing filming the scene of Jesus calming the storm, we had a wind machine explode. It was a wonderful bit of Moroccan ramshackle Heath Robinson jerry building, with an old aircraft propeller welded onto a car engine with a wire cage around it for some sort of safety. Again, thankfully, no one was hurt and we had finished filming, but it didn't half make a big bang.

There were hundreds of weird and surreal moments. For example, when we filmed the crucifixion we had to have Selva 'fitted' for Jesus's cross so that he could comfortably stay upright in the crucifixion position for the hours it would take to film him. I can now tell you that it involved a small bicycle seat covered in soft fur. But, at the time, rather than being amusing it simply brought home what a truly brutal and terrifying death that must have been.

When Jesus is crucified he is placed between two thieves also on crosses. Our two thieves were local extras as little real acting was involved. As with almost every man in Morocco they were smokers and between each take their cigarettes would miraculously appear, having been hidden away in their cloth nappies. They would puff merrily away, legs crossed, waiting for me to shout action again. It was almost Monty Python.

Our John the Baptist actor – who was a brilliant actor by the way and looked just as I imagined 'John the B' to look like – turned out to be the Oliver Reed of Ourazazate in that he liked a drink or two or ten and could get quite rowdy with it. He was never drunk on set, but I was told there was always a chance he might not make it back in one piece after a day off. All was fine until the final shoot when we wanted to redo a couple of his scenes, only to discover that in the intervening weeks he had been involved in a huge bar fight and was currently lounging at his Moroccan Majesty's pleasure in the Ourazazate jail! In terms of what actually happened to John when Herod threw him into prison, it was weirdly appropriate – and at least ours didn't have his head cut off.

Animals appear regularly in the gospel stories. Have you ever tried to direct a flock of Moroccan sheep or get doves to fly in the right direction? It's not easy … While shooting the Nativity I discovered just how smelly and obstinate camels can be; and I never want to see another Gadarene swine. And when we filmed the triumphal entry into Jerusalem, the first time Jesus got on his donkey it was most definitely not very triumphant as he promptly fell off. We also had to find an extra large donkey so that Selva's long legs did not drag comically in the dust.

And that brings me on to miracles and how you film them. For me, not a regular church goer and a fringe Christian at best, it is miracles and how they are portrayed and used (and sometimes abused) that causes problems. In our mission to make this as authentic as possible, I wanted to leave the notion of miracles as ambivalent and ambiguous as I could to allow the audience to make up their own minds as to what exactly took place. Miracles are mentioned so often and with such passion that something extraordinary clearly happened, but we can argue and debate forever exactly what. For me, what was more important than the actual moment of the miracle was its effect on the people around Jesus, both the person being healed and those watching. So our simple way to portray miracles was, wherever possible, to play them out in the eyes of the beholder. In that sense we may stop being obsessed with the actual miracle itself – and Hollywood's usually failed attempts at clever digital trickery – and concentrate more on its consequences.

Perhaps the biggest question I am asked by Christians who have seen this film – especially Evangelical Christians – is why didn't I cast Christians in all the parts? Surely it is wrong to have non-Christians playing Jesus and his disciples and all the other parts? Wouldn't a completely Christian cast give a deeper understanding to the story? My answer is always an emphatic No'. Put aside the practical financial reasons that we could not afford to fly in a Christian cast from the UK, and that there just are not enough Christian actors and extras in Morocco. There is a much more profound reason here. Jesus was not a Christian. The word Christian describing a new religion based around the teachings of Jesus did not come in until a long time after Jesus' death. Throughout his life on earth Jesus was a Jew, as were all of his followers and all of the people in that first-century world, except of course the Samaritans and the Romans. So if we are being truly accurate on that front all the cast should actually be Jewish or Roman or Samaritan, which is of course faintly ridiculous and missing the point.

What matters is the cast's acting ability and how they perform the various scenes. The fact that they do not know or understand the full story until they encounter it and have to try and make sense of it, just as the people at the time did, can actually be a bonus in terms of getting the right performance out of them. And I can tell you, from filming with all these Moroccan actors and extras over the last five years, that the large majority of them have been on multiple biblical films of one sort or another and are hugely knowledgeable about the subject and would often make great suggestions about how to film things. So I for one have never bought that argument about the need for a wholly Christian cast.

So, to summarize, we have produced a series of four films, one for each gospel. The Gospel of John has already been released on Netflix in the US and on the BBC in the UK. It will be followed by Luke, then probably Mark, and finally Matthew over the next 18 months or so. The producers' intention is initially to release two versions of each – the New International Version and the King James Version, but later down the line we will release other versions and crucially in other languages too. The joy of this is that we can lay any version we like into the film. From Spanish to Swahili, from Chinese to Russian, from Korean to Hindi. Any language. Any version. And eventually, once the producers have recouped some of the money it took to make it, they have said they will release it for free on a new app called YouVersion. Based on the online Bible, YouVersion is a free mobile Bible that can be installed on almost any phone and has hundreds of different versions to choose from. Our Bible films will eventually provide users of that app with a visual version; and it will be completely free. To date, the app has been downloaded by over 140 million people and the Greens are hoping our films will be viewed by as many people as the famous 'Jesus film' made in 1979, which the New York Times now claims is the most watched film in history.[13] So if we are only half as successful in terms of viewers, it will be a massive achievement in terms of raising biblical literacy.

13. On this film, see https://en.wikipedia.org/wiki/Jesus_(1979_film).

Chapter 5

SCHOLARS WORKING IN TELEVISION: SOME PERSONAL REFLECTIONS AND ADVICE

Joan E. Taylor

A long time ago, when I had finished my first degree at Auckland University and wondered what I should do with my life, I got a job at New Zealand's foremost film company: the New Zealand National Film Unit (NFU), as it was then. This was a government-sponsored production company making short documentaries, primarily for movie theatres, at a time short films were often shown ahead of the main feature, and the NFU also made films for TV on subjects of New Zealand life and history. I was sent on a television and film production short course, and was moved around into different areas of production, learning various skills, mainly film editing, though I was based in the stock footage library (supplying material to advertisers, as well as to documentary and movie makers).

As part of my training I had the opportunity to do some pieces of writing, and this led to one of the directors asking me to write the narration for a half-hour documentary. He had his own rough script to which the film had been cut, but he needed the narration (voice over) written properly, and he said that I had a nice voice and could read it in the sound box when I had finished, and he'd see how that went. It was quite frightening. Here I was, given such a fantastic job at a young age, and it seemed that if they liked my script and my voice maybe it would mean they would keep both on the finished documentary.

I worked hard to translate the director's notes and match my script with the film with the right timing for each scene. I recorded the narration in the sound box as required, and then I waited for the director's verdict.

It was quite slow in coming, but finally he said that he liked what I had done but he had a few changes after viewing it with his consultant audience. I was anxious – did he want me to make the changes, did he want me to re-record the narration?

A week later I discovered that my narration over the rough cut was a stage in the process, and the narration had been done, after some editing, by Dougal Stevenson, New Zealand's foremost newsreader, using a modified script from the one I had prepared. When I eventually saw the film, I listened to an authoritative male voice, and in the credits I was not listed.

How did I react? I felt slightly embarrassed, and stupid, to think that I had imagined that the director might even remotely have thought I could read the narration. It was a misunderstanding. He'd given me an opportunity, and my voice was used just to get a sense of how the narration sounded, for timing and content, and for screening it to the consultants. Why would anyone credit a production trainee, or want the voice of a young woman, for that matter? I did not have gravitas.

Now, very many years later, this story makes me reflect on what it means for me to be classified as an authority in a way that my voice is useful in documentaries, but Dougal Stevenson's newsreader voice echoes in countless documentaries to this day.[1] There are still not enough women narrators in documentaries, or women shown as experts in those that we see. When we do appear, television favours younger women.

Gender and Television

The question that arises for me then is how women can be shown as experts – with gravitas – in a way that would be equivalent in weightiness to those (men) deemed authoritative, and yet also be – fundamentally – *ourselves*. Authority is often linked up with a certain masculine bearing. How do we do it? The BBC news anchor Fiona Bruce and women journalists and actors have cultivated something of the smooth and weighty voice, for their voice-over work. I notice it involves low tones, and a certain steady intonation that is close to masculine. I suspect that I have learnt in academic environments to do the same thing with my voice, since the field of Biblical Studies and early Christian history remains male-dominated: the issue remains one of gravitas.

1. Interestingly, he is deemed 'the voice of authority' by Keith Sharp in the New Zealand TV Guide, http://www.stuff.co.nz/entertainment/tv-radio/8736149/Dougal-Stevenson-The-voice-of-authority.

This is quite important, in that I have noticed that some men are particularly sensitised to a type of woman's voice that they find irritating. In my experience, I have never heard a woman complain that a man's voice is irritating. At a British New Testament Conference a few years ago, a senior male biblical scholar commented in session about annoying high-pitched – 'shrill' – women's voices saying the liturgy in church. The higher the pitch, apparently, the more irritating our voices might be to male ears. Thus, the Fiona Bruces go for low, steady and mellow, and get work as narrators in documentaries. In the US, Signourney Weaver's voice has been chosen for a number of nature-oriented documentaries.[2]

In terms of presenters, both men and women are found on our screens engaging with audiences to create a great sense of engagement and animation. David Attenborough does this with a combination of enthu-siasm and gravitas. Can a woman do that, in the same way? Whenever I have been on television, I find myself very aware of needing to create a distinctive kind of authority figure for myself: one that is alongside the viewer, knowledgeable and sharing ideas. People often note that I seem calm, interested and informed. But I don't think I have gravitas.

The intellectual woman remains a slightly tricky type: we can easily fall into traps of being judged on our looks, our voices, our clothes, rather than on what we say. And it is not so often we see older women on television: the Miss Marples are usually absent. A female equivalent of a presenter like David Attenborough needs nurturing, and sustaining through different television series, from youth to old age. Cambridge professor of ancient history Mary Beard has not had that, though she is probably now the leading UK female presenter. She comes across as smart, keen, comfortable with herself and down to earth. But she is not as well loved as Attenborough. She has been mercilessly critiqued, and has been called 'too ugly for television',[3] which shows how audiences will first appraise a woman's looks before what she says. The 'bright young woman' type of television presenter is safer for television. It is more than about being televisual: an attractive young woman, as every advertiser knows, sells products. We are in the world of the infamous 'male gaze',[4] and most production teams are male, so they are finely attuned to it, often

2. The documentary *Planet Earth* was narrated by David Attenborough for the BBC but by Sigourney Weaver for the Discovery Channel's US version.

3.   *The Telegraph*,   26   July   2013,   http://www.telegraph.co.uk/culture/tvandradio/10204252/Mary-Beard-I-will-never-have-a-makeover.html.

4. First defined by Laura Mulvey, 'Visual Pleasure and Narrative Cinema', *Screen* 16, no. 3 (1975): 6–18.

unconsciously.[5] Whereas a man can progress smoothly from being a cool, attractive and interesting enthusiast, as David Attenborough was in his youth, to the older man with gravitas, a young woman presenter does not necessarily acquire gravitas with age. As she ages, knowledgeability may seem just a bit 'know-it-ally' and opinionated. There is something that people may even find a bit threatening about an older, clever woman.

Advice on Different Ways of Being on Television

In the past 20 years I have been fortunate to work in various different capacities within television and radio. Every experience is different. The talking head interview is one thing. Filming on location is another. Sometimes I need to fit into a slot: to give sound bites that will work in a narrative crafted by the production team. I have also been a script consultant, a historical consultant and I have worked with Helen Bond as co-creator and co-presenter of an hour-length Channel 4 documentary (Minerva Productions): *Jesus' Female Disciples: The New Evidence* (Producers J. C. Bragard and Anna Cox). Engaging in script consultancy is interesting because it means you can spot errors (sometimes in what interviewees say – even experts can make mistakes) and shape narration. Being a consultant from the inception and first funding of a programme through its design and into its completion, with a chance to modify the programme at the editorial stage also, is satisfying work to do, since here I have been able to participate creatively.

Having worked in a documentary production company myself, I know about the different parts of the creative process and the different roles people have. A film production team involves a great deal of collaboration and respect for everyone's distinctive crafts. I have enormous respect for film-makers and what they do. Each documentary is a kind of campaign, in which every element has to fit together perfectly. The amount of skill and design work is huge, and people work under strict deadlines. Those who enter this profession are invariably extremely committed and intelligent people, who can work at very high levels of intensity and energy, and when you as an expert participate in the process you are expected to perform at the same level, as a professional in an environment in which everyone is giving their best.

---

5.   http://www.theguardian.com/lifeandstyle/2010/feb/04/older-women-too-old-for-tv, accessed 25 April 2014.

The total package of the documentary involves getting funding on the basis of a treatment or outline, with a proposed budget. The producer and director often work together to create this, with a clear sense of audience and potential distribution through a television network. At this stage, scholars can be called upon to help with the development of an idea, through to a pitch to a television channel, with an expectation that you might well later be called upon as an interviewee if the pitch to a network or other funder is successful.

Many colleagues are a bit mystified by this process. It will often be the case that you get an email out of the blue by some researcher in a production company, with a paragraph on what they are hoping to do, asking to have a phone chat. If you accept that, then it is always a good idea in my experience to say that you have 10, 20 or 30 minutes (absolute maximum) to discuss, and often saying you have 10 minutes is quite wise because if it turns out you have more confidence in what they are trying to do then you can always say you have a bit more time, but if you indicate you have 30 minutes then it is harder to get away. It is a good idea to ask questions of them before they start asking questions of you. Find out what they have done before, to see whether you are dealing with a reputable company. It is good to know whether you are talking with a very experienced and successful team or people that are just starting out. Discover where they are hoping to place the programme in terms of a network, and check them out online. You will never get paid for this kind of phone conversation, and much of the time, I have to say, you will never hear from these people again. This is because they have not managed to get funding for their documentary, or they have decided not to interview you when they do. This is just them soliciting you for free advice.

Another kind of email followed by phone conversation is often from production companies who have got funding and are now in the process of finalizing who will be interviewed as a talking head in a programme that has already been quite well scripted, after the initial treatment/outline has successfully found a network home and funding. Sometimes filming has already begun and they are very serious and focused. The production assistant/researcher/director here is liable to sound a lot more confident, and sure about the overall shape of the documentary, and explain where they see you fitting in. They want to know your ideas, and how these might work with those of other scholars they are thinking of using. Often they want different perspectives, so they will ask you questions and take note if you are saying something unlike others. Sometimes they want you to say something highly specific, and if you don't come up with this, then they might not want you to participate. They will not tell you what they are wanting, but if you hit the right notes, they will often be jubilant.

Once they say they would like you to be in the documentary, and send you an email confirming that, this is where scholars are at a critical juncture, and we need to learn from people who are savvy about how the performance industry works, because what you are now going to be doing is a performance on camera for a commercial product: a documentary film. Your image and voice are going to be used, as will the content of what you say, and you will be signing a release form allowing the production company to do what they want with these.[6] Some release forms are long and complex, and we are sometimes asked to sign them just as someone is mic-ing us up, so the chances are you will not read them thoroughly. But you essentially become a kind of product within the overall product of the film itself. They can cut your words to size and fit them where they want. They can use your image for publicity. Anything you deliver is theirs.

Before you sign this you should actually have negotiated what the production company will pay you, in terms of expenses, a *per diem* or a fee and so on. It is a legal document that outlines what your entitlement is as a 'contributor'. You won't get paid for a news story, or for US public television, but you should otherwise.

Scholars themselves frequently configure their participation in documentaries as a kind of public talk, or seminar, an extension of teaching even, all for the public good as part of their duty, but it is a different kind of creature altogether. You are a resource, without which this particular kind of documentary itself could not exist. In my view, it is important that scholars do not offer their services in commercial TV for free. Most production companies know that they need to provide a small fee or honorarium for their interviewees, as well as covering all expenses (e.g. getting to and from the filming location). After all, we are asked to give our time and often we need to do some preparation. Some scholars have become so savvy about their roles in these that they have agents. One of my colleagues working in archaeology is so often in documentaries on location in Israel-Palestine he has an agent that gets 10% of whatever fee he gets, and he tells me that his standard is $100 an hour on set. Being filmed in an interview for an hour is quite intense, hard work, and I think this sum is quite fair.

You will often be asked to send an invoice, which for scholars puts many of us into a bit of a spin, but this is a very basic life skill. In the Appendix to this chapter is a model invoice to help with this. If sending an invoice makes you feel a little uncomfortable, since it seems you are working outside your regular employment, remember that any royalties

6. See http://www.bbc.co.uk/filmnetwork/filmmaking/guide/production/legal-guide-production-agreements, accessed 25 April 2015.

you get for your academic writing is also money earned outside your regular employment. Universities can have regulations about not having a second job aside from your full-time job with them, but this does not preclude you from earning money through academic consultancies or from royalties paid from your books. In fact, major academic consultancies in the business world are being increasingly encouraged by British universities.[7] What we do in television is a small foray into that. However, we tend to do so feeling our way in the dark, being extremely grateful to anyone in television who might be remotely interested in what we have to say. But just believe in the value of what you know.

Some production companies are on a very tight budget as a result of minimal funding, and in some cases I have waived any request for a fee, because I like the project. It may help me in some way explore an idea and television work is fun, but in principle I do feel quite strongly that we should not be asked to be resources for documentaries – working as performance artists as 'contributors' – without any remuneration. Everyone else in a documentary is being paid, including actors that are used to play the parts of Jesus, the apostles and the disciples, in biblical re-enactments. It is unfair if the only people who are not paid are the academics who are taking time away from their very busy schedules in order to provide a kind of service to an industry that is manufacturing a commercial product. We get no bonuses from our university employers for working in television; it counts as nothing in promotion, or for the departmental finances or for our scholarly CVs – we do it because we like it, we feel glad to be asked (even flattered) and we have this sense of public responsibility, of wanting to share our learning with the world. But we are consultants and performers who should be remunerated like everyone else in the production.

I felt particularly perplexed with CNN, who commissioned a British production company to make a series of documentaries, *Finding Jesus*, apparently with no budget for remuneration to interviewees other than for expenses, but this series ended up being one of the most watched on cable in the USA. A network like CNN, which makes its money on advertising placed within the documentary, effectively makes millions from this kind of product.[8] Viewers' ratings dictate the amount of advertising revenue they can obtain. Not to give interviewees a *per diem* or a fee, when we have given up our time to work for them, seems particularly bad form.

7.   http://www.kcl.ac.uk/innovation/business/support/partnerships/consultancy.aspx, accessed 25 April 2015.

8.   http://cnnpressroom.blogs.cnn.com/2015/03/02/cnns-two-new-cnnorigseries-findingjesus-and-thewonderlist-debut-as-1-in-cable-news-last-night-full-release/, 25 April 2015.

Nevertheless, often as a scholar you don't need to ask: the production company will say in their email letter of agreement that you will be paid such and such an amount and expenses, and they hope this is agreeable. It is usually not very much, but enough to make you feel recognized and valued. My friend's $100 an hour on set is quite generous. If you are on location, as he is often, this sum can add up over a few days of shooting. If you have no *per diem*, claim expenses on receipts.

Being Interviewed: Practical Aspects

In terms of practical considerations when being interviewed, there are some important things to know. You may be filmed in a studio or in a quiet space set up for filming. Production teams often favour filming in very cold churches, even crypts, for biblical subjects, so it is worth bringing reasonably warm clothing to wear, so as not to shiver visibly as much as for your own comfort. But, in a studio space, have a lighter option available in case you find it warm under the lights. You also do not want to sweat visibly, and sometimes people will come up and powder your nose if you do. Better, have powder of your own. Check your face.

Since the backgrounds are usually dark, it is wise not to wear clothing that is also dark, or you will look like a head suspended in space. The old adage is that you should not wear stripes or dots, because they can bleed and jiggle on a television screen, but actually with HD screens this is unlikely to happen. Very busy patterns might well be an issue, but you do not have to be pattern free. White used to be avoided too, but this likewise is less of a problem now. All the same, a non-patterned medium-toned shirt or top is usually advisable.

This brings me to image. For a man, clothing and hair are not often noticed or commented upon. A man can go for a suit, or something smart-casual like a shirt or a jumper of some kind, and that is fine. For a woman, dressing to be on television involves all kinds of decisions. Women's hair is often longer than men's hair, and what we do with it is noticed. If we are out on location, in the open air, it can be a problem if it is loose, by blowing in all directions. Continuity issues can arise when they are editing what we say, if our hair is different in each sequence, behind our ears one moment, and in front of our ears the next. More importantly, what we do with it, what colour it is, what we have as our hair style, are all things that are noticed.

Earrings, jewellery, scarves will all define a woman speaker, in a world very far from gender equity. I've had someone take the trouble to email me simply to ask where I got the scarf I was wearing. Looking glamorous can be good, as long as it fits with a professional image. Looking 'girlie', being too feminine, again raises the issue of authority (since this is usually defined as masculine). Male production crews and viewing audiences can enjoy the notion of a young, sexy, woman academic, and in a hot climate you may feel 'holidayish' and opt to wear more revealing clothing simply for comfort, but in my experience this is generally not a very good idea, as showing too much skin, especially cleavage and legs, detracts from the content of what we are saying. Looking at yourself in terms of the 'male gaze' can be jangling. I would love to see more of us being naturally ourselves on television, but we need to do this knowing what we are up against. In today's world how women look is noted before what women say

I don't think I have ever seen myself on a documentary and thought positively about my image, but this is probably because most women do the same critical appraisal of themselves in front of a mirror. This brings me to make-up. I have discovered that it is almost impossible to wear too much make-up on television. Being televisual is about having defined features, with contrasting colouration, and make-up can enhance that. My colouring is rather bland on television, and my features do not stand out, so make-up can make my face less wishy-washy. Strong studio lights or outdoor sun will nevertheless erase even what I think is quite a lot of make-up, and I will just look dowdy. The low-key make-up we might use professionally needs to be applied three times more intensely to make any difference on screen.

Many years ago, when I was in Jerusalem as a scholar at the British School of Archaeology, I met Margaret Thatcher, then Prime Minister of Great Britain, who was on an official visit to Israel. Up close, I was amazed at the caked-on make-up she had on her face, almost like it was applied for her going on stage. Her hair was held in place by a mountain of hairspray, so that nothing moved. In person, that was not a good look. On the TV news that evening, when I saw what had been filmed of this, she looked, as usual, very professionally polished. You could recognize that she was wearing make-up, but it was not excessive; she looked simply tidy and well turned out. This is what the camera does to our faces.

Once you are ready and about to do the interview, you will have a small microphone clipped to a part of your clothing, and this is often passed through from below, from the lower part of your top or shirt, or from the bottom of your dress. A sound technician should allow you to go under your clothing yourself. You might like to think about where they will clip the mic before you choose what to wear. Other times, the mic will hang above you, especially on location, looking like a small furry animal. Remember to ignore it.

Interviews in the studio are straightforward. You will be seated, with lights positioned on your face from the side, and these can sometimes catch your eye. Don't look at these lights, but rather at the questioner (the director, or a production assistant) who will be seated a little to one side of the camera before you, with a load of papers on their knee. They might have shared the questions they want to ask with you beforehand, and they will have built these up on the basis of phone chats with you, and the overall shape of the documentary, with its key focus points.

When they ask you a question, make sure you include an element of this in your answer, because that makes editing work easier. So, if they ask, 'Where do you think Jesus was born?' don't answer, 'In Bethlehem of Judaea, according to two of our gospels', but rather, 'According to two of our gospels, Jesus was born in Bethlehem of Judaea'. Given this question, you might think of how others might answer it, and add, 'Some scholars think that Jesus was born in Nazareth, and that the Bethlehem stories are invented, but I myself trust this identification'. These sorts of statements are sound bites. They can be cut and pasted in different places. In the editing process, your statements can be placed back to front and out of sequence, and much can be jumped over. Always keep things fairly simple.

I try to make answers relatively short, and create pauses, but sometimes the questioner allows you to ramble on, waiting to see what you might turn up. If that does happen, be aware that they will quarry your ramble for those small sound bites and a few interesting things they can use. They will not give you time to make a long speech in a finished documentary. What you say will not have the context of a before or after, or any nuanced qualifications, and what you say can be used in any order of small bites.

Endeavour to relax and enjoy the experience. Being in the hot seat, with lights and camera right in front of you, and a number of people staring at you fixedly a short distance away, does not lend itself to that, especially if you let audience numbers come into your head (biblically themed documentaries can have total viewing figures in the millions), but the more you concentrate on the subject matter and doing a good job the better. Pretend you are just talking with a couple of friendly people. Be friendly.

It is always obvious when scholars are nervous on camera. They look rigid, and slightly like a possum in headlights. They speak without much animation. Unfortunately, television is a medium in which stage nerves cannot easily be hidden. In fact, in the Stanislavsky technique of acting, an actor is encouraged simply to feel an emotion and trust that the camera, in close up, will pick it up. Great film actors just go with the feeling.

Therefore, feeling nervous inside will definitely show on the surface. There is no distance between you and your audience. It will also make it harder for you to formulate your thoughts neatly and clearly.

The best thing if you are feeling nervous is to take a few breaths before you sit down and think, 'hey, isn't this fun?' or some such. Take it as a nice experience, and it will be. Film crews are nice people. The television audiences are too. Loosen up, and let go. Don't worry. Smile. You've got some great things to say. And the good news is that if you fluff your words, you yourself can say, 'hold it, I need to say that again' and you can do another take of the same thing. Do not be afraid to say this and take a moment. Live television is another matter, but usually you are making a recording. But do always be polite and co-operative.

Sometimes they will ask you to say the same thing ten times for different sized bites, between 15 seconds and 45 seconds. It is not because they think you are not doing well that they keep doing it again, but they want different options for editing. You have to think fast and be very focused.

On Location

All this advice is for studios or in sets in buildings, but if you are called out to film on location somewhere around the Mediterranean this is the cream of our kind of television work. You get a free ticket (and hopefully also a *per diem* and fee) to an invariably sunny spot packed with interesting historical significance and archaeological remains, and you can spend days, or weeks, working with the film crew in different places that have been worked out beforehand, sometimes with your input. Location work is always fun and interesting, in my experience, but it can be hard as well, especially if it is very hot, or if the days are long. You will get up before dawn, and often not finish until dusk, because every day of a shoot on location costs a lot of money, and the production team will want to make use of you to the maximum. Make sure you eat well, and get as much rest as you can beforehand (not easy as an early start in Israel-Palestine, at 5.00 am, translates to 3.00 am British time). Take a bag with water, wet wipes, make-up, snacks, sun cream, sunglasses, hat, headache pills, anything to make yourself comfortable. I also take a camera.

Location work requires enormous concentration, since you will usually need to respond to questions by a presenter while dealing with aspects of your surroundings. I have been the questioner, which also involves a lot of careful thought and alertness. It is one thing to be sitting in a chair with lights shining in your face, a stable environment, with somone asking you questions several times over in the hope of getting the perfect sound bite. It is another thing to say more or less the same thing to a presenter-questioner walking beside you, while going down a set of slippery steps, remembering to turn right at the end and point to the relevant archaeological feature as you go. When you have done this ten times, because there is an intrusive noise, the presenter's hat falls off, the film cartridge runs out, you almost slip over, etc., your insightful and enthusiastic words of wisdom (repeated more or less in the same way) start to sound a little hackneyed. It is at such a time that you recognize most keenly that you are indeed a performance artist putting on a show, using your intellect and knowledge as a resource. No matter how much fun you are having, you have definitely earned your fee.

Consultancy

Script/historical consultancy involves a different set of skills. You might have been interviewed as well in the programme, but this job gets you behind the creative process. You can be involved right at the start. I have been in a meeting with funders, in which my input was part of the total pitch. I have worked closely with producers and directors, crafting the overall programme. I have helped design things for a celebrity presenter speaking words we had written for him to say. The audience often assumes such a celebrity presenter has done this work him/herself, but this is not often the case. It is when you get an expert in the field (for example Mary Beard) that this actually happens.

Before being engaged as a consultant you should always negotiate a fee. As with the fee for being interviewed, the production company will often suggest it. In this business, it is not unusual to ask for something higher and no one minds, even if they might reject it. After you have completed the job, then you send your invoice for the agreed amount.

Generally script consultancy involves going over what is a transcript rough cut of the documentary with interviewees' sound bites and suggested narration. It takes a few hours to go through, noting where interviewees or narration is wrong, with suggestions for replacement wording. The production team then have the job of acting on your critique and amendments, and may send you then a reworked version for final approval.

Designing your own programme is of course a wonderful thing. In 2008 I worked on a fifteen-minute segment in a two-part documentary, in which I could choose who was interviewed, define filming locations and advise on content. It was shot on location, and I loved being driven to places and exploring ideas with people. It actually helped me with my own research, and allowed me to take some great photographs I use in classes. This gave me the yen to do more, which is why I teamed up with Helen Bond to pitch *Jesus' Female Disciples*.

But to get your own documentary idea taken up by a production team is a challenge. After Jean-Claude Bragard of Minerva Productions decided to take on our idea for the documentary, he shot a short film to interest a network. He spent hours with me and Helen, out in the Scottish countryside one warm summer day, filming us in conversation about the subject matter, as a kind of taster to use as part of the pitch for possible funders and networks. He spent a great deal of time distilling what Helen and I wanted into something he believed would be good for a documentary, and interest a channel or network. He finally suceeded in attracting the support of Channel 4 (UK). It is very satisfying to have a real say in the design of a programme, hatching it from the egg of the concept and nurturing it through to funding, placement and production. Even still, it is the film company that makes the programme, and one has to respect their craft, their decisions.

What I wonder about more and more is how we as academics can feed our ideas into production, to create relevant and interesting projects that will engage the public. Every time you see a programme on television, you need to ask – who came up with this idea? Who funded it? If you have a great idea for a programme, try to find a production company and see if you can get someone interested. The world is ever hungry for good quality, well-informed and stimulating television documentaries.

Conclusions

Working in television is a treat. It allows you to get ideas out to the general public, and involves you in a great contemporary art form. But it is usually commercial work, and you should be remunerated for what you do. What I have provided here are a few personal reflections and some advice on being a scholar on television, particularly as it relates to biblical and historical programmes. While much of what I have reflected on applies to both men and women, I remain particularly concerned about how to be a woman on television, as I noted at the beginning. It is part of a wider category of being a woman in public, and being an intellectual woman in any form of media requires some experimentation, both in terms of staying authentic and getting things right in terms of public expectations. Being professionally prepared and sharing knowledge to do this job well is one of the ways we can help each other.

Appendix

Invoice

From: Prof. A. Person, consultant/contributor, address, email
To: Television Company, address, email
Reference: make up something like TV1-A
Date:

Date of Work:
Description of work:
  script editing
  historical consultancy
  interview
  presenting
Expenses: amount with receipts
Fee: amount as agreed
Total: amount

Please pay the above amount requested to the following bank account:
A. Person
Bank:
Address:
IBAN/Swift:
Sort code:
Account no.

Many thanks.

[Provide signature here]

Chapter 6

CRITICAL BLACK CHRISTIAN BODY:
OPPOSITION AND RESISTANCE
IN THE RELIGIOUS DOCUMENTARY

Robert Beckford

As a black liberation theologian and a veteran presenter of over twenty-five religious documentary films, I am often asked by students and colleagues, 'how did you get into documentary film business?' My standard response is to explain how in the late '90s a television interview on Channel 4's 'Right to Reply' television programme inspired me to pitch documentary ideas to commissioning editors, the people responsible for what appears on our television screens.

Fortuitously, a few years later one of my ideas was incorporated into a series on the history of slavery ('Britain's Slave Past' 1999). More in hope than in expectation that the person I am speaking to wants to have a nuanced conversation about representational politics in the British media, I always steer the conversation away from the 'how' to the 'why'. I continue with, 'I got into documentary filmmaking to change things, you know'. The shift in the direction of the conversation usually prompts a more interrogative question, such as 'Oh … what did you want to change?' I respond with, 'I wanted to challenge representation and present an alternative image of black Christianity on television'. After a pause in conversation, the few conversationalists that are genuinely interested in my second answer, as the politics of 'race' and religion is often a conversation stopper for all but the most erudite or politically motivated, go on to ask me one of the two following questions. 'What is wrong with the way black Christianity is portrayed on television?' Or 'Were you successful in your quest to change things?' Emboldened by the arrival of this third round of questions, I move on to a lengthier and fuller response to the either question.

I am presuming, as you the reader have chosen to read this chapter, that you are also interested the 'third round' of questions and want to enter into a conversation of the motivations that lies behind a black liberation theologian presenting religious documentary films on mainstream television in Britain.

The communicative-theory underpinning this chapter foregrounds the role of authors to disrupt the postmodern hegemony of texts and audiences in the production of meaning. The auteur is not dead.[1] However, I am not seeking to consign meaning exclusively to one location in the communication circuit, but instead, move towards a holistic interpretive impulse.[2] With the particularity of this chapter, I am suggesting that, in relation to the Bible documentary, we must *read* the presenters, because presenters also make meaning. I hint at this reality in the introduction to the Bible documentary, 'Who Wrote the Bible?' (Channel 4, 2004). In the film, I begin the journey by locating myself in a dialectic between the university and black church. In this chapter, I place myself within a broader social history, to reveal how subjectivities produce meaning.

This chapter is a disclosure, an enunciation of motivation. Methodologically, I am appropriating aspects of auto/ethnography, specifically, the use of autobiographical material to 'unveil' personal motivation in the form of two critical experiences.[3] This is to fill in the gaps between presenting, production and broadcast by naming the *politics of affect* which underscore presenter reflexivity.[4]

---

1. R. Maule, *Beyond Auteurism: New Directions in Authorial Film Practices in France, Italy and Spain Since the 1980s* (Chicago: University of Chicago Press, 2013); A. Ashby, ed., *Popular Music and the New Auteur: Visionary Filmmakers After MTV* (Oxford: Oxford University Press, 2013).

2. See a comprehensive method in Gordon Lynch, *Understanding Theology and Popular Culture* (Malden, MA: Blackwell).

3. H. Rosen, *Speaking from Memory: The Study of Autobiographical Discourse* (Stoke on Trent: Trentham Books, 1998), 30; T. Muncey, *Creating Autoethnographies* (Los Angeles, CA: Sage, 2010); Y. Lincoln, eds, *Handbook of Qualitative Research* (Thousand Oaks, CA: Sage, 2005), 959–78.

4. Brian Massumi, *The Politics of Affect* (Cambridge and Malden, MA: Polity Press, 2015); Marta Figlerowicz, 'Affect Theory Dossier: An Introduction', *Qui Parle* 20, no. 2 (2012): 3–18.

Experience Matters

The first experience is conscientization of the contradictions at *play* in the media practices of black television presenters, namely how presenters position themselves in relation to television's racial politics.[5] Two negotiations of this predicament are foregrounded in a television debate in which I participated, on Channel 4's 'Right to Reply' in the mid-'90s. I frame these practices through the lenses of the 'politics of containment' and 'misrecognition'. These discourses demarcate the limitations and co-option of black bodies in television space. In response to the inevitability of industry confinement/misrecognition, I decided to position myself within the resistance to it – on the borderlands, the diversity and anti-racism campaigns. In other words, in the Bible films, I seek to represent what Kehinde Andrews terms 'black radicalism'.[6]

The second experience concerns the specific question of black Christian representation on British terrestrial television. There are very few images of black Christians in this media, and the dominant images are racialised: either musical or troublesome. 'Black folks who love Jesus' either sing well or 'got problems'. To combat these stereotypes, I was determined to embody a counter image to the choir and conflicted black bodies, by developing what I term a 'critical black Christian body'. This second position is performed in documentary aesthetics and narrative content.

While communication carries no guarantees,[7] there is evidence that segments of the audience received *aspects* of the preferred message. To evidence the reception and to complete the chapter, I will identify reviews of my films which I suggest acknowledges *aspects* of this new position in black Christian representation.

5. Gavin Schaffer, *The Vision of a Nation: Making Multiculturalism on British Television* (London: Palgrave Macmillan, 2014); Jamie Doward and Burhar Wazir, 'British Television Accused of Institutional Racism', *The Guardian*, Sunday 25 August 2002.

6. Kehinde Andrews, *Back to Black: Black Radicalism for the 21st Century* (London: Zed Books, 2018).

7. Stuart Hall, 'Encoding and Decoding in the Television Discourse: Paper for the Council of Europe Colloquy on Training in the Critical Reading of Television Language' (Centre for Contemporary Cultural Studies, University of Birmingham, 1973); Paul Jones and David Holmes, 'Encoding/Decoding', in *Key Concepts in Media and Communications* (London: Sage, 2011), 74–80.

Right to Reply

To explain the first motivation, it is necessary to recap a seminal experience in television, my first appearance on a television show. This experience inspired me to challenge what I perceived to be a contradictory existence of black television presenters, and also set in motion my development as a television presenter.

My entry into television documentary was not as a consequence of talent spotting, nepotism or a latent black theological megalomania. Neither was it a result of an explicit theological concern. Instead, my first foray into television was to express my dissatisfaction with the representation of black people on Channel 4 television, on the viewers' complaint programme, 'Right to Reply'. I went on the programme in the mid-1990s because of a growing frustration over a subtle change of emphasis in black programming at the channel. By the mid-1990s I perceive a shift towards an imbalance of negative *racialised* representations.

Racialised representations on British television are not new, but in the case of Channel 4, this shift was significant. Like many black people of my generation, I grew up admiring the channel because, after its launch in the early 1980s, it became a leading space to explore complex issues confronting black people including the dynamics of racism(s) and African diaspora cultural politics. Committed to constructive but critical explorations of black history, culture and politics, the channel commissioned programmes such as the magazine 'Black on Black' and the black political show 'The Bandung File'. These programmes provided a balance to the normative domestic neo-colonial representations of black people, which, according to television critic, Sarita Malik, dominated the late twentieth century.[8] In addition to these magazine programs, the channel also broadcast a raft of documentaries exploring a range of popular and esoteric themes in black history from the domestic and international arenas. Thus, for a decade, the channel devoted a significant amount of time and resources to examining black people's perspectives in the mainstream. In the first decade of Channel 4 it was not usual to hear black people of all classes discuss in public and private spaces the political value of Channel 4.[9]

8. S. Malik, *Representing Black Britain: Black and Asian Images on Television* (London: Sage, 2002), 70–1.

9. S. Lambert, *Channel 4: Television with a Difference?* (London: British Film Institute, 1982), 144–6; D. Hobson, *Channel 4: The Early Years and the Jeremy Isaacs Legacy* (London: I.B. Tauris, 2008), 68–70.

By the mid-1990s, 'the gloves came off', and the previously supportive perspectives with their explicit anti-racism were beaten aside. In their place emerged a new gaze on black social and cultural life – a move from critical solidarity to a conservative critique. While not completely denying the efficacy and existence of racism, the new emphasis de-emphasized its importance. While the motivations for this cultural shift at the channel remain opaque, I suggest that the change bears an uncanny resemblance to a political philosophy called 'post-racial liberalism'.[10] Post-racial liberalism arises in late modernity from liberal political thinkers in Western societies with long histories of racial discord. While proffering a complex articulation of 'race'-relations, this discourse is accused of reducing the importance of 'race' as a factor in black disadvantage. It demotes the efficacy of 'race' by promoting diversity rather than equality, colour-blindness rather than affirmative action and 'culture of poverty' theories (the idea that disadvantage is fundamentally an individual matter related to a lack of education and bad life choices rather than structural and historical analyses). An indication of this new outlook was evident in a number of documentary films broadcast on subjects as diverse as the problem of black single parenting, the proliferation of mixed identities and black criminality. On the cusp of this change was the emergence of 'Badass TV'.

Badass TV was a magazine show that combined satire, parody and late-night titillation. The programme series embodied post-racial liberalism's sensibilities by its aversion to the briefest historicization of cultural forms and the precedence of oppressive structural forces. In other words, black cultural artefacts were presented as ahistorical and asocial – despite these two conceptual frameworks being integral to meaningful interpretation and re-articulation of blaxploitation, especially its complex use of hyper-real and black power motifs. In their defence, we may argue that Badass was satirical and therefore not subject to the same critical exegesis of current affairs or documentary films. However, the program was billed as being slightly more critical that previous programmes of its ilk. The initial advertising suggested a critical tension in the series, a narrative struggle personified by West Coast gangster rapper Ice T and black British presenter Andrea Oliver. These presenters were to assume the roles of the protagonist and antagonist respectively. Unfortunately, the balancing act

---

10. M. E. L. Bush, *Everyday Forms of Whiteness: Understanding Race in a 'Post-Racial World'*, 2nd edn (Plymouth: Rowman & Littlefield, 2011); W. C. Rich, *The Post-Racial Society is Here: Recognition, Critics and the Nation-State* (London: Routledge, 2013).

never materialised. Ice T's sharp pithy statements, machismo and educated taste in all things blaxploitation were privileged in the studio links, and set the tone for the series. Consequently, viewers expecting some element of critical investigation of the genre were disappointed. Instead, the producers served up a weekly diet of ahistorical, salacious voyeurism of hyper-real sexualities and a bizarre ghetto-centric cultural production. Even artists rooted in serious black artistic endeavours could not escape these production values. Take for instance the programme's discussion of the work of the award-winning artist, Chris Ofili. His artwork was presented to the audience as a modern-day example of blaxploitation because of his use of elephant dung. The programme, however, failed to fully acknowledge why he used the waste product – a pragmatic African philosophy undergirding his aesthetic.[11]

I decided to complain about the series and left a voice message on the channel's viewer complaint line. To my surprise, I was invited to present my case to 'Right to Reply'. This weekly programme aimed to achieve broadcaster accountability by allowing viewers to challenge filmmakers, thereby making visible, to a degree, behind-the-scenes decision-making. I went on the show to register displeasure at the move towards a more antagonist approach to black programming and a specific objection to Badass TV. Alongside Bola Fayola, another concerned viewer, I tackled the Commissioning Editor for Youth Programmes, David Stevenson, and co-presenter Andrea Oliver. Our segment on the show was a mere 10 minutes, recorded live and broadcast the next day.

The ensuing discussion brought to the fore contrasting views of the program and also, more importantly for me, the question of how presenters navigate contradiction.

The discussion began with Bola claiming that the programme was negative, especially in relation to the portrayal of black women. Andrea, consistent with her viewpoint in the series, countered by arguing that the programme was satire. She gave an example of how an interview with African American rapper 'Sir Mix-A-Lot' lying on a bed, carousing with semi-naked women, was a sophisticated attempt to unmask and ridicule his misogyny. Then David, supporting Andrea, chipped in to argue that such images do not stereotype black men as hyper-masculine but attempt to portray them through the programmer's 'multi-textured approach'. I was not convinced, so to support Fayola's gender critique, when asked by the show's presenter, Roger Bolton, about my concerns, I said:

11. Bush, *Everyday Forms of Whiteness*; Rich, *The Post-Racial Society is Here*.

> In the first programme, five out of the seven items ... looked at black women
> and sex. Now to me that was an overwhelming attempt to represent black
> women as sexual objects, as commodities to be exploited. And I think that's
> very dangerous on television.

I continued by gesturing towards a wider discursive impact of these
representations:

> I think this [kind of programme] is dangerous in a climate where negative,
> racialized images are used to justify the mistreatment of black people. If you
> present black people as being no more than people who are somehow patho-
> logical, who have something internally wrong with them, then you run the
> risk of enforcing views which are held by parts of the [national] community
> we would not want to be associated with.

Both David Stevenson and Andrea Oliver denied this was the case and
that the programme was in no way 'racialized'. However, in the green
room after the discussion, Oliver conceded that the show did engage in
stereotypes and racial tropes. The contradiction was telling and caused me
to think about the politics and positioning of black broadcasters, and how
they navigate racial politics to stay employed.

On the tube to central London, Bola and I were struck by the representational politics that were played out in and out of the studio discussion. We
considered ways to interpret what happened during and after the filming.
One theory was signifying. The defenders of the show were 'playing fool
to catch wise'. That is to say, they were cognizant of the racial tropes but
'played' innocent. But we did not feel this subaltern resistance strategy
was the dominant negotiation. Instead, we decided to read the defence
through the politics of containment and misrecognition.

According to Patricia Hill Collins,[12] the politics of containment
describes how black people have to comply with prevailing racialised
norms in the workplace, no matter how incongruous. A select group of
black people are foregrounded as examples of achievement, hard work
or meritocracy, but their presence is also a form of surveillance, a polic-
ing of black bodies to ensure compliance.[13] At the nub of containment is
a contradiction: the relative visibility of black people in the work place

---

12. P. H. Collins, *Fighting Words: Black Women and the Search for Justice*
(Minneapolis: University of Minnesota Press, 1998), 14; for a broader perspective
see, Simone Browne, *Dark Matters: On the Surveillance of Blackness* (Durham, NC:
Duke University Press, 2015).

13. Browne, *Dark Matters*.

masks exclusionary practices. Faced with these confines, black people have to navigate situations that claim to be empowering, which in reality are sites of disadvantage. But there is also another predicament that lacks the reflexivity exhibited in those negotiating the politics of containment, and that is misrecognition.[14]

Misrecognition is a form of forgetting within a cultural context, wherein individuals in question collude with the hierarchical order of things and unwittingly legitimate their own oppression:

> The agent engaged in practice knows the world ... too well, without objec-
> tifying distance, takes it for granted, precisely because he [*sic*] is caught up
> in it, bound up with it; he inhabits it like a garment ... he feels at home in
> the world because the world is also in him ...[15]

Misrecognition is acceptance and consent of the way things are. It is as equally as dangerous as the politics of containment. It may lead to 'symbolic violence', or 'the violence which is exercised upon a social agent with his or her complicity'.[16] What this means in everyday life is that, unwittingly, by failing to recognize oppressive forces, some individuals leave themselves open to manipulation by them. In relation to the defence of the programme on 'Right to Reply', misrecognition as an interpretation of events registers the possibility of complicity.

In sum, folding the politics of containment into misrecognition to interpret the first experience led me to the conclusion that black presence in the media is a negotiation of survival in a hostile environment. I opted to resist it.

To oppose the politics of containment and misrecognition, I committed myself to addressing issues of racial bias and discrimination at every level of operation in the media. I aligned myself with every media equalities group, and whenever possible participated in panel discussions or private discussions on matters of inclusion and diversity in the media. I always positioned myself at the most critical or radical position possible in order to 'out' racialized oppression at every level of operation. For instance, during a diversity meeting at Channel 4 in 2011, I confronted the leadership with evidence of the broadcaster's 'cultural illiteracy' and lack of 'moral courage'. Intriguingly, a few months after, I won an award for

---

14. P. Bourdieu, 'Thinking about Limits', *Theory, Culture and Society* 9 (2002): 37–49.
15. Ibid.
16. Ibid.

Best Presenter from the TV Collective, a guild established to represent the interests of black presenters and television professionals. My suspicion was that the award was given for my moral courage in the face of the liberal white media hegemony, rather than for my skills as a television presenter! However, taking a critical view of the politics of 'race' in the media can be commercially counter-productive in contemporary Britain. The difficulty is due in part to an institutionalization of ignorance of the historical workings of British racism(s). Ignorance produces negative knee-jerk reactions rather than considered reflection.[17] As cultural theorist bell hooks notes, in societies structured around racial ignorance, the rewards and promotions, more than often, go to the those who choose to 'see, hear and speak' *no* truth to power.[18] By taking a radical stance, however, I sought to defy the politics of containment by making clear that my participation was part of a struggle for black inclusion in the media rather than a 'fig leaf' of respectability for institutional inactivity and obfuscation. This was my challenge to representation.

I also desired to embody an alternative representation of black Christian tradition in Britain, and this second motivation led to a new positioning, beyond the two dominant images of black Christians as the choir and conflicted individual.

The Choir

Arguably the most popular image of black church life on television since the 1990s is the choir. Whether in a semi-comedic television commercial (cereal or mobile phone adverts), backing a musician or band on a popular music television show or singing the Spirituals on a 'special edition' of the BBC's Songs of Praise, the choir has come to personify the black church. While it is true that the choir is an important component of black church worship (especially Pentecostal and evangelical traditions) it is not the only facet of the black church. So why the media preoccupation with the choir? There are aesthetic and commercial priorities. The quest for the sublime so inextricably interwoven with African diaspora choral music has wide appeal. Black choirs have inspired and entertained the British

17. Paul Gilroy, *After Empire: Melancholia or Convivial Culture?* (London: Routledge, 2004).

18. See bell hooks's discussion of 'the gaze' as black kinesis in b. hooks, *Black Looks: Race and Representation* (Cambridge, MA: South End, 1992); K. R. Johnson, 'Black Kinesics – Some Non-verbal Patterns in Black Culture', *Florida F/L Reporter* 9, nos. 1 and 2 (1971): 17–20.

public since the tour of the African America Fisk Jubilee Singers in the late nineteenth century. Back then, as now, the choir is an easier 'sell' for mainstream culture compared to other aspects of the black church tradition, such as prophetic preaching or supercharged Holy Ghost worship. There are very few Pentecostal churches featured on BBC worship programmes. As a result of their over-representation in mainstream British culture, the choir is synonymous with black Christianity.

The choir is more than an aesthetic or genre. In Britain it also has a social and didactic function. Socially speaking, choirs were established as means of securing church and denominational solidarity, particularly among young people. Later, interdenominational choirs provided an occasion for informal ecumenical links that were forged between second- and third-generation black British people. For instance, the London Community Gospel Choir (LCGC) was founded on a desire to unite in musical harmony young people from across the black churches in London. In recent years, this inclusive impulse has led to Christians from white and other church communities joining what were once exclusively black choirs. Furthermore, we should not forget that in the black Atlantic, the gospel choir has a pedagogic role: it is a musical mediation of deep spiritual truths. While in the UK context, the teaching role of the choir is collapsed into ecumenical solidarity, in contrast, despite the evolution of the form, in North America there is a long history of choirs maintaining historical memory of the Spirituals, including the esteemed tradition of the double-meaning.[19]

There are two *readings* of the black choir in the mainstream that I want to advance. On the one hand, the over-representation can be read as a success story – it exemplifies the way that yet another black culture, rooted in the slave sublime, has infiltrated and reshaped mainstream culture. On the other, the choir, when decontextualized, de-historicised and depoliti-cised, is reduced to a type of 'blackface'. 'Blackface' describes a complex history of black representation based on the caricature or stereotype of a black person. Blackface can apply equally to whites imitating blacks as well as blacks imitating blacks.[20] Either way, blackface seeks to project a 'laugh at us' rather than a 'laugh with us' orientation. I am not suggesting that black choirs perform with the express aim of demeaning or denigrating black people, but I am gesturing towards a representational

19. S. A. Smith, *British Black Gospel: The Foundations of this Vibrant UK Sound* (Oxford: Monarch Books, 2009).

20. E. Lott, *Love and Theft: Blackface Minstrely and the American Working Class* (New York: Oxford University Press, 1995), 15–18.

politics in the media which inadvertently produces images of the black choir, with resonance with racialised musical discourses of black musical performance. In this case, the choir is 'blacked up'. As a stereotype of the black church, the representation of the choir has power; it establishes differences and these differences allow judgements to made and exercised over black Christianity. In this case, the stereotyping of the black church as smiling, clapping, singing black Christians reduces a complex religious tradition and its intersections with slavery, community and resistance to nothing more than dark-skinned people who 'sing so well'.

The Conflicted

The conflicted black Christian body describes a black Christian body in turmoil and conflict – either emotionally, ethically or physically.[21] This representation arises out of a simplistic interpretation of black Christian ethics. The media logic is this: the traditional preaching and teaching of the black church, particularly its traditional affirmation of non-market values of conservative morality and personal integrity, are portrayed as reactionary and contradictory, especially through the prism of a post-Christian, secular society. Folding black Christianity into an unreliable fundamentalism connotes duplicity, contraction and blind faith in action. I suggest, with few exceptions,[22] it is only the black Christian body that is marked in this way. In contrast, the white Christian body on screen, while also the subject of stereotype and even ridicule, does not suffer from being both 'raced' and duplicitous.

The conflicted black Christian body is particularly prevalent in drama series and comedy productions. Arguably it makes its television debut in the only black soap of the in 1990s. In 'Brothers and Sisters', a soap opera set in a black church, the twist in narrative was the 'coming-out' of a gay black minister. In this case the conflicted black Christian body is represented in a conflict over sexual ethics. More recently, the conflicted black Christian body appears in 2007, in the BBC drama series Casualty, where a black Jehovah's Witness family was faced with the dilemma/conflict of a blood transfusion. After a significant amount of criticism of their beliefs, the hospital had to discover a way of allowing the family to retain their principles but save their daughter. Questions of violence and the black Christian body emerge in 2010, in the BBC's soap opera 'Eastenders'.

21. C. Jackson, *Violence, Visual Culture, and the Black Male Body* (London: Routledge, 2010), Introduction.
22. For instance, in the Sean Bean film, 'Broken', the black character Daniel Martin (Danni Sapani) defies stereotype.

Here a character who was murderous, duplicitous, self-righteous and mad was also deeply Christian. Black performers are not averse to capitalising on the conflicted black Christian body for sardonic effect. For instance, in one of most successful black British comedy series of the 1990s, 'The Real McCoy', a regular sketch was of a black preacher played by deceased comedy genius, Felix Dexter. The black preacher character gained laughs by the fact that he was always torn between professing moral virtues while unsuccessfully failing to contain a lust for the unholy. Again, the black Christian body was a site for signifying loss of trust. Another conflicted black Christian body is presented in the comedy series 'The Little Miss Jocelyn Show' (2009). A black church sister, 'Miss Kingston', with a propensity for unpredictable verbal profanity, was a staple of the series. With the dye now cast, it was no surprise to see a crooked 'ambulance chasing' preacher as the subject of one of the skits on new wave black comedy show, 'The Javone Prince Show' (2015).

The 'wounded black' motif is a useful way of explaining why black bodies in conflict are reproduced in mainstream culture.[23] The 'wounded black body' is an ambivalent practice – incorporating both resistance and complicity. As resistance, the wounded black body is a way of providing non-market images of the black body to counter the hyper-real, hyper-sexed black bodies that circulate as commodities in Western music, fashion and arts. Conversely, the 'wounded black body' registers patholo-gization – an over-representation of black bodies as weak, conflicted or contradictory to index inferiority. The figure of the wounded black builds on cultural ideas that equate bodily difference with inferiority. The wound serves as the mark of difference. "Lurking beyond the wound is the notion of the not wounded, the intact, normal body by which the wounded body is measured insufficient."[24]

Reading the conflicted black Christian body through the lens of the wounded black motif leads to the conclusion that the representation is either support for 'the multi-texted approach to black representation' argued by David Stevenson above or a nuanced pathologization of the black body. In this case black Christian bodies are defective.

Critical Black Christian Body

To distance myself from the blackface of the choir and also the wounded black motif, I decided to embody another embodied form of black

---

23. Jackson, *Violence, Visual Culture, and the Black Male Body*, 6.
24. Ibid.

Christian identity, that is, the tradition of black Christian resistance. Black Christian resistance, while a complex tradition of thought and action, describes black religious opposition to oppression, whether 'race', class or gender exploitation. The black church as an arbiter of black resistance has a long history in the English-speaking Caribbean. Reaching a high point in the nineteenth-century Christian slave revolts, black Christianity, particularly non-conformist, was at the forefront of anti-slavery and anti-colonial struggle. Take for instance the role of the native Baptists in Jamaican uprisings in 1831 and later in 1865. Resistance in black Christianity in Britain is opaque. While explicit public resistance has not characterised black churches in Britain, implicit forms of resistance are present in its worship culture.[25] Embodying black Christian resistance or projecting a critical black Christian body was a covert visual and audio practice. I explored signifying resistance in and through the visual aesthetics ('Black Suite Matters', 2009)[26] but more importantly, inscribing black liberation theology in the narrative aesthetic of the vast majority of documentary films I presented (*Documentary as Exorcism,* 2014).[27]

Renaissance Man?

Was this mission a success? Is there any evidence of a change of perception of black Christianity in the mainstream media? If so, what are some of the outcomes for interpreting the Bible documentary on television? I want to illustrate the range of responses to my representational politics based on reviews of my films in the national press in Britain. As shown above, television genres have a long history of positioning black Christians negatively as either musical blackface or conflicted bodies; however, authorial intentions in broadcasting come with few guarantees – the audience may not always understand the message as the receiver intended, and this is also the case here. I suggest that while the responses vary, they nonetheless demonstrate a meaningful shift in perception.

First, and closet to my intended message, are the preferred readings within the print reviews of my films. Intriguingly, these responses came

25. Robert Beckford, *Jesus is Dread: Black Theology and Black Culture in Britain* (London: DLT, 1998); Robert Beckford, *Dread and Pentecostal: A Political Theology for the Black Church in Britain* (London: SPCK, 2000).

26. R. Beckford, 'Black Suit Matters: Faith, Politics and Representation in the Religious Documentary', in *Black Theology and Aesthetics*, ed. A. Pinn (New York: Palgrave, 2009), 135–51.

27. R Beckford, *Documentary as Exorcism: Resisting the Bewitchment of Colonial Christianity* (London: Bloomsbury, 2014).

from the black press in Britain. The weekly 'Voice Newspaper', Britain's best-selling black newspaper, ran positive and constructive reviews of my films. More importantly by positioning my films as a critique of the black church, the religious affairs journalist for the newspaper, Marcia Dixon, acknowledged a shift in black church representation from entertainment to current affairs – a change I interpret as recognition of the critical black Christian body motif. However, there are also critiques of this position from within the church community. For instance, the Evangelical Alliance, an umbrella organisation for evangelical and Pentecostal churches, put out a press release, criticising my critique of African Christianity in the documentary, 'God is Black' (2004).[28]

Acknowledgement of a change in direction is also reflected in an interview in the black women's magazine 'Pride' in 2006. The title of the article, 'Dr Robert Beckford: Renaissance Black Man' spoke to a transformation of representation of black Christianity in the mainstream, including the black church as seat of learning:

> As far as the black intelligentsia goes, there are only a few whom we know about, let alone see on the screen. Robert Beckford is one of them.[29]

The article went on to consider the importance of a critical black voice emanating from the church and some of the drawbacks for those critiquing 'race' in the mainstream.

A second strand of reviews acknowledge the new position but failed to consider the implications for the black church. Instead the new representation was placed in a wider context and compared with a previous generation of religious broadcasters. For instance, a major review of 'God is Black' (2004) in *The Guardian* by Mark Lawson *played* on these historical presenter differences, to affirm a new direction in Christian broadcasting.

> Dreadlocked and demotic, Dr Robert Beckford may have little obviously in common with the late Dame Thora Hird. A meeting between the two might make a good Dead Ringers sketch. But a documentary series beginning this week suggests that Beckford may be the future of religious broadcasting on television, now that Thora has gone to find out if the heaven she so believed in is there.

28. 'Evangelicals Criticise Channel 4 Documentary about the Bible', *Ekklesia*, 19 December 12, www.ekklesia.co.uk.

29. *Pride*, Special Issue, 2006, 120–1.

The new black position was subsumed under a media perception of my presence as a new direction for religious broadcasting. In this guise, my critical black theological perspective was read as a general academic critique. One outcome of subsuming the black perspective was that I 'read' as a theologian or Anglican theologian rather than a 'black theologian'.

As I am neither an Anglican nor, as mentioned above, colluding with the politics of confinement/misrecognition, the moniker of 'Anglican' raises a new set of questions. For instance, was it possible to position myself as critical and still be considered a black Pentecostal?

Finally, a third strand of reviews repositioned the new position in black Christianity inside old racialised tropes. In other words, the new position was problematised as 'controversial'. For example, *The Guardian* newspaper's education supplement ran a full-page feature on my work as a part of a regular review of the work of publicly engaged academics. The review's subheading read:

> Theologian Robert Beckford is nurturing a new generation of African-Caribbean academics with his controversial views.[30]

So, what were these dangerous views? Liz Ford, the interviewer, referred to my critique of the collusion of English Christianity with empire as controversial! In the article, my response to the label she projected on me was to ask the readers to consider how critical black bodies are mis-read in the mainstream media as controversial, whereas bodies which are not marked in the same way, but which are equally challenging, are viewed as progressive or 'ground breaking'. Reading the new position as 'controversial', whatever its empirical merits, was, I suggest, on another level a re-inscribing of the wounded black motif. In this case, the appearance of the black Christian body signified danger, concern and ultimately difference.

In conclusion, the Bible documentary, like many visual texts, is mostly interpreted and read according to postmodern interest in textual or audience interpretation. Textual readings allow us to makes sense of an assemblage of narratives and perspectives on a biblical theme, and similarly, audience reception further enhances our ability to explore the impact of a film. However, the motivations explored in this chapter suggest that we cannot discount the motivations of the author of the programme and the discursive practices that engulf them. I have shown from the

---

30. Liz Ford, 'Robert Beckford: A Voice in the Crowd', *The Guardian*, 17 May 2005.

newspaper reviews that, like all representational politics, the motivations of presenters are never guaranteed to be received in the way that receiver intends for the audience. Much depends on where the audience positions themselves in relation to what they see and hear, and their cultural and theological awareness of the themes at play.

Chapter 7

THE NATIVITY ON TV

Helen K. Bond

The birth of Jesus is surely the best known – and most loved – of all the biblical stories. Shepherds, wise men, and a host of singing angels converge on a stable in Bethlehem to worship a tiny baby born to peasant parents. The evil plots of the wicked King Herod are thwarted, and goodness and innocence clearly triumph over greed and worldly desire. Every Christmas season countless primary schools and churches recreate their own version of the tale, under the watchful guidance of kindergarten teachers and Sunday School leaders. Some of these aspire to a 'traditional' retelling, following the biblical story closely and spending time on costumes and glow-in-the-dark stars. Others take more artistic license, aiming to shake up the old story with a new angle, extra characters or a novel twist to the plot. All the while, misty-eyed parents and adoring grandparents watch as their children prance across the stage wearing tea-towel headdresses, tinsel halos and assorted animal-inspired 'onesies'.[1]

But what about television adaptations? How has the story of the nativity fared on the small screen? TV programmes about the nativity can broadly be divided into two groups: (1) documentaries that ask about the 'real' birth of Jesus, offering scholarly analysis of the 'virgin birth' and various other aspects of the story (the Bethlehem tradition, the star, the census, the stable etc.), and (2) dramatizations of the biblical story. In

---

1. Anyone who has not experienced this first-hand might want to watch Debbie Isitt's film *Nativity* (2009), based around the experiences of a junior-school teacher.

this chapter, I shall examine one example from both categories. My aim is not at all to be exhaustive, but simply to focus on two TV programmes with which I have been involved. As a representative of the first group, I shall look at BBC's *Virgin Mary* (2002); I appeared on this programme as a 'talking head' and was approached by a number of radio stations and newspapers afterwards to defend the views expressed in it. As an example of the second type, I shall discuss the BBC's *Nativity* (2010), for which I acted as historical consultant. In each case, I am interested both in how these programmes can help us to understand the biblical story itself and also in how they reflect our contemporary culture.

The Virgin Mary

This documentary was a BBC/Discovery Channel co-production, in association with Jerusalem pictures, and first aired the Sunday before Christmas 2002 at 8pm. It was presented by actress Sue Johnston (well-known for her roles in *Brookside* and, more recently, the *Royle Family*), and produced and directed by David McNab (*The Planets*, 1999; *Equinox*, 2005).[2] The question the documentary posed was a simple one: what can we know about the real mother of Jesus? The aim was to reach back, behind the Virgin Mother of Christian piety, to the young woman from a Galilean village.[3]

My own involvement in the programme had come several months earlier when I was telephoned by one of the researchers. I had appeared on a handful of documentaries already, but still felt fairly new to the whole process. The researcher wanted to know what I thought about the 'real' Mary, what her life might have been like and whether I thought there was any historical truth in the birth narratives now preserved in the gospels of Matthew and Luke. By training I'm a biblical historian, with a focus on the people and politics of first-century Judaea, so the search for 'real human beings' was very much something which resonated with me. Of course, the truth is that we know virtually nothing about Jesus' mother, but scholars have pieced together an increasingly complex picture of what the life of a peasant woman in rural first-century Galilee might have been like. Although it would be a mistake blindly to apply all our insights to Mary,

2. Executive Producers were Jean-Claude Bragard and Alan Bookbinder. The film also thanks Prof Geza Vermes (Oxford) and Dr Sarah Boss (UK Centre for Marian Studies).

3. See the official press announcement, http://www.bbc.co.uk/pressoffice/pressreleases/stories/2002/12_december/12/mary_pack.shtml.

it gives us a very good picture of how her life is *likely* to have been, and certainly saves us from projecting our modern assumptions onto her. We know, for example, that young girls tended to be married early (anything after the onset of puberty, which was taken to be around twelve and a half), that infant mortality rates were extremely high, that childbirth itself was a risky undertaking and that the average life expectancy for women at the time was around 30 years of age. We know that women were largely engaged in domestic activities, child rearing, cooking and the making and mending of clothes, though women of higher social status and greater financial independence might exercise a great deal more autonomy in the public and even religious sphere.[4] We also know a reasonable amount about the political situation at the time: the end of Herod I's successful yet repressive reign, the revolts which erupted all over the country in 4 BCE (around the time of Jesus' birth) and the brutal Roman reprisals, and the reasonably competent rule of Herod's son Antipas.[5] I spoke to the researcher about all of these things at some length; then, as often happens, all went quiet.

In the summer of 2002, I was invited for an interview at Yarnton Manor in Oxford. The imposing panel-lined rooms were to be the backdrop for all three British contributors – myself, Mark Goodacre and Chris Maunder (James Charlesworth, Tal Ilan and Miriam Peskowitz were filmed elsewhere). My own interview lasted around two hours and I have to admit that it was one of the most difficult I've ever had to do. David McNab (the director) asked me a question and I responded, then he asked me to give my answer again but with the components rearranged. So, for example, in answer to the question 'Is it likely that Herod killed all the young boys in and around Bethlehem?' I might say 'There are a number of reasons why I think it unlikely that Herod killed the young boys. One is that the report is only in Matthew's gospel, another is that Matthew is keen to link Jesus with Moses and this story sounds suspiciously like the

---

4. Useful analyses of women in first-century Israel can be found in Tal Ilan, *Jewish Women in Greco-Roman Palestine: An Inquiry into Image and Status* (Tübingen: Mohr Siebeck, 1995); R. S. Kraemer, *Her Share of the Blessings: Women's Religions among Pagans, Jews and Christians in the Greco-Roman World* (Oxford: Oxford University Press, 1992); and R. S. Kraemer and M. R. D'Angelo, eds, *Women and Christian Origins* (New York/Oxford: Oxford University Press, 1999).

5. See, for example, L. Grabbe, *Judaism from Cyrus to Hadrian* (London: SCM, 1994); M. H. Jensen, *Herod Antipas in Galilee: The Literary and Archaeological Sources on the Reign of Herod Antipas and its Socio-Economic Impact on Galilee* (Tübingen: Mohr Siebeck, 2006).

story of Pharaoh's vendetta against the Jewish boys in Exodus, and the
third reason is that the Jewish historian Josephus, who gives a detailed
account of the last years of Herod's reign, doesn't mention it.' 'Great',
David said in response, 'now say it again starting with Moses ...' (or
Josephus, or Matthew). By the end of two hours my head was completely
spinning and I flew back to Edinburgh with very little sense of whether
my contribution was any good or not. Once the documentary aired, I saw
exactly why we'd all had to repeat ourselves so many times. The scholars
featured in the programme were slotted together so that often one person
started the thought, another continued it and a third finished it off. That
was why we had needed so many different versions of each answer! The
resulting collage gave a strong sense that what we were saying wasn't
just our own opinion but represented the scholarly guild – something for
which I would later be grateful.

A few weeks before Christmas I began to get some inkling that the
programme might make a stir. Representatives from the BBC asked if I
would be willing to speak to the press about the views expressed in the
documentary, and I agreed. At first things were fairly easy going. The
Saturday Mail ran a feature on Mary, quoting from a telephone interview
they'd done with me, and *The Guardian* asked me to write an article on
'The Real Mary'.[6] On 11 December *The Daily Telegraph* ran an article
headlined 'BBC Says Christ was Born in Nazareth'. The article quoted
two of the contributors – Mark Goodacre and Christopher Maunder –
and noted that the programme would upset 'traditionalists'.[7] Already
the papers had someone ready to be offended: Canon Professor Edward
Norman, the Chancellor of York Minster and a modern church historian,
attacked the programme as sensationalist, declaring 'I see no reason to
doubt the traditional account'.[8] Tara Conlan in the *Daily Mail* reported
that the Vatican had weighed into the controversy. Reacting to a claim
that the programme discussed whether Mary had been the victim of rape,
Vatican spokesman Cardinal Martins Jose Saravia accused the BBC of
'silliness', perpetuating 'old stories that every now and then resurface and
that have never had any historical support'. He added: 'As a Christian, I

6. H. K. Bond, 'Who was the Real Virgin Mary?' *The Guardian*, 19 December
2002, http://www.theguardian.com/world/2002/dec/19/gender.uk1.

7. For Mark Goodacre's reflections on the storm caused by the programme (and
the fact that he was never asked to preach again in his church), see http://www.
sbl-site.org/publications/article.aspx?articleId=239.

8. The article can be found at http://www.telegraph.co.uk/news/uknews/1415755/
BBC-says-Christ-was-born-in-Nazareth.html.

am simply mortified that something like this should be shown so close to Christmas'.[9]

Foremost amongst detractors, however, was the Catholic Bishop of Portsmouth. The Right Reverend Crispian Hollis had three primary objections: first, that the programme queried the 'virgin birth';[10] second, that we had raised the possibility that Mary had been raped by a Roman soldier; and, third, that (in his view) we had treated Mary with a lack of respect. 'As Mother of God', he noted, Mary 'is honoured and venerated by millions of Catholics and other Christians within these islands and all over the world'. He summed things up in the following manner:

> To include, within a historical examination of her life, confused and unfounded guesswork, which carries with it crude and offensive speculation is not only unscholarly but runs the risk of undermining the very integrity of the project itself.[11]

Reports of the 'offensive' programme quickly spread throughout the internet, particularly within Catholic circles. The UK-based contributors were asked by the BBC to speak on behalf of the programme; Mark Goodacre was a guest of Edwina Curry's late night show on Five Live and over the next few days I was invited to a series of radio interviews. Fortunately, the production team sent me a video copy of the documentary so that I – unlike my opponents – had at least seen the programme.

The fact that so many people were ready to condemn a programme they had never seen struck me as one of the oddest features of this whole episode. In the end, over 500 people complained to the BBC, making it the year's most complained about programme.[12] But the vast majority of those

9. T. Conlan, 'BBC Faces Fury for Portraying Virgin Mary as Rape Victim', http://www.dailymail.co.uk/news/article-152617/BBC-faces-fury-portraying-Virgin-Mary-rape-victim.html.

10. Technically, of course, we were discussing the *virginal conception* of Jesus, but I have retained the more popular phrase as it was used at the time.

11. Bishop Hollis was chairman of the Church's Strategic Media Committee and an ex-BBC producer. For coverage at the time, see http://news.bbc.co.uk/1/hi/uk/2598357.stm.

12. On 23 December 2002, the number was reported at 500; see O. Gibson, 'Record Complaints for BBC's Virgin Mary', *The Guardian*; http://www.theguardian.com/media/2002/dec/23/bbc.broadcasting. By 11 January 2003 the number was reported at 'more than 1000'; see J. Petre, 'Viewers Attack Virgin Mary Documentary', *The Telegraph*, http://www.telegraph.co.uk/news/uknews/1418553/Viewers-attack-Virgin-Mary-documentary.html. Both papers note that most complaints were made before people had seen the programme.

complaints (around 80%) were made *before* the show aired, meaning that most of the people who contacted the BBC had not actually seen the programme! Undoubtedly some of the complainers took their lead from the Catholic clergy and what they had read about the programme in the media. Others, however, seem to have been part of a more calculated plan of action. The American Society for the Defense of Tradition, Family and Property announced the 'insulting' documentary on its website. In addition to holding protest rallies outside the BBC's US headquarters, the society

> immediately activated its phone and email protest network. Hundreds were called within 48 hours. Each activist was requested to call BBC to express their rejection of The Virgin Mary program, plus call 10 more friends and urge them to do the same. In this manner, the protest quickly snowballed.[13]

The group's stated aim was to prevent the documentary from ever airing in the US. Again, none of these people knew exactly what they were complaining about, but were only too willing to believe the worst of the BBC. Once the documentary had aired, the number of official complaints tailed off considerably. The negative publicity, however, may have taken its toll on viewing figures – despite its prime time slot and well-known presenter, only three million people tuned in (roughly 10% of the viewing audience that night).

So what did the programme actually say? Despite all the hype and controversy, the documentary simply pointed out what biblical scholars have known for years. It referred to Mary throughout by her Jewish name, Miriam, and filled out the meagre biblical details from what we know of the lives of Jewish peasant women in the first century. The programme picked up her story as a girl of perhaps twelve or thirteen, finding herself unexpectedly pregnant just as she was about to be married to a much older man. Alternative explanations for Mary/Miriam's mysterious pregnancy were considered, including the possibility that her son might have been illegitimate (a charge which may lie behind Jn 8:41) and the suggestion that she may have been raped by a Roman soldier (a claim which goes back at least to Celsus in the second century CE). Those scholars who appeared on the programme were unanimous in judging these to be unlikely historically. In all probability, it was concluded, Jesus' father was none other than Joseph. Three of the interviewees, however, openly declared their own Christian commitment, and the tension they felt as

---

13. The quotation is taken from the Society's own webpage: http://www.tfp.org/ current-campaigns/2002/american-catholics-reject-bbc-pseudo-documentary.html.

both Christians and historians. The Bethlehem tradition and the story of Herod's slaughter of the young boys were also discussed, though in less depth. Once again, both were said to be unlikely historically, though the programme offered good reasons for their rejection (specifically the desire to link Jesus with the City of David, hence the Bethlehem tradition, and Moses, hence the Herod story with its strong links to Exod. 2).

Considering Mary's later life, the programme paid some attention to Joseph's death, noting the plight of a widow in biblical times, and the expectations which must now have rested on Jesus as head of the household. This led to a discussion of the tension between Jesus and his family suggested by Mk 3:21, 31-35. Despite raising the possibility of difficulties, however, the film still maintained the traditional view that Mary accompanied her son to Jerusalem for his last Passover, and left the viewer with the impression that it was more than likely that she would have been at the cross (as Jn 19:25 maintains). Finally, the film reflected on the tradition of Mary's perpetual virginity (a non-biblical belief which started to emerge around the second century) and the assumption into heaven of her incorruptible body after death (which only became dogma in 1950).[14]

The film was a clever blend of personal reflection and questioning from the presenter, interspersed with academic 'talking heads' and dramatic reconstructions of biblical events. The dramas were shot in Morocco, and featured a middle-eastern cast in clearly peasant surroundings. While there was no direct interaction between Sue Johnson and the scholars, she often appeared to observe the dramatic reconstructions, watching events unfold and reacting to what she saw. Particularly striking, too, was the strong visual contrast between a serene 20-year old Mary in her traditional blue robe (invariably accompanied by tranquil music) and an alarmingly young, much darker peasant girl in dirty clothes who was cast as Miriam (accompanied by the sounds of a busy Arab home and oriental music). While the 'traditional' image of Mary glided effortlessly through her surroundings, young Miriam was very much part of the dangerous and chaotic political upheaval of her times. The purpose of the programme, however, was not to *replace* one woman with another, but simply to suggest that there may be more to the story of Mary-Miriam than the church's recollection of her. This is made quite explicit in the closing reflections, when Sue Johnson says that she has

---

14. The findings of the programme are broadly summarised in a factsheet, 'The Real Mary', provided by the BBC at http://www.bbc.co.uk/pressoffice/pressreleases/stories/2002/12_december/12/mary_pack_realmary.pdf.

found two women – the Mary of faith, and the real woman at the centre of later Christian reflection. There is no sense that one is 'better' than another; the point is rather that they provide two differing images which will resonate in various ways with different people.

The Miriam of history/Mary of faith distinction is reminiscent of the common scholarly distinction between the Jesus of history/Christ of faith. Strangely, TV audiences seem to be much more able to separate out their Jesuses from their Marys. Perhaps this is because of the sheer volume of documentaries that have concentrated on the Jesus behind the myths – not least *Jesus the Evidence* almost twenty years previously. The idea that there might have been a 'real' first-century Jesus behind the Christ of the church seems to be one which a majority of people are willing to accept. Another reason might be that there is much more material to work with for Jesus, and TV documentaries, however sensational, rarely depart too drastically from a broadly traditional picture.[15] An attempt to separate the Miriam of history from the Mary of faith is hampered by the fact that the available material is so slight and is itself so heavily permeated with theological and Christological concerns. It was only by stripping these away that we could hope to find the historical Mary, but it was precisely in this process that we challenged what many held most dear about her.

There were other things, too, which caused offence. Despite its relatively early scheduling (8pm), the programme contained a fairly graphic scene of Mary giving birth to her son. Nativity scenes don't tend to focus on the squalid surroundings, the agony of childbirth and the danger of the whole undertaking in one so young. The programme pointed out, too, that Joseph was likely to have been much older than Mary. This is a perfectly accepted part of church tradition, included in the second-century *Protoevangelium of James* (in which Joseph is an elderly widower with children from a previous marriage). But when viewers actually *saw* a girl of around thirteen with a man who was clearly much older (and who, it has to be said, often seemed to have a worldly wise, even lascivious, smirk on his face), it was perhaps inevitable that the clear overtones of paedophilia provoked a shocked reaction.

Cultural prejudices may also have played their part. Most people know intellectually that Mary was a Jewish girl from a peasant home, and that she would have looked very different from her usual depictions in Western art. It is a very different thing, however, to see her 'otherness' brought

---

15. One of the few which does is Simcha Jacobovici and James Cameron's *The Lost Tomb of Jesus* (2007), which not surprisingly caused an outcry (given that it claimed to have found the tomb of Jesus).

to life on the screen. More curiously, as James Crossley has observed, the programme draws not so much on *Jewish* stereotypes as *Arab* ones: characters have rotten teeth, seem to exhibit unbridled lust, treat their women as drudges, cover their heads and generally display wild and ungoverned speech and behaviour.[16] Shortly after 9/11 and the early stages of the 'War on Terror', the documentary highlighted Mary's 'otherness' by aligning her with the new enemies of the West. The holy family are rescued to some extent from their oriental otherness: Mary does not cover her head, Jesus is clean-shaven or sports a neatly trimmed beard and Joseph mellows into a loving father.[17] Yet the shock that some viewers felt at seeing them projected into an alien culture which was associated in the daily news with terrorism is easy to appreciate.

Of course, I was aware that the programme's subject matter was going to be controversial. Although I'm from a Protestant tradition, I attended a Catholic Convent school until I was ten, so I'm quite aware of the prominence of the Blessed Virgin Mary within some church traditions (Mary's own immaculate conception and dormition were firmly established items on my own curriculum). Perhaps because of my early schooling I would consider myself more ready than most Protestants to give the mother of Jesus a crucial role in his upbringing and formative years. Yet I was still surprised by the levels of hostility that the programme aroused, and deeply shocked and hurt by the letters and emails that I received personally (which included death threats and what would probably be considered 'hate mail'). While many people enjoyed the programme, finding the consideration of Mary as a real historical woman both liberating and enlightening, some had clearly found it too threatening to stomach.

Reflecting on it later, a number of things occurred to me. First, although I would stand by the film's content in its entirety, I can appreciate that challenging ideas were presented rather too quickly. If I were teaching the gospel birth narratives to a class of first year undergraduates, I would present things very differently. I'd get them to compare the account in Matthew 1–2 with Luke 1–2, taking into consideration points of agreement/disagreement and matters of chronology (for example, the facts that Herod died in 4 BCE while Quirinius's census took place in 6 CE). I'd get them to observe how each account fits nicely with the concerns of each evangelist (Jesus as a second Moses and King for Matthew, an interest in the poor and oppressed for Luke). Finally, I'd ask students to think about

16. J. G. Crossley, *Jesus in and Age of Terror: Scholarly Projects for a New American Century* (London: Equinox, 2008), 103–5.

17. So also ibid., 104.

the more philosophical problem of whether an event has to be historical for it to be 'true', and to ask whether an account can convey theological truth even if historians are doubtful that it ever took place. All of this, of course, takes time and sensitivity, and these are not often features of a one-hour documentary.

I did end up feeling some frustration that while we had dismantled the historical framework of the traditional Christmas story, we were not given enough space to suggest anything more positive. James Charlesworth briefly suggested that the virgin birth story might be seen as 'symbolic', but the thought was not developed. In many ways this was quite understandable; the focus was on the historical Mary, not the birth stories themselves, Yet the overall result tended to be rather negative, and stopped short at providing people with the tools they might need to articulate their faith in a different way ('picture language', 'metaphor' etc.). Interestingly, the programme coincided with a survey carried out by the *Sunday Telegraph* which suggested that 27% of Church of England clergy did not believe in the virgin birth.[18] Two years later, a similar poll of Church of Scotland ministers found that 37% interpreted the virgin birth metaphorically rather than as a description of an actual event.[19] Trained in universities and theological colleges, these clergy presumably accepted the mainstream scholarly approach expressed by the programme, but it would have been interesting to see whether any of them used the documentary to start a discussion within their churches about how important history is to faith – or whether they simply shied away from the whole issue.

The same might also be said of the more vocal detractors. Reading through the press cuttings more than a decade later, I still feel that the ideas and opinions of a range of scholars were trivialised and belittled by Bishop Hollis and others. Presumably they felt they were defending their faith against heresy and attack, which they had every right to do. But to label our scholarship 'confused and unfounded guesswork' was not only deliberately offensive towards those who had consented to be on the programme, but also deeply misleading. Had the bishop taken the time to

18. C. Hasting and F. Govan, 'Quarter of Clergy do not Believe in the Virgin Birth', 22 December 2002; http://www.telegraph.co.uk/news/uknews/1416824/Quarter-of-clergy-do-not-believe-in-the-Virgin-Birth.html.

19. V. Cleary and H. Marney, 'Virgin Birth not taken as Gospel', *The Sunday Times*, Scotland, http://www.timesonline.co.uk/. Not surprisingly perhaps, there seemed to be a geographical split with those in the Highlands and Islands favouring a more literal approach and those in the central belt tending towards the more metaphorical.

read one of the most significant books on the gospel birth stories, written by Catholic scholar Raymond Brown, he would have found similar views (albeit couched in rather more careful language and accompanied with a full suite of footnotes).[20] Rather than brand scholars and the BBC as 'anti-religious', it might have been more fruitful for Christian leaders to begin an open conversation on how we might understand texts like the gospel birth stories in a modern, scientific society. The virginity of Mary might be a part of the creed, but it is surely useful to reflect on the fact that two of our earliest Christian writers, the apostle Paul and the evangelist Mark, seem quite ignorant of the tradition. The importance which this particular Christian belief has attained in some quarters would doubtless have struck both New Testament authors as remarkable.[21]

A final point concerns timing. The Vatican spokesman suggested that Christmas was the very worst time to air a programme exploring the 'real' Mary, but when would have been better? For the majority of people (including protestant believers), Christmas is the only time throughout the year when Mary achieves any kind of prominence. Would the same programme have been received differently if it had been broadcast over the summer? I doubt it, though there might perhaps have been less news coverage.

What my participation in *The Virgin Mary* taught me was that it is not always easy to turn biblical scholarship into a TV documentary. Many (perhaps the majority?) will find the discussion fresh and liberating. Others, particularly at Christmas, want only to be reminded of the mystery of the birth of Jesus Christ. For them, a Bible documentary is at best an irritant, at worst a programmatic attack on their faith. But what about the other kind of biblical programme, the type that aims to dramatize the text in a historically credible way?

The Nativity

This TV miniseries first aired on the BBC in December 2010, going out in four half-hour episodes each evening at 7pm in the run-up to Christmas.[22]

20. R. E. Brown, *The Birth of the Messiah: A Commentary on the Gospels of Matthew and Luke* (London: Chapman, 1993).

21. For a balanced appraisal, see now the thoughtful and thorough study by A. Lincoln, *Born of a Virgin? Reconceiving Jesus in the Bible, Tradition and Theology* (London: SPCK, 2013).

22. The series was shown again the following year, this time in two hour-long episodes on 24 and 25 December, and in the US (on BBC America) as one two-hour block in 2012.

It was written by Tony Jordan, a writer on the hugely popular soaps *Eastenders* and *Brookside*, and the series *Hustle* (from 2004) and *Life on Mars* (2006).[23] The series was produced by Jordan's own production company, Red Planet Pictures, and was filmed in Ouarzazate, Morocco. It was directed by Coky Giedroyc (*Women Talking Dirty*, 1999; *The Virgin Queen*, 2005), and starred Tatiana Maslany (*Orphan Black*) as Mary and Andrew Buchan (*Garrow's Law*, *Broadchurch*) as Joseph. The miniseries was an instant hit, attracting 5.21 million viewers in the UK alone (representing an audience share of 20.3%).[24] Widely acclaimed as a gritty yet moving portrayal of the traditional story, the series emerged as the clear winner at the annual Sandford St Martin Trust religious programme awards and was voted best religious programme of the year by *Radio Times* readers (both 2011).

My own involvement with the project went back to 2005. It all started with an email from Simon Winstone, Head of Development at Red Planet Pictures. He had seen me on a few TV documentaries and knew from my webpage that I was a biblical historian with a particular interest in Roman Judaea and Christian origins. He told me that Red Planet was hoping to dramatize the story of the birth of Jesus for the BBC, and that they were looking for someone to act as historical consultant. I've always been fascinated by the gospel accounts of Jesus' birth, and the chance to work on a dramatization of them was one that I couldn't easily turn down. But I was also slightly bemused: as already noted, I don't think that there is a great deal of history in these stories, and the difficulties only increase when you try to put the Matthean and Lukan versions together. Do you set the story in the final years of Herod I, around 6 BCE (so Matthew), or at the time of the census in 6 CE (so Luke)? Does the holy family have to make a special journey to Bethlehem (so Luke), or are they resident there already (so Matthew)? And is the newborn visited by shepherds (so Luke), or Magi (so Matthew) – or both?

In January 2006, Simon arranged to come up to see me in Edinburgh along with the writer, Tony Jordan, and the three of us met in an Italian restaurant to talk things through. I remember turning to Simon early in the conversation and suggesting that they dramatize just one of the birth stories – either Matthew's version or Luke's. The advantage, I argued, was that each one has its own integrity, its own 'world' which could much more easily be mapped onto a historical framework. Without a

23. Jordan would continue the biblical theme with his script for BBC's *The Ark* in 2015.

24. Paul Millar, '4.3M see "Miranda" Xmas Special', http://www.digitalspy. co.uk/tv/news/a294384/43m-see-miranda-xmas-special.html.

moment's hesitation, Simon patiently explained that the composite picture was part of our modern birth story. Each and every detail (irrespective of which gospel it came from) was a crucial component in the contemporary Christmas-card, nativity-play view of the birth of Jesus. Shepherds, wise men, Herod, the census, even down to the star – the finished product was going to have them all. In retrospect (and much as it pains me to say it), he was right. There's a place for academic treatments of the birth story (such as the documentary mentioned earlier), but this wasn't it. In a dramatization destined to air at peak time in the run-up to Christmas, viewers don't want to be challenged by nit-picking academics. What they want to see is the story they have known ever since they were children, with all its magic and mystery.

But where did that leave my role as historical consultant? As a historian, I don't imagine that there was a census which required Galileans to return to Bethlehem, nor do I believe that Herod killed all the toddlers in and around Bethlehem (as we've seen already, the detail is meant to link him to the Pharaoh of Exod. 2, and so to present Jesus as a second Moses). I think that these stories are true in a very profound, theological way, but I don't think that the birth of Jesus happened as either Matthew or Luke tell it. So I clearly had to decide whether I was up for a project like this or not. It didn't take long to decide that I was. The basic storyline was a given (irrespective of my view of its historical nature). My job was going to be one of providing local colour, adding historical detail, perhaps even adding plausibility to some features of the story and generally helping the whole thing to evoke the cultural world of first-century Israel.

And that's what we talked about at that first meeting. Tony wanted to know what it would have been like for a young unmarried girl to find herself pregnant in first-century Judaea; what a carpenter would have done; where on the social pecking order a shepherd belonged; what people thought about Rome and taxes, and a host of other things. I told him about Herod I, only to be rather deflated when he said that Herod probably wouldn't make an appearance, and that his presence would be much more menacing and brooding if we didn't see him on screen (actually, we did see an ill, sore-ridden Herod in the finished product). I also told him about Nicolaus of Damascus, Herod's court secretary and advisor, who eventually made it into the drama as Herod's right-hand man (and as a Greek provided an important outsider perspective). I also stressed the shame that a young girl would have felt in an ancient context, and the consequences that her pregnancy could have had for the whole family (this was used to good effect in the Bethlehem scenes, where Joseph and Mary are unable to find a room because of the dishonour they have brought to their families, rather than simply a lack of space). The afternoon passed quickly as we tried to imagine ourselves back in those ancient times.

After that I heard nothing until June 2007, when Simon contacted me with a script which he wanted me to look at and the news that the idea had gone to the BBC commissioners. He noted that it was now 'somewhat traditional rather than historically accurate', which is only what I'd expected after that initial meeting. Still, there were a number of places where small revisions would give the work a more historical edge, and I sent back a list of these. In April 2009, I heard that the drama had been commissioned, that work on the script would now proceed quickly and that it would go out in December 2010.

Over the next year or so I saw two further versions of the script, one in April 2009 and another (the pre-production) just before filming started in March 2010. Most of my input was in the form of emails or telephone calls to Simon Winstone, who would then convey suggestions to Tony Jordan. In some ways emails were the easiest way of communicating; they might be quite lengthy, but I could explain exactly what I meant and Simon could simply forward them on. Once filming was underway, Simon occasionally asked my advice on particular points. For example, as they were about to film the betrothal ceremony he wanted to know if a bride would wear a veil (I thought she would), whether people would be seated or standing to pray (I thought standing), how a Herodian soldier might salute (this was trickier, but I thought the same way as a Roman), whether a rabbi would have had prayer beads (I thought not, just a fringed shawl perhaps) and what they might have eaten after a betrothal (obviously kosher, but perhaps the men and higher status individuals might have taken their food first). The answers to many of these queries are far from clear – all I could do was to suggest what seemed likeliest to me, based on my general knowledge of the first century, and I certainly learnt a lot myself.

The comments I had on the scripts were generally of two types. First were the small details which could be changed easily without any detriment to the script, things which would add a greater sense of authenticity to the story. So, for example, the Magi talked of the 'King of Israel', but the evidence we have suggests that this phrase was only used by Jews themselves – outsiders talked of the 'King of the Jews'. An early script suggested that it took Joseph several months to make the 50-mile journey to Bethlehem; I thought a few weeks would have been enough to get there and back. We also had some discussion as to what level of taxation Thomas the shepherd would have paid. Originally he was due to pay five shekels, but this seemed high to me (particularly considering that the Temple tax was only half a shekel each year). The difficulty was knowing what to replace it with – a burly soldier asking for half a shekel (though a large amount in reality) somehow didn't sound very threatening. I suggested using one of the other coins in use in Judaea at the time – either the small bronze *lepta* (the widow's mite) or perhaps better the Greek *drachma* (one *drachma* = one *denarius* = a quarter of a shekel). The advantages with a drachma were that people have heard of it and the burly soldier could ask for a few of them! (In the end, however, the shekels remained.) There were other things too. Someone was described as a zealot (in the sense of a nationalist), when our evidence suggests that this group only emerged in the Jewish war of 66 CE; early scripts showed Galileans drinking Roman wine (the upper classes might have done this, but ordinary folk would have been more than content with their own local wines); people were drawing their water from a pump (more likely simply a well); and Mary called her father 'papa' (*abba*, I suggested, would be more authentic). These are all small details in themselves, but when there are significant numbers of them they can make a huge difference to the feel of the whole thing.

The second group of comments were much more significant and could potentially have a bearing on the plot itself. One problem that I always have with historical dramas is explaining that Roman soldiers weren't actually in Galilee in the time of Jesus. Herod I had his own army, largely drawn from the pagan cities of Caesarea and Sebaste, along with a few foreign mercenaries. Although he was a Roman appointment, the king didn't command any *Roman* soldiers.[25] The only place in the whole nativity story where legionaries would make sense is in connection with the census, where they would have been the men of Quirinius, the legate of Syria. If the story was going to have any verisimilitude, this was something that needed sorting out (and to be reflected in the costumes).

Another aspect of the story which concerned me at first was the role of the synagogue, which was being presented very much as a modern church. Mary went to the synagogue every day to sit and reflect, and the Rabbi referred to it as the 'house of God'. This might have been appropriate for the Temple in Jerusalem, with its high levels of purity and its aura of sanctity, but it didn't seem to capture the much more communal, practical role of the synagogue in an ancient Jewish village.[26] The Rabbi, too, was

25. On Roman troops under Herod, see B. Isaac, *The Limits of Empire: The Roman Army in the East* (Oxford: Clarendon, 1990).

26. On the ancient synagogue, see A. Runesson, *The Origins of the Synagogue: A Socio-Historical Study* (Stockholm: Almqvist & Wiksell, 2001).

cast as a modern Rabbi (or even a Christian minister), entrusted with the full-time care of his flock; whenever anyone wanted to see him, they simply made their way to the synagogue. Despite my efforts, I don't think that the synagogue ever really achieved much historical verisimilitude in the programme, but what it did do was to underline the piety of Mary (at least as far as Christian viewers were concerned).

There were also a couple of times when the pregnant Mary said that she was ready to 'go it alone', and later on her father (Joachim) asked Joseph to take her to Bethlehem with him so that she could 'start a new life'. Both of these struck me as very modern concepts – there would be no possibility of a woman and a baby surviving on their own in the ancient world. Even if her parents gave her money, the shame would be too much. Widows were always seen as the most vulnerable group in ancient society, and a woman with an illegitimate child all the more so (presumably prostitution or slavery would be her only options). I suggested that Joachim make arrangements for Joseph to take her to Bethlehem where she might be met by Elizabeth. As far as I could see, life with a sympathetic family would be the best option that Mary and her baby could hope for. In the end, two 'go it alone' passages did remain, though the expression on the faces of the actors did convey a sense of the futility of the situation.

My greatest worries, however, centred around the Magi. Part of the problem was that they seemed extremely well informed for Persian astrologers: they had an intimate knowledge of the Jewish Scriptures, recognized the star of Balaam straight away and were able to quote passages at will. More seriously, they also seemed well informed regarding later Christian ideas. At one point in an early script Melchior explains that the expectant Jewish Messiah was to be 'God in human form'.[27] Historically, there were a range of differing views regarding the Messiah amongst first-century Jews (a kingly leader? a priestly ruler? a prophet? God's envoy?), but there is no evidence whatsoever that anyone expected him to be 'God in human form'. The Magi had an uncanny knack of quoting exactly those passages that Christians would later draw upon as pointers to Jesus, and Melchior at the end (echoing Gabriel) describes Jesus in terms drawn from John's gospel. This was a particularly difficult issue as the Magi act in many ways as the 'religious interpreters' of the whole thing – they make sense of the story theologically, showing how

27. On messiahs in the first century, see G. S. Oegema, *The Anointed and his People: Messianic Expectations from the Maccabees to Bar Kochba* (Sheffield: Sheffield Academic, 1998); J. J. Collins, *The Scepter and the Star: Messianism in the Light of the Dead Sea Scrolls* (Grand Rapids: Eerdmans, 2010); and M. V. Novenson, *Christ Among the Messiahs* (New York: Oxford University Press, 2012).

events are all part of God's plan, foretold from ancient times.[28] If the Magi didn't know the significance of what they were seeing and simply went to Jerusalem to have a closer look at an interesting conjunction, we would miss a crucial dimension of the whole story. Someone else would have to supply the theological underpinning, but no one else was quite so well suited for this role as the exotic men from the East. In the end, the Magi's great knowledge stayed in the script. It was one of the things that the series was criticized for, particularly by biblical bloggers (who love to point out historical faults), but I don't really think that there was much alternative. Without it the whole story would have lost a great deal of its religious meaning.[29]

What struck me most about the final script was the strength of the characterization. Biblical stories are not easy to retell, and characters can all too easily descend into implausibility and woodenness. The film *The Nativity Story* (released in December 2006), was full of nativity clichés – soaring musical scores and angelic choruses – and presented a Mary who could have stepped straight out of a Christmas card. At the other extreme, we've already seen that *The Virgin Mary* went almost too far, casting Mary/Miriam as a character almost too 'other' for contemporary Western women to identify with. One of the aims of the BBC production was to avoid crass stereotypes. In fact, the reason for approaching Tony Jordan in the first place was because he was known for some of the 'edgier' plotlines on TV soaps. The idea was that the drama would be gritty, the characters complex and believable and the plot would be a deeply human story. And this of course meant getting as far away as possible from the Christmas card tableaux

28. The sense of 'everything written in the stars' was highlighted by a number of computer-generated shots of planets moving into conjunction, about which Jordan is said to have consulted NASA.
29. Similar worries surrounded Elizabeth. In any early script, she has a scroll of Isaiah in her house and is able to consult it and find the prophecy of Isa. 7:14 in which a virgin is said to conceive a child. There were a number of difficulties here: given low literacy rates, is it likely that Elizabeth could read? Would many people have owned an Isaiah scroll? And – most important of all – did anyone, prior to the late first century, read this passage as a prophecy of the expected Messiah? In the end, her husband Zechariah (now struck dumb by his encounter with an angelic messenger) writes the Isaiah passage on a wax tablet for her to read. A slightly better scenario, perhaps, but the basic problem of interpreting Isaiah in the manner of later Christians still remains.

In many respects, the nativity story has all the hallmarks of a TV soap opera.[30] There's the young, unmarried girl who finds herself pregnant; her devastated fiancé, whose first instinct is to break off the engagement and lash out; and a range of ordinary folk like shepherds and the inn-keepers trying to keep their heads above water. Even the decision to first broadcast the drama in four 30-minute slots on consecutive evenings, and to end each one on a cliff-hanger, mimicked the typical transmission of a TV soap. As Jordan said himself, the challenge was to retell the nativity in a way that would 'still surprise and move you'. And it seems to have worked. The effect of fuller storylines, quirky retellings and the stripping back of at least some of the traditional religious veneer did mean that people tuned into the programme in large numbers.

Making Mary into a credible character was no easy task. We're introduced to a delightful, playful, caring, pious young girl who, the programme is keen to tell us, is already sixteen ('a woman') and ready to marry. This is still young by contemporary standards, but not excessively so,[31] and while we may worry about a young girl who gives birth so young, there is no hint of paedophilia in this presentation (the possibility of marriage to a much older toothless man is quickly, and rather humorously, dispensed with). The most difficult aspect of Mary's story is dealing with the annunciation. How should the supernatural be portrayed? And how likely is it that any young girl (however pious and saintly) would really believe Gabriel's incredible message quite that quickly? Jordan's annunciation scene is extremely well done. There's no flashing light or searing music, but instead a rather strange night-time encounter in the family garden between Mary and an enigmatic, serene stranger. Mary is scared; she can't really believe what she's hearing and asks the mysterious man to leave. It's only when he tells her to shut her eyes and to look deep inside herself that she begins to believe that what he says might be true, and only when she goes to visit her cousin Elizabeth that she finally starts to accept that she has been chosen to be the mother of the promised Messiah. The mingling of joy and terror, coupled with a growing sense of her own destiny, make this Mary every bit as pious as the traditional Virgin, while the greater level of uncertainty underlines the personal cost demanded from her, and imbues the whole portrait with new depths. Tatiana Maslany spoke of her experiences as Mary, finding her fallible

30. Also noted by Matt Page, http://biblefilms.blogspot.co.uk/search/label/BBC%27s%20The%20Nativity.

31. The age both of marriage and consent in the UK is 16.

and complicated, 'a girl with innocence, confusion and doubt, and also great courage and faith'. An ordinary child faced with 'an extraordinary journey'.[32]

The traditional portrait of Joseph is also problematic. Even allowing for angelic communications, there's something rather unreal about the speed and ease with which he accepts the fact that his fiancée's baby is from God. The biblical narrative hints at a greater degree of soul searching on Joseph's part (Mt. 1:19), a hint exploited to the full by Jordan's rewriting. In this retelling, Joseph does not believe that the child is from God until the very end. His initial thoughts are all too understandable: has Mary had too much wine and slept with someone? Was she raped? And how will he bear the shame of what she's done to him? He is persuaded to take Mary with him to Bethlehem by her father, and much against his own inclinations. In fact, the programme starts with the tense relations between the two of them on the way to Bethlehem, a tension which is gradually explained through a series of flashbacks. As the journey progresses, however, Joseph begins to change. He has a dream about Mary, but says that he does not have enough faith to believe what he is told. As he watches events in the stable, however, he finally believes. Overall, Joseph is a thoroughly credible character; not too bright, perhaps, but courageous, loyal and keen to do the right thing.

Jordan broke down the nativity story into three major strands:

-	At the heart of it all was the love story between Mary and Joseph, two ordinary people caught up in an extraordinary story. The climax of the whole drama wasn't just the birth of the child, but the moment when Joseph took Mary's outstretched hand in his as she gave birth to Jesus. All his blistering doubts, anger and rejection suddenly evaporated in a tidal wave of pure love.
-	Intertwined with the main story was the journey of the Magi, astrologers who made their way '1000 miles' from the east, chasing Balaam's star and searching for the promised messiah. This was probably the most 'traditional' strand of the drama, providing the motif of the 'quest' which is resolved at the end.
-	And finally was the story of Thomas, an overtaxed shepherd with a sick wife, struggling to make ends meet and finding himself drawn inexorably into rebellion against Rome. This strand allowed the story to be grounded in the realities of Roman-occupied Judaea;

32.	http://www.bbc.co.uk/blogs/legacy/tv/2010/12/tony-jordans-nativity-mary.shtml.

it gave a sense of the frustrations and limitations of most people's lives, and offered a less theologically charged idea of what 'salvation' might have meant in that context. In many respects, Thomas stands for us all, trying to make sense of the world around us.

All three strands come together at the end in the stable, forming the Christmas card cameo that we expect. But this is the only concession to sentimentality, and each character's journey to that ending is anything but clichéd. I was lucky enough to be invited to a screening in London a few weeks before the drama went out. It's even more powerful when you see all of it together in a two-hour block – and I don't think I was the only one to have tears streaming down my face by the end.

Jordan has spoken of his own personal journey as he brought these characters to life. He was frustrated by scholars who (like me!) told him it was all historically problematic, and yet at the same time he could see the inconsistencies in the accounts. In good scholarly fashion, he came up with a criterion for deciding how to get to the heart of things. He assumed that the tale had been passed down orally for decades, perhaps by shepherds around the campfire. It was inevitable that stories were tweaked, that dates got lost and that details were forgotten. So, for example, the Magi story as it is traditionally told is problematic. If Herod was so perturbed by their news, why did he not simply have the Magi followed? Why trust them to come back? The answer, he surmised, was that the Magi had not actually met with Herod, but with his envoy, Nicolaus of Damascus, who rode out to them as they camped on the outskirts of Herod's territory. Recognising the danger that they were putting the child in, the Magi pretended to pack up camp and leave by night (fooling Herod's guards) while secretly three of them made their way down to Bethlehem to see the newborn baby. Told around a campfire, however, this rather complicated chain of events was simplified,

> Would a shepherd take the time to mention that Herod sent an envoy to challenge the Magi, or would they simply say it was Herod himself? Those shepherds also wouldn't know who or what the Magi were, so how would they describe them? Wise men? Kings?[33]

By the time he'd finished the script, Jordan says, 'I believed that it did happen and it was a true story'.

33. Interview in *The Daily Mail*, http://www.dailymail.co.uk/home/moslive/article-1338840/Nativity-The-truth-story-according-Life-Mars-writer-Tony-Jordan.html.

The BBC took great care to ensure that the drama did not cause offence. In addition to a historical consultant, they also made sure that practising Christians were involved in the production, looking at scripts and attending the opening preview. For the most part, the efforts paid off. Most believers were delighted with the programme. It won praise from the Roman Catholic archbishop of Westminster, who noted that while there was clearly some dramatic license, there remained 'an overall fidelity, not only to the Gospel accounts but also to traditional imagery'. Similarly, the Evangelical Alliance called it an 'utterly moving piece of television'.[34]

But there were some detractors. Even before the programme had aired, the *Express* ran a story with the headline 'Fury over BBC's Nativity Insult'. What it all boiled down to was that a certain Stephen Green of a group calling itself 'Christian Voice' had objected to Joseph's assumption that Mary had been 'whoring' or even raped, and the insults cast on Mary by her neighbours. Mr Green opined that:

> [The Bible] doesn't suggest any physical or verbal abuse. It's typical of the fertile imagination you need for something like *EastEnders*. The kids that do nativity plays in school will be perplexed that someone has come up with this revisionist, puerile idea. The BBC can't help themselves. Three quarters of our population are Christian. At the BBC, this proportion is reversed. You have a huge proportion of militant, liberal atheists who are keen to dump on Christianity.[35]

The story was picked up by *The Way: Christianity without Walls*, an online Christian news site, with the headline 'Christians Outraged with BBC Nativity Drama'.[36] They quoted Green, adding comments by an ex-BBC presenter, Don Maclean, who claimed that the BBC failed to show churches in a positive light, saying: 'They seem to take the negative angle every time'. Interestingly, the comments section of the webpage was deluged by Christians who wrote in support of the series (by this time the first programme had aired).

---

34. Both noted by Riazat Butt in *The Guardian*, https://www.theguardian.com/media/2010/dec/23/bbc-nativity-drama-anti-jewish.

35. http://www.express.co.uk/news/uk/218290/Fury-over-BBC-s-Nativity-insult; dated 19 December 2010. According to Wikipedia, Christian Voice is a Christian advocacy group, whose stated objective is 'to uphold Christianity as the Faith of the United Kingdom, to be a voice for biblical values in law and public policy, and to defend and support traditional family life', http://en.wikipedia.org/wiki/Christian_Voice_%28UK%29.

36. http://www.theway.co.uk/news-8303-christians-outraged-with-bbc-nativity-drama.

Criticisms came from Jews too. *The Guardian* ran a story midway through the four episodes in which Rabbi Jonathan Romain (of the progressive movement Reform) complained about a scene in which a Bethlehem rabbi had denied shelter to a pregnant Mary. 'The Gospels tell us there was no room at the inn', he is quoted as saying, 'not that a rabbi kicked Mary out of a synagogue. Having survived Mel Gibson's anti-Jewish Easter onslaught *The Passion* [*of the Christ*] now the season of goodwill has been spoiled'. The BBC countered rabbi Romain's complaint by noting that everyone in the village reacted with hostility towards the pregnant Mary, and in fact the rabbi is the only character who shows her some compassion (he does at least allow her to escape the angry crowd by offering her a route to safety through the synagogue).[37]

Overall, the series was a huge success. What (small) criticisms there were seemed to centre on the fact that the plot line had gone beyond the biblical evidence. Two things need to be said in response to this. First, a dramatization which followed only the biblical script would not only be very short but would be virtually unwatchable due to its lack of psychological verisimilitude. Much that would be apparent to a first-century audience needs explaining in our own time: the penalties for adultery, the shame of Mary's predicament and so on. Second, those who responded rather snootily to the show's artistic license might want to consider that rewriting biblical passages for a new generation has an extremely long and distinguished pedigree. The category 'rewritten Bible' was coined by Geza Vermes to cover any rewriting of a scriptural text and covers material as diverse as rabbinic *midrash*, various books from the Pseudepigrapha (*Jubilees*, *1 Enoch* etc.) and works by Josephus and Pseudo-Philo.[38] Whether or not this body of literature forms a distinct 'genre', it seems to have been particularly popular in the late Second Temple period.[39] Often works are close to their scriptural source, but at other times they make quite significant additions or omissions. Sometimes the retelling is shaped and governed by intra-Jewish polemics, but at other times it seems largely to be a question of explaining material which is unclear, or updating it for a new generation. Of particular interest here is the retelling of the

---

37. Visit http://www.theguardian.com/media/2010/dec/23/bbc-nativity-drama-anti-jewish.

38. G. Vermes, *Scripture and Tradition in Judaism: Haggadic Studies* (Leiden: Brill, 1961), 67–126; for a recent review, see D. A. Machiela, 'Once More, with Feeling: Rewritten Scripture in Ancient Judaism – A Review of Recent Developments', *JJS* 61 (2010): 308–20.

39. See the discussion in M. Zahn, 'Genre and Rewritten Scripture: A Reassessment', *JBL* 131 (2012): 271–88.

Hebrew Scriptures by Josephus, something which occupies the first half of his *Jewish Antiquities*. Josephus explains away apparent contradictions, eliminates much of the supernatural, and stresses qualities in his heroes likely to commend them to his Graeco-Roman readers (for example, their courage, nobility, hospitality, great learning, beauty, etc.).[40] As Molly Zahn notes, 'What these texts do is provide a version of past tradition that better reflects the concerns and ideology of their community'.[41]

By updating the biblical text and explaining contradictions and difficulties, these later rewritings enabled the earlier texts to speak to contemporary readers. In many respects, what Jordan has done with *Nativity* is to produce a 'rewritten Bible' for today. His version of the story makes certain omissions (the supernatural is toned down considerably), explains apparent difficulties (the problem caused by Herod's rather naïve trust in the Magi is eliminated), provides greater rationales for the behaviour of central characters (Mary and Joseph respond to events in a much more credible manner) and generally updates the story for a modern audience.

Final Reflections

If *Nativity* can be seen as standing in the line of ancient rewritten Scriptures, it also has a much more modern counterpart in Dorothy L. Sayers's celebrated radio drama, *The Man Born to Be King* (1941/2).[42] Radio was the perfect place for stories, and television was perfect for *visual* stories, for shots of the Holy Land with its deserts and camels, Jerusalem's old city and other exotic locations.[43] As a genre, the gospel drama has proved incredibly popular, engaging with both churchgoers and a wider audience. The historical context is foregrounded, but in a non-threatening way, and the supernatural cut down to modern tastes. Viewers encounter the biblical stories anew, repackaged in a fresh way for a modern generation, and simply take them as timeless moral tales. In the face of political

40. See here the two works by L. H. Feldman, *Studies in Josephus' Rewritten Bible* (Leiden: Brill, 1998) and *Josephus' Interpretation of the Bible* (Berkeley: University of California Press, 1998).

41. Zahn, 'Genre and Rewritten Bible', 286.

42. See the discussion in Kenneth Wolfe, 'The Bible and Broadcasting', in *Using the Bible Today: Contemporary Interpretations of Scripture*, ed. D. Cohn-Sherbock (London: Bellew, 1991), 47–67; also Richard Wallis, Chapter 1 above.

43. This visual potential was exploited to the full by Zefirelli's *Jesus of Nazareth* (1977), BBC's *The Passion* (1999) and History Channel's *The Bible* (2013).

uncertainties, fragile stock-markets and uncertain futures, there is something deeply reassuring in the power of an ancient story.

And yet there is surely a problem here for biblical scholarship. These dramas condense the four gospels into one harmonious narrative, airbrushing out significant differences in perspective, and eliminating ambiguities. By toning down the supernatural and turning the biblical characters into the people next door, the biblical narrative is domesticated, deprived of its ability to shock or perplex. There is no room in all of this for Markan priority, the Q hypothesis or complicated theses of orality, still less feminist and postcolonial approaches to the Scriptures. Viewers might be emotionally moved, but they are not particularly challenged, nor asked to wrestle with the complex theological development that marked the early years of the church.

All of this means that the gap between biblical scholars and the general public continues to expand. While dramas might be a safe way for commissioners to fill their religious programming requirements, it is important for biblical scholars to continue to contribute to documentaries and to push for more factual-based programming on biblical themes. At a time when biblical studies is rarely taught in schools (as opposed to simply reading Bible stories), and churches are often reluctant to engage with more challenging questions, biblical documentaries may be one of the few ways in which scholars can promote the discipline to a wider audience. And if that sometimes means that we have to live with controversy and debate, often with people who haven't even bothered to watch the programme under discussion, then that is something we may simply have to live with.

Chapter 8

PUTTING PAUL ON TV:
THE CASE OF *DAVID SUCHET: IN THE FOOTSTEPS
OF ST PAUL**

Edward Adams

The apostle Paul has not received a massive amount of attention on
mainstream TV, but he has by no means been neglected either.[1] I acted
as academic consultant for one of the most recent attempts to put Paul
on TV: *David Suchet: In the Footsteps of St Paul* (hereafter, *DSFSP*), a
documentary series consisting of two hour-long episodes, first broadcast
in the UK on BBC1 in 2012. In this chapter, I look at how *DSFSP* deals
with Paul. I consider its approach to Paul in terms of its format as a
'footsteps of Paul' travelogue and as a quest for Paul's character; its
handling of the New Testament sources for the apostle; its use of interviewee contributions; and its coverage of the subject. I begin with basic
information about the series.[2]

* I would like to thank Ray Bruce and Martin Kemp for their help as I prepared
this chapter, and my co-editor for reading several drafts of it.
   1. Aside from the series under discussion in this essay, there have been three
other notable documentary productions on Paul on mainline British TV within the
past 20 years: *John Meets Paul: A Mediterranean Journey*, a six-part documentary
series hosted by John McCarthy, broadcast in 2003 on ITV; *Saint Paul*, a one-hour
documentary presented by Jonathan Edwards, shown the same year on BBC1; and
a one-hour episode on the apostle, led by Tom Holland, within the series *The Bible:
A History*, shown in 2010 on Channel 4. The apostle was also the subject of a major
BBC Radio 4 series, *In the Footsteps of Saint Paul*, broadcast in 2002, written and
presented by Edward Stourton.
   2. I am grateful to Caroline Matthews of CTVC for supplying me with press
information and viewing figures.

Basic Series Information

DSFSP follows the distinguished British actor David Suchet, famous internationally for his portrayal of Hercule Poirot in the long-running TV serial *Agatha Christie's Poirot*, on a journey from Jerusalem to Rome inspired by Paul's travels. Visiting Pauline places, viewing relevant archaeology and speaking to a host of 'expert witnesses', Suchet seeks to learn more about the apostle, especially the kind of person he was. Suchet is not simply filling the role of a celebrity presenter; as he explains at the beginning of the documentary, he is himself a Christian who owes his faith to Paul. It was through reading Paul's letter to the Romans in 1986 that Suchet was converted to Christianity.[3] Ever since, he has been fascinated by the apostle, and as an actor he would have liked to play him. Suchet's journey is thus, as he puts it, 'a very personal quest' for him, fulfilling a long-held ambition to walk in Paul's footsteps.[4]

The journey undertaken by Suchet structures the series. Episode 1 begins with Suchet in Jerusalem, where we first encounter Paul in the Acts of the Apostles, and ends with the actor crossing over into Europe. In Episode 2, Suchet follows Paul's route through Greece, vising Philippi, Thessalonica, Athens and Corinth; he returns to Jerusalem, visits the remains of the ancient city of Caesarea, and finally goes to Rome, where we last find Paul in Acts and where, according to early church tradition, he died as a martyr.

DSFSP was made for the BBC by CTVC in association with Jerusalem Productions. It was produced by Ray Bruce and Hannah Holloway and written and directed by Martin Kemp. The series was Suchet's own idea which he pitched to Bruce and CTVC, and Bruce pitched it to the BBC (the commissioning editor at the time was Aaqil Ahmed). Production took place between October 2011 and March 2012; filming was conducted over a six-week period in November and December 2011, with a crew consisting of Kemp, Paula Nightingale, who was the assistant producer, the late Lawrence Gardner, who was the director of photography, and Timothy Watts, who was the sound engineer. On his website, Kemp explains that

---

3. Suchet has expanded on his Christian conversion in a number of published interviews. See, for example, Justin Brierley, Interview with David Suchet, *Christianity*, February 2013, 16–19, esp. 18.

4. Suchet's 'journey of discovery' in *DSFSP* is of course carefully crafted for TV, but it is no charade. In his interview with Brierley, Suchet refers to his Pauline expedition as 'one of the most important experiences for me both as a person and as an actor'. As one of Suchet's interviewees in *DSFSP*, I can confirm the authenticity of his quest. Off-screen we chatted for hours about Paul: he was genuinely seeking to expand his knowledge of the apostle.

shooting the series in the Mediterranean so late in the year meant running the risk of delays to filming due to bad weather. Amazingly, though, not a single day was lost. 'The sun shone more or less constantly'.[5]

The series formed part of the BBC's religious output over Christmas 2012. It was heavily promoted, with Suchet giving a raft of media interviews in the lead-up to broadcast,[6] and it was highlighted in various TV viewing schedules (*Radio Times*; *TV Times*; *Daily Mail*; *The Telegraph*; *The Mail on Sunday*; *The Sunday Telegraph*; *The Sunday Times*). The first episode was screened on (Sunday) 23 December at 9am; the second was broadcast the next day, Christmas Eve, at the same time. The two programmes were repeated on BBC HD a week later (30 and 31 December).

Consolidating the original and repeat airings, each episode was watched by 3 million viewers. The series was positively reviewed, and it won two major awards: the 2013 Sanford Premier Award for religious television and the 2013 Radio Times Readers' Award. In the wake of its success, a sequel series with Suchet on St Peter was commissioned and broadcast (*David Suchet: In the Footsteps of Saint Peter*, BBC1, 2015). *DSFSP* was shown again on BBC1 during the Christmas period of 2015.[7]

Approach to Paul

The series' approach to Paul is governed by its format as a 'footsteps of Paul' travelogue and by its angle of enquiry as a quest for Paul's character.

A 'Footsteps of Paul' Travelogue

DSFSP adopts the format of a 'footsteps of Paul' travelogue, a traditional and once highly popular genre of writing about Paul in which a contemporary traveller recounts their experiences of following an itinerary based on Paul's movements, visiting sites associated with him.[8] The most famous example of the genre is H. V. Morton's *In the Steps of Saint*

---

5. https://www.martinkemp.tv/david-suchet-in-the-footsteps-of-stpaul.

6. He gave interviews to the *Daily Express* (10 December 2012), *Daily Mail* (15 December 2012) and *Lonely Planet Traveller* (December 2012). He appeared on ITV's *This Morning* (19 December 2012) and BBC1's *The One Show* (20 December 2012). He was interviewed on BBC Radio 4's *Loose Ends* (8 December 2012), and on 21 BBC local radio stations.

7. https://www.bbc.co.uk/programmes/b01pq9h5/broadcasts/2015/12.

8. On the growth and popularity of the genre in the nineteenth century, see Michael Ledger-Lomas, 'In the Steps of Saint Paul', in *Travel Writing, Visual Culture, and Form, 1760–1900*, ed. Mary Henes and Brian H. Murrays (Basingstoke: Palgrave Macmillan, 2016), 156–74.

Paul.[9] It was reading this book that instilled in Suchet the desire to go on his own Pauline pilgrimage.[10]

The format is a good fit for TV, and *DSFSP* is not the first TV production on Paul to adopt it.[11] It partially aligns with the established and popular TV genre of travel documentary, since to follow in Paul's footsteps 'is to be taken on a wide-ranging tour around the lands of the Mediterranean'.[12] Suchet's tour takes in fascinating cities such as Tarsus/Mersin and Antioch/ Antakya, famous landmarks such as Mars Hill in Athens, and wonderful archaeological sites such as Ephesus and ancient Corinth. The travel-documentary aspect is advantageous for attracting viewers who might not otherwise watch a TV show on Paul. In his interview in this volume, Bruce stresses the importance of making a Bible-based documentary 'appeal to a broad constituency, not just people of faith'.[13] The aesthetic potential of the format is brilliantly exploited by Gardner, who has furnished *DSFSP* with stunning location photography, and Gardner's photography is complemented by Howard Davidson's atmospheric soundtrack.

The format is a convenient one for relating the events of Paul's life, and Suchet captivatingly tells the story of Paul as he goes. Also, it facilitates an exploration of Paul in relation to the world in which he lived and moved. There is, of course, the danger that the locations become the centre of attention. But Suchet's personal quest keeps the focus on Paul, only rarely digressing to take in tourist attractions unconnected with the apostle,[14] and while the actor wants to get a sense of what Pauline places were like in Paul's own time, it is with a view to getting a better understanding of Paul himself.

9. H. V. Morton, *In the Steps of St. Paul* (New York: Dodd, Mead & Co., 1936). The book was an instant hit. It appeared in the month of October, and sold over a quarter of a million copies by the end of the year (Ledger-Lomas, 'In the Steps of Saint Paul', 156). Though the genre's heyday has long passed, 'footsteps of Paul' books continue to appear, though they are more travel guides than travel memoirs. For a recent (and excellent) example, see Peter Walker, *In the Steps of Saint Paul: An Illustrated Guide to Paul's Journeys* (Oxford: Lion Hudson, 2008)

10. Brierley, *Christianity*, 19. Suchet here calls Morton's volume 'one of the great books about Paul'.

11. *John Meets Paul: A Mediterranean Journey* is also in the style of a 'footsteps of Paul' travelogue. Stourton's *In the Footsteps of Saint Paul* clearly assumes the format too.

12. Walker, *In the Steps of St Paul*, 7.

13. See p. 85 in this volume.

14. As when he takes a boat trip along the Corinth canal, constructed in the late nineteenth century. An attempt was made under Nero to cut through the Isthmus of Corinth (Suetonius, *Life of Nero* 19), which Suchet mentions to justify his trip, but Nero's venture was an unmitigated failure.

A Quest for Paul's Character

Suchet's quest focuses especially on Paul's *character*, in line with the presenter's interest in Paul from an actorly point of view. He wants to know: What sort of person was Paul? What motivated him? What made him tick? He conducts his pursuit of the apostle as if he were researching a subject he is going to play. In his book, *Poirot and Me*, Suchet explains that as a character actor, he doesn't want to pretend to be someone else; his goal is rather 'to inhabit them, to bring them to life'.[15] He tells how, in preparation for his role as the famous detective, he read through all Agatha Christies' Poirot books, compiling a 'dossier of characteristics' in which he recorded every detail of Poirot's character,[16] so that he could 'project Poirot's behaviour precisely as Dame Agatha had described it'.[17] In *DSFSP*, he takes a similar approach to Paul, jotting down in a notebook things he learns about the apostle.[18] In narration and pieces to camera, he updates viewers on the personality profile he is building.

The emphasis on Paul's character works well for TV. It is well established that viewers connect with characters,[19] and so majoring on 'Paul the character' is a nice way of eliciting and sustaining viewer interest. Suchet's attempts to inhabit Paul – trying his hand at weaving (in which Paul as a tentmaker may have been skilled), imagining how Paul might have felt viewing an object, trying to capture Paul's gait – make entertaining viewing.[20] The character angle also works well for developing the subject, taking the exploration beyond a survey-level treatment of Paul's life into a deeper form of engagement with the apostle.

Use of the New Testament Sources for Paul

At the beginning of the documentary, viewers are informed that our historical sources for Paul are the Acts of Apostles and Paul's own letters,

15. David Suchet and Geoffrey Wansell, *Poirot and Me* (London: Headline Publishing Group, 2013), 21.

16. E.g. Belgian not French; will drink black coffee, but prefers tisane; wears pointed leather shoes; bows when shaking hands; reads his Bible every night before going to sleep. Suchet and Wansell, *Poirot and Me*, 23–4.

17. Ibid., 40.

18. Adopting this approach was actually Kemp's idea. He suggested it to Suchet a month or so before filming started.

19. Victoria O'Donnell, *Television Criticism*, 3rd ed. (Los Angeles: Sage, 2017), 90.

20. Suchet's deduction that Paul must have been a speedy walker (to cover the distances he traversed) actually makes good sense!

and these are the main sources upon which the series draws.[21] Broadly speaking, Acts is the principal source for Suchet's story of Paul, while Paul's letters serve as the main biblical repository for his examination of Paul's character.

Acts

The story of the apostle recounted by Suchet follows Luke's account of Paul in Acts.[22] Suchet's story is a heavily condensed version of the Acts narrative of Paul. He leaves out a lot of material in Acts, and he abbreviates much of what he takes over. Yet, he is faithful to the text of Acts; he does not embellish what Luke describes. Thus, when relating the riot at Ephesus, Suchet follows Luke's account, reading out word-for-word the speech of Demetrius the silversmith in Acts 19:25-27. Artistic license is used, though, when representing Paul's itinerary. In Acts, Paul goes on three large journeys to extend his mission. The first (Acts 13:4–14:26) takes him from Antioch in Syria to Cyprus and then to cities in southern Asia Minor. In the second (Acts 15:36–18:22), he travels from Antioch through Asia Minor and advances into Europe, moving through Macedonia and Achaia. He then returns to Antioch via Ephesus and Caesarea. In the third (Acts 18:23–21:17), he proceeds from Antioch through Asia Minor to Ephesus, where he remains for around three years. He crosses over to Europe again, travelling through Macedonia to Achaia, before making his way back to Jerusalem. In *DSFSP*, Suchet narrates a simpler missionary

21. Additionally, reference is made to the *Acts of Paul and Thecla*, part of the composite work, the *Acts of Paul*, on which see now Richard Pervo, *The Acts of Paul: A New Translation with Introduction and Commentary* (Eugene, OR: Cascade, 2014). Seeing the image of Thecla alongside that of Paul in the Grotto of Saint Paul in Ephesus prompts Suchet to read her story in this apocryphal narrative. What stands out for him in this text is its famous description of Paul's appearance (*Acts of Paul and Thecla* 3), which he reads to viewers in a piece to camera. He finds in the statement that Paul sometimes appeared like a man, and at other times like an angel, a fitting description of Paul's personality. Suchet also talks about 'the church tradition' of Paul's martyrdom in Rome, without referring to any specific ancient authority. Scott Brodeur, in his interview, states that Paul was beheaded but likewise makes no mention of any specific source. The execution of Paul by decapitation is described in the *Martyrdom of Paul* (also part of the *Acts of Paul*).

22. Acts is generally treated by Suchet as a reliable historical resource (though he seems to adopt a slightly more questioning attitude when dealing with Luke's account of Paul's conversion). On the trustworthiness of Acts as a source of information about Paul (which I would strongly affirm), see Stanley Porter, 'The Portrait of Paul in Acts', in *The Blackwell Companion to Paul*, ed. S. Westerholm (Oxford: Blackwell, 2011), 124–38.

itinerary whereby Paul travels progressively westward from his base in Antioch, first through Asia Minor and then over to Europe, moving down through Macedonia and Achaia (visiting Philippi, Thessalonica, Athens and Corinth, as noted above), before going back again to Jerusalem.[23] The simplified itinerary is obviously easier for viewers to follow. It also matches, and is indeed heavily dictated by, the actual, linear journey Suchet is making (apart from his returns to Jerusalem). While it compresses and conflates the missionary journeys of Acts, it at least captures the broad progression of Paul's missionary movements.

Paul's Letters

Paul's letters, I am told (by Bruce), don't make great source material for TV. They are non-narrative in form and, from a TV point of view, lacking in drama and excitement. But *DSFSP* manages to include a fair amount of content from them. This is largely due to Suchet's special interest in Paul's character. While Acts offers a 'gripping narrative'[24] of Paul's life, it is well recognized that if you are specifically interested in Paul's personality you have got to turn to Paul's letters, since, as John Knox puts it, besides being from Paul himself, they 'are so rich in indications of what kind of man he was and of what was going on in his mind and heart'.[25] Suchet cites from Paul's letters regularly as he carries out his character analysis of Paul. Citations serve to illustrate or illuminate the apostle's temperament, attitudes, patterns of conduct, ambition and mind-set: his zeal (Gal. 1:13-14); his liberality (Rom. 14:13); his determination to work for a living rather than depend on handouts from his converts (2 Thess. 3:8); his tactical flexibility (1 Cor. 9:21-22); his ambition to preach the gospel in unevangelized areas (Rom. 15:20); etc. Citations are used for other purposes as well, such as to show how the Graeco-Roman symposium tradition negatively affected celebrations of the Lord's Supper among some of Paul's Gentile converts (1 Cor. 11:20-22).

In all, Suchet quotes or partially cites 18 different Pauline passages (a couple are cited more than once). In addition to the citations, he recites, at the end of the series, an extract from 1 Corinthians 15 'in character' as Paul. Usually when a Pauline passage is quoted by Suchet, the words

---

23. To fit the steady westward progression, Paul's mission to Ephesus (culminating in the riot) is taken out of its place in the travel sequences of Acts (Acts 18:19-21; 19:1–20:1) and presented as occurring before his pioneering mission into Europe.

24. As John M. G. Barclay (*Paul: A Very Brief History* [London: SPCK, 2017], 4) puts it.

25. John Knox, *Chapters in a Life of Paul*, rev. ed. (London SCM, 1989), 18.

appear as a caption on the screen, with letter, chapter and verse/s indicated, giving the quotation a visual prominence.

Pauline quotations are deployed in a proof-texting manner, i.e., without reference to the literary context from which they are drawn and without interpretative comment. From an exegetical point of view, this would be considered bad practice, but the use of the Bible on TV must not be judged by exegetical criteria. TV is not a medium for Pauline exegesis! The quotes are used accurately enough, broadly in line with their contextual intention.[26]

A consequence of *DSFSP*'s engagement with Paul's letters through selected and isolated quotations is that viewers unfamiliar with the apostle's writings don't get any sense of the overall shape of a Pauline letter; nor do they get an idea of the distinctive character of any individual letter. The varied quotations do, though, give such viewers a flavour of Paul's words, and it is clearly Suchet's hope that after watching the documentary, they might go and read his letters for themselves.

Use of Interviewee Contributions

Interviewee contributions play a large part in *DSFSP*. Suchet's 'expert witnesses' comprise local guides, church leaders and especially academics – historians, archaeologists, New Testament scholars and a psychoanalyst. Interviewees supply Suchet – and viewers – with important locational and background information (especially the state of a particular place when Paul was there), and/or with perspectives and insights on Paul. The late Jerome Murphy O'Connor talks about Paul's early life, Shmuel Erlich gives a psychological assessment of Paul's 'conversion' experience, Helen Bond discusses Paul's teaching and why it was so controversial, and so on.

Local archaeology figures in many of the contributions, and Suchet gets to see some new archaeological discoveries potentially relevant to his quest, such as the recently uncovered portrait of Paul in the Catacomb of Saint Thekla in Rome, which is now the earliest extant, artistic representation of the apostle.[27] This artefact is of particular interest to Suchet

---

26. The exception is the citation of Rom. 15:23 at the end of Episode 1. Paul's statement that there is 'no further place for me in these regions' in its epistolary context relates to the completion of his mission to plant churches from Jerusalem to Illyricum. Having accomplished this task, he can set his sights on Spain by way of Rome (Rom. 15:24, 28). In *DSFSP*, the verse is applied to the re-imagined completion of the mission in Asia Minor.

27. On the value of having a strong archaeological component in TV Bible-based documentaries, see Bruce p. 3 in this volume.

because he has long believed that he looks like Paul as the apostle has been portrayed in art, and this belief encouraged him to think that he was right for the part of Paul. When he sees the picture, he is reassured to find that it conforms exactly to the classic image of Paul. But he gets a shock when Fabrizio Bisconti, the archaeologist who made the discovery, tells him that the standard image of Paul is unlikely to be a true likeness of the apostle; rather, it was probably inspired by the image of the third-century philosopher Porphyry!

Interviewees speak in a conversational, unscripted way. Academic contributors avoid technical jargon, speaking, for example, of Paul's expectation of the 'end of the world', rather than his imminent eschatology. Several conversations reflect recent emphases and lines of interest in Pauline studies: Paul and women (Ekaterini Tsalampouni); the social level of Paul and his converts (Guy Sanders); Paul and Empire (Scott Brodeur). Bond nods at the 'New Perspective with Paul',[28] without actually referring to it – linking Paul's message of salvation to the issue of the terms on which Gentiles are included in the Jesus movement. Suchet takes on board what he hears; he does not challenge any of his interviewees, nor does he seek another opinion on the matter under discussion. This approach is suited to a fairly fast-moving documentary which doesn't want to get bogged down in scholarly debates. Even so, it would have been good to have had an alternative view on one or two topics, such as Paul's 'conversion',[29] and what Paul looked like![30]

28. The 'New Perspective on Paul' is the wave of scholarship initiated by the publication of E. P. Sanders' *Paul and Palestinian Judaism* (Minneapolis: Fortress, 1977).

29. On which there has been a great deal of scholarly discussion since the seminal essay by Krister Stendahl, 'Paul and the Introspective Conscience of the West', *Harvard Theological Review* 55, no. 4 (1963): 199–215. See Larry Hurtado, 'Convert, Apostate, or Apostle to the Nations: The "Conversion" of Paul in Recent Scholarship', *Studies in Religion* 22 (1993): 273–84. For a recent account of Paul's conversion, see N. T. Wright, *Paul: A Biography* (London: HarperOne, 2018), 41–59.

30. In a paper delivered to the British Society of New Testament Studies in Bristol in 1999, Philip Esler refuted the suggestion that the classical image of Paul is based on sculptures of Porphyry. In an email to me, he comments, 'Why would any Christian in the late third or early fourth century CE (for that is when it must have been on this view) use Porphyry as a model for Paul?! Not only did he write against the Christians (for which he was banned by Constantine!) but I think there is evidence that he held some sway with Diocletian, well known Christian killer. The fact that there is a resemblance between the Pauline images and the sculptures of (so unsavoury a figure as) Porphyry is strong corroboration that this is indeed what Paul looked like.'

Coverage of the Subject

Given the limited running time, *DSFSP* covers the subject pretty well. The coverage extends to three areas of the study of Paul: Paul's world; his life, travels and mission; and his character.

Paul's World

The series does a good job of conveying a sense of Paul's world, both at a wider and a localized level. Viewers get an idea of general features of Paul's Graeco-Roman environment, such as the prevalence of the gods, the fusion of religious and socio-economic life and the scope and strength of Roman rule, and they gain an appreciation of what particular cities that Paul visited or stayed in were like in his day, perhaps qualifying existing ideas they may have had of such places. Thus, Suchet points out that the Rome to which Paul came was not classical Rome as is commonly pictured, since many of the city's 'iconic monuments' – the Coliseum, the Pantheon and most of the triumphal arches – 'had not yet been built'. The series shows Paul interacting with the Roman world both positively and critically in the course of his mission. On the one hand, he exploited the empire's famed network of paved roads and shipping lines to aid his evangelistic travel.[31] That same network also facilitated the transport of his letters, enabling him to stay in touch with the communities of believers he had founded. On the other hand, he was deeply antagonistic towards the idolatry he encountered as he travelled, and his proclamation of Jesus as Lord 'set him on a collision course with the power of Rome'.

Paul's Life, Travels and Mission

The story of Paul told by Suchet spans the general course of the apostle's life, and key events in it – his involvement in the stoning of Stephen, his conversion, the Jerusalem Council, etc. – are explored in conversation with interviewees. The series enables viewers to follow the broad lines of Paul's geographical movements, and they are able to get a good grasp of the mission with which his travels were bound up. Key features of Paul's missionary strategy are highlighted: his focus on strategically located cities; his tactic of preaching and holding meetings in a house (which 'not only afforded a venue, but also gave him access to a wider network

---

31. The perilous nature of travel is not really brought out. See Ryan S. Schellenberg, 'Danger in the Wilderness, Danger at Sea: Paul and the Perils of Travel', in *Travel and Religion in Antiquity*, ed. Philip A. Harland (Waterloo, ON: Wilfrid Laurier University Press, 2011), 141–61.

of family and friends who could help spread the word');[32] his practice of sharing his faith while working at his craft; his use of letters to foster communities he founded. The role of women, as converts and co-workers, within Paul's mission is emphasized. His insistence that Gentiles were to be accepted into the Jesus movement without being required to adopt core Jewish identity markers, especially circumcision (in the case of males), is singled out as decisive in enabling their recruitment in large numbers.

Paul's Character

Suchet offers his own take on Paul's personality, drawing on what he hears from others. He finds in Paul 'a man of total conviction and extremes of behaviour'. His conversion completely transformed his worldview, but it did not, in Suchet's view, change his personality. He put his zeal into a different cause. Growing up in Tarsus, a multicultural city, as a Jew and Roman citizen may have given Paul in his early years 'a confused sense of identity', but the tolerant atmosphere of the city may have rubbed off on him, helping to prepare him for his role as a bridge-builder between the Jewish and non-Jewish worlds. Paul was not anti-women. He reflected to an extent the attitudes of his time, but he was also convinced that there is neither male nor female in Christ (cf. Gal. 3:28), and so didn't make a distinction between men and women. In conducting his mission, two personal attributes stand out: his tactical adaptability and his extraordinary persistence. As to what motivated his 'fanatical drive and energy' as a missionary – 'he genuinely believed that Jesus was going to come back soon'.[33]

What about Paul's Theology?

There is a rather obvious deficiency in *DSFSP*'s coverage of the subject: the series is very thin on Paul's theology. There is no mention of core Pauline doctrines such as 'justification by faith', 'participation in Christ' or the church as the 'body of Christ'. It was clear from the outset of production that the documentary was not going to deal, at least explicitly, with Paul's theology. Indeed, Bruce did not want the phrase 'Paul's

---

32. On the 'household context' of Paul's churches, see Wayne Meeks, *The First Urban Christians* (New Haven: Yale University Press, 1983), 75–7. For a measure of critique, see my *The Earliest Christian Meeting Places: Almost Exclusively Houses?* (London: Bloomsbury, 2015).

33. The eschatological motivation, in retrospect, receives too much emphasis. Other motivating factors, not least his sense of having been commissioned to his missionary task directly by Christ, could have been given more consideration.

theology' to appear in the script.[34] The issue, it seems, is that Paul's theology is too conceptual for TV, which is a visual medium.[35] However, *DSFSP* is not entirely devoid of theological content. In her summary of Paul's message, Bond makes clear Paul's emphasis on salvation through faith in what God has done through Christ, specifically his death and resurrection. Practically, this meant that Gentiles did not need to keep the Law to be accepted by God. Also, one feature of Paul's theology is repeatedly mentioned: his imminent eschatology.

Conclusion

DSFSP is a successful attempt to engage with Paul on TV. It meets recognized criteria for good TV:[36] it is well produced, is visually appealing, tells a story, connects with viewers and provides entertainment. At the same time, it offers an informative and responsible treatment of the apostle. Viewers who know very little about Paul get to learn quite a lot about him by the end of the series, and many of those well-versed in Paul would come away with some fresh insights.

The secret of *DSFSP*'s success lies of course in Suchet himself. The series was commissioned on the strength of his involvement and ability to draw a large viewing audience. But his value to *DSFSP* goes far beyond his pulling power. He is a wonderful guide to Paul and a compelling advocate for him. The actor has long wanted to play Paul, but he thinks that moment has passed since he has now become too old for the role.[37] It's a great pity he never got the opportunity he craved. He may well have been the face of Paul for a generation.

34. In the end, though, though, it did effectively make it in – not once but twice. Suchet refers to 'Paul's own theology' in conversation with Tsalampouni about Paul's view of women, and later on he describes Romans as the letter in which Paul sets out 'his theology'.

35. For an effective attempt to do theology on TV, see *The Day Jesus Died*, BBC 1, 2010. In this documentary, Bettany Hughes digs deeply into the Christian theological understandings of the meaning of Jesus' death.

36. O'Donnell, *Television Criticism*, 206, 224.

37. Interview by Brierley, *Christianity*, 19. According to Barclay (*Paul*, 11), Paul may have been only in his fifties when he was executed.

Chapter 9

HOW DO 'BIBLE-USERS' RESPOND TO
THE BIBLE ON TV?*

Cherryl Hunt

Introduction

Newspaper headlines such as 'Fury over BBC's Nativity insult'[1] and
'Row over BBC drama which shows Jesus crucified in a foetal position',[2]
might convey the impression that televisual, or at least BBC, adaptations
of biblical accounts generate much controversy and are often met with
hostility by those viewers for whom the Bible is significant. However,
a closer and wider examination of responses by these viewers reveals
a more complex and nuanced range of approaches towards attempts to
portray the Bible on the small screen.

This chapter seeks to explore some of the themes apparent within
such responses. To do this, and in an attempt to gain an impression of the
opinions of a wide range of viewers, I draw on a sample of responses,
mainly from online resources including blogs, reviews, comments and
some magazines and newsletters produced by Christian communities. I
have examined those comments whose authors and contributors are self-
identifying as 'Christian', or as a user of the Bible, either by the identity

* Some of the data considered here came from a project partly funded by the
Bible Society and St Luke's College Foundation, for which I would like to express my
thanks. I am also grateful to Louise Lawrence and David Horrell for their comments
on an earlier draft of this chapter.

1. D. Stephenson, 'Fury Over BBC's Nativity Insult', *Express* 2010, http://www.
express.co.uk/news/uk/218290/Fury-over-BBC-s-Nativity-insult.

2. P. Revoir, 'Row over BBC Drama Which Shows Jesus Crucified in a Foetal
Position', *Mail Online* 2008, http://www.dailymail.co.uk/tvshowbiz/article-535748/
Row-BBC-drama-shows-Jesus-crucified-foetal-position.html.

of the site used or by some content in their response.[3] On more generic sites used by the general public, including those hosted by the BBC itself, there is some possibility of 'contamination' by respondents who are not in fact Bible-users; nonetheless, where comments appear concerning spiritual response or regarding how closely the film matched the biblical text, it seems reasonable to suppose that the comment originates with someone who could be designated a 'user' of the Bible. The other sources used here arose in the context of a Bible Society project, 'Pathfinder', which included small church groups of different denominations using two of the BBC productions as resources for biblical engagement; I evaluated responses to these through the use of focus groups and interviews.[4] The focus group materials differed from the online sources in two important respects: they arose within intra-group discussions and debate, sometimes revealing contrasting responses, and they followed upon watching the television programmes within those same small groups, often in homes but sometimes on church premises. Online comments sometimes arose in the course of online debate but often in isolation, rather than face-to-face and, presumably, many of the authors watched in domestic settings. However, while there is a significant difference between watching at home and in a cinema,[5] and group dynamics may affect the ways in which people respond, no obvious demarcation was observable between the comments made in the two different contexts, as examples below will illustrate.

3. I have not consciously drawn on academic theological blogs. Although some academically authored reviews aimed at general readers are included, I have also tried to gain an impression of opinions across non-academic sources although, of course, in many cases the origins of online reviews, blog posts or comments are not clear. As noted by Clive Marsh, the strategy of 'eavesdropping' on online responses has its limitations since it 'only brings scholars into contact with those who write reviews and want to express ... what they felt and thought' within that arena; 'Audience Reception', in *The Routledge Companion to Religion and Film*, ed. J. Lyden (London & New York: Routledge, 2009), 255–74 (255). Moreover, given the volume of material online it is impossible to be comprehensive; consequently, I make no claims for this survey being more than a sampling of an available source of responses and the exercise is making no attempt to be quantitative other than providing an indication of the relative prevalence of some themes across the data gathered.

4. This project is discussed in my PhD thesis, 'Promoting Biblical Engagement Among Ordinary Christians in English Churches: Reflections on the Pathfinder Project' (see http://hdl.handle.net/10871/23365). From this, some related data may be found in C. Hunt, 'Seeing the Light: Ordinary Christians Encountering the Bible through Video', *The Expository Times* 129, no. 7 (2018): 307–16.

5. E. Siegler, 'Television', in *The Routledge Companion to Religion and Popular Culture*, ed. J. C. Lyden and E. M. Mazur (London & New York: Routledge, 2015), 41–46 (42).

The programmes being considered here are all BBC productions. The two for which I have responses from the Pathfinder focus groups are the earlier programmes, to which I found fewer available online responses. *The Miracles of Jesus* (*Miracles*), first shown in 2006, comprises a set of three documentaries presented by Rageh Omaar, which include period dramatizations of incidents from the gospels acted out in Aramaic with English sub-titles.[6] Although Omaar does suggest some prosaic explanations for the miracles he is not really concerned with whether or not they happened as written but with their significance in first-century Jewish thought and what they might show us about contemporary opinions of Jesus. *The Passion* is a four-episode drama produced in 2008. The BBC calls this a 'fresh re-telling of the story of Jesus's [*sic*] final days on Earth, inspired by the Gospels and other contemporary historical sources, and seen from the perspective of all the main figures involved'.[7] Bible Society describes it as 'a unique, dramatic and inspiring perspective on the person of Jesus, Holy Week and Easter and the Christian faith' for which they had developed support materials for churches and schools, on a CD-ROM.[8] The other two productions, for which only online responses are considered, are *The Nativity*, shown in 2010 and 2012, 'revealing the human story beneath the classic biblical tale, from the courtship of Mary and Joseph in Nazareth to the birth of Jesus in a Bethlehem stable'[9] and *The Ark* (2015) 'telling the human story of Noah: a man who risks everything to save the people he loves … fusing elements from the Bible and the Qur'an to tell a universal story of faith and love'.[10] Both the latter were scripted by Tony Jordan.

The responses from the sources were coded thematically using NVivo software, particular notice being taken of themes found occurring across all the four BBC productions and those most prevalent across the data. In common with responses from people not identifying as Christian and not giving any indication of being a user of the Bible, some comments made in response to these programmes related generally to issues of cinematography and special effects, or to the acting abilities and casting

6. BBC Press Office, 'The Miracles of Jesus', 2006, http://www.bbc.co.uk/ pressoffice/pressreleases/stories/2006/07_july/12/jesus.shtml. These programmes were supported, in the focus groups, by downloadable materials for church settings devised by Bible Society, 'The Miracles of Jesus', 2007, http://web.archive.org/ web/20120724044405/http://www.miraclesofjesus.co.uk/.

7. BBC, *The Passion*, 2009, http://www.bbc.co.uk/programmes/b009mgrw.

8. Bible Society, *The Passion*, 2009, http://web.archive.org/web/20110809035809/ http://www.biblesociety.org.uk/products/518/49/the_passion_the_film/.

9. BBC, *The Nativity*, 2010, http://www.bbc.co.uk/programmes/b00x15ny.

10. BBC, *The Ark*, 2015, http://www.bbc.co.uk/programmes/b05psczv.

decisions.[11] Unsurprisingly, in view of the fact that evidence of being a user of the Bible was one of the criteria used in selecting the responses, the issue of how the production 'agrees' or not with the biblical text was the most frequently occurring theme I found in the sources examined, although the nature of the perceived disagreement varied; this is discussed in the first section below. However, examination of the comments also suggested that, for a majority of Bible-users, faithfulness to the parent texts was not seen as the most important factor in judging the productions; some programmes perceived as flawed in their 'agreement' with the Bible were nevertheless seen as being of value. The second section below on 'Responses' discusses the range of attitudes expressed among the sources, from rejection of the programmes as unbiblical, through acceptance of a degree of dramatic license, to appreciation for the ways in which the Bible on TV can bring its ancient texts alive for contemporary viewers.

In, Out, Shake it All About: 'Disagreement' with the Biblical Text

Some viewers of these BBC programmes commented favourably on the presentation of an episode of the biblical narrative being portrayed in a manner which, in their opinion, closely adhered to the biblical texts. Others pointed out various points at which they had noticed some discrepancy between the texts and its representation on TV. The latter group of comments could be grouped under three headings: those which noted *insertions* of extra-biblical storylines or extended dialogues *into* the biblical account, those which pointed out events or significant points of biblical dialogue that had been left *out* of the televised drama and others that discussed where biblical narratives had been 'shaken about', for instance into an alternative chronology, through use of paraphrasing to render the biblical dialogue in a contemporary idiom, or through the manner in which the textual account was portrayed visually. Since there is some overlap between the latter grouping and the others I will first discuss

11. For example, I found a few comments relating to the effects produced by James Nesbitt playing Pilate with an Ulster accent (see M. Page, 'Drama Goes the Extra Mile in Recreating the Story of Jesus', *rejesus*, 2008, http://www.rejesus.co.uk/site/module/the_passion/P6/; P. Malone, 'BBC's "The Passion" Viewed by Peter Malone', *SIGNIS: World Catholic Association for Communication*, 2008, http://www.signis.net/spip.php?article2143) and several referring to racial stereotyping (see, with reference to *The Nativity*, Joy on 23-12-2010 [Hopkins 2010] and concerning *The Ark*, M. Page, 'The Ark', *Bible Films Blog*, 2015, http://biblefilms.blogspot.co.uk/2015/03/the-ark-2015.html. These kinds of comments could also be found in sources not identifiable as Bible-users.

the comments that perceived the text as having been disrupted in some way by its presentation on screen.

Shaken About: Issues Around Presentation of Events or Characters

Unexpected visual presentations were noticed by some viewers. For example, the rigorous raising of the widow's son in *Miracles* was seen as 'a classic sign of CPR gone a bit overboard' by one of the focus group members, although another thought the turning of water into wine was cleverly handled 'because all they did was focused on his eyes, and I thought, "Oh well, that's a novel way of doing it"'.[12] Other programmes generated comments on how angels were portrayed, with Mark Woods noting that the one who appeared to Noah in *The Ark* was 'very ordinary-looking'.[13] With *The Nativity*, Matt Page finds the handling of angelic appearances one of the strengths of the production:

> When Gabriel appears to Mary it's very low-key. There's no dazzling light, indeed as he appears to Mary outside, and during the night, it leaves open the slight possibilities that this might not be an angel at all or that she may only be dreaming. Joseph's encounter is stripped down even further. Gabriel remains off-screen, so we only hear about what has happened because Joseph tells us next morning. This, for me, is actually one of the best and most inventive parts of the series, holding very closely to the biblical text, and yet offering a very fresh interpretation of it that seems very plausible in such a sceptical age.[14]

As these comments indicate, episodes that the Bible portrays as in some way supra-natural present a particular challenge for producers of

12. Pathfinder focus group data. 'CPR' refers to cardiopulmonary resuscitation.

13. M. Woods, 'BBC's The Ark Stayed Afloat, Just About', *Christian Today* 2015, http://www.christiantoday.com/article/the.ark.noah.drama.to.show.on.bbc/49831. htm. Interestingly, I came across a couple of American Christian review sites complaining that the angel addressing Noah was an inaccurate portrayal of the text which has 'the Lord' speak to Noah (T. Chaffey, 'Movie Review: Noah's Ark', 2015, *Answers in Genesis*, https://answersingenesis.org/reviews/movies/noahs-ark/, and J. W. Kennedy, 'TV Review: UP TV's "Noah's Ark"', 2015, *beliefnet*, http://www.beliefnet.com/columnists/faithmediaandculture/2015/03/tv-review-up-tvs-noahs-ark.html, but I did not find any comments about this feature within the British sources. (*The Ark* was shown as *Noah's Ark* on the UP network on 23 March 2015.)

14. M. Page, 'Review: *The Nativity* (BBC1)', *Bible Films Blog*, 2010, http://biblefilms.blogspot.co.uk/2010/12/review-nativity-bbc1.html. See, in contrast, comment 187 on the BBC blog; T. Maslany, 'Tony Jordan's Nativity: I play Mary', *love TV*, 2010, http://www.bbc.co.uk/blogs/tv/entries/9020307a-e4b5-3044-ae72-d11a3350540d.

programmes aimed at the general public rather than a specifically Christian audience. But this problem is perhaps most acute in the portrayal of Jesus' miracles and resurrection; Brendan O'Regan refers to the 'naturalistic approach' of *The Passion* and notes that, while Jesus 'says to this man that his sins are forgiven, ... there's no talk of taking up the bed and walking'.[15] Similarly, Michael Kirwan detected 'a clear avoidance of Jesus as worker of signs and wonders, apart from his prediction that he will rise again after his death'. Although he understood this decision in light of the intended audience, he felt that it resulted in 'an impoverished view of Jesus' miraculous signs: detachable from his authority and message, dispensible [*sic*] for a sceptical age'.[16]

The portrayal of the person of Christ was the topic of a small proportion of responses to these BBC productions, with some respondents commenting on how he was portrayed physically, and how charismatic he appeared, and several reflections on how well particular productions had conveyed the humanity and the divinity. These comments were mostly unrelated to any textual issues, but the Pathfinder focus groups took exception to the temptation of Jesus in the desert, as portrayed by *Miracles*, with one respondent noting that there had been 'some quite violent views on that' because 'it was going too far, really, as to Jesus being powerless and sort of overwhelmed by everything, which didn't really match the Bible accounts'.

With both *The Passion* and *The Nativity* there were a few comments, some from sources identifiable as Catholic, concerning the degree to which the portrayal of Mary was in agreement with the biblical account, specifically comments about her reaction to her role. These varied from blog comments noting the omission of Mary's *fiat* and the *Magnificat* from *The Nativity*[17] to complaints about Mary's attitude and responses in *The Passion*: one blogger found her too 'bitter' and 'resentful' and notes where she says that Jesus was in her belly before she knew it, although they also admitted that 'this doesn't necessarily clash with the biblical

15. B. O'Regan, 'Reviews of The Passion (BBC) – From Blog Entries', *FaithArts*, 2008, http://www.faitharts.ie/bbcpassion.html 2016.

16. M. Kirwan, 'The Passion, Part Two: "A Passion Tailored For Our Times"', *Thinking Faith*, 2008, https://www.thinkingfaith.org/articles/20080317_1.htm.

17. See comment 23 on the BBC blog; Maslany, 'Tony Jordan's Nativity'. See also A. Dickson, '"The Nativity", Part Two: A Familiar Story from a New Perspective', *Thinking Faith*, 2010, http://www.thinkingfaith.org/articles/20101221_1.htm, and an account of the debate at the pre-screening where this issue is also raised (R. Butt, 'Judgment Day for BBC's Premiere of the Passion', *The Guardian*, 2008, https://www.theguardian.com/media/2008/mar/01/bbc.religion).

version – maybe this is something that Mary says in the heat of the moment, under the pressure of seeing her son heading inexorably towards a horrible death'.[18]

Out: Omission of Textual Events on the Screen

Since *Miracles* was interspersed with individual dramatized sections portraying specific events there was not so much cause for viewers to complain that any particular event had been omitted although, even then, one blogger complained that the story of Jesus walking on water (Mt. 14:22-32) missed out Peter going out to walk to Jesus.[19] The other three presentations all portray specific biblical story-lines and, as such, are open to accusations of leaving out events which viewers might see as integral to the narrative. However, the omission of biblical material did not seem to be a prominent topic among responses to these programmes, aside from the types of comment above, on the omission of Mary's *Magnificat* and Jesus' miracles, one or two observations on the absence of *some* post-resurrection appearances from *The Passion*[20] and varied sources noting a dearth of animals and flooding in *The Ark*![21]

In: Addition of Back-story and Dialogue to the Text

If leaving things out of a filmed version of biblical texts generates few comments from Bible-users, the insertion of non-biblical storylines to add drama, or as explanatory back-story, stimulates more comment, although this is by no means all negative. Several sources noted *The Passion*'s portrayal and fleshing out of the minor characters in the Bible stories, especially Barabbas, Pilate, Judas and Caiaphas.[22] One Pathfinder focus

18. O'Regan, 'Reviews of The Passion'.

19. Anonymous, 6 August 2006, *Man in a Shed*, http://atoryblog.blogspot.co.uk/2006/08/bbc-1-sunday-miracles-of-jesus-part-1.html.

20. O'Regan, 'Reviews of The Passion'.

21. See, for example, comments by Russon and Armstrong responding to review by 'Matt D' (2015), 'The Ark Review: David Threlfall, Joanne Whalley Shine in this BBC Biblical Drama'. Unreality TV. http://primetime.unrealitytv.co.uk/the-ark-review-david-threlfall-joanne-whalley-shine-in-this-bbc-biblical-drama/, and comment by 'Mark B', on 1 March 2016, on the Amazon site, *Noah's Ark DVD*, 2016, https://www.amazon.com/gp/customer-reviews/R3PHGQEGWX0AHR/ref=cm_cr_arp_d_viewpnt?ie=UTF8&ASIN=B017S3Z1IW#R3PHGQEGWX0AHR.

22. Page, 'Drama Goes the Extra Mile', writes 'Barabbas re-emerges from the shadows of the Gospels. No longer is he just a figure accused of some kind of robbery / insurrection / murder before getting off the hook and making it home in time for tea and hot cross buns'.

group member reported that they had 'started looking at all the different people, ... which we'd never done before, well I hadn't. Pilate and Herod and Judas and how they reacted and it actually sank in their part in it, instead of, you know, you read about Herod, Pilate and concentrate on Jesus; it all fitted together'. For this viewer, the production resulted in them changing their view of Judas.

Similarly, *The Nativity* generated comments on the insertion of material relating to how Mary's pregnancy was perceived by Joseph and her neighbours, in particular showing Joseph as suspecting her of being unfaithful to him and taking some time to accept Mary's account of her pregnancy. This sub-plot had generated one of the negative headlines noted above, when Stephen Green of Christian Voice had suggested that this extrapolation from the gospel account was unjustified and too imaginative. This became a classic case of Chinese Whispers; having been reported in *The Express* as a 'TV drama *in which the Virgin Mary is branded* a prostitute and sex cheat',[23] which then made clear this was an accusation coming from characters within the drama, the same story was described in *The Way*, a conservative evangelical website, as 'a BBC *production which portrayed* the Virgin Mary as a prostitute' (my emphasis).[24] Interestingly, given the theological 'flavour' of this website, only two of the 62 comments following this article were unfavourable; most respondents enjoyed the production and found nothing offensive in it, although one commented on the 'anachronism' of Joseph not accepting Mary's account earlier in the storyline. But the 'back-story' of Mary's struggle to convey her account was accepted by most:

> I don't doubt that in times such as those when Jesus was born that people would be very suspicious of a woman who fell pregnant by anyone other than their husband, as they are today, be it the man next door or the Holy Spirit. Nothing the BBC has shown has taken anything away from the wonder of Jesus's birth, or the importance of the message he brought. And if we have trouble thinking of the mother of God and her son as human people haven't we entirely missed the point of the Nativity? Mary was nobody special and as such would have faced the full wrath of society's judgement. That's the point.[25]

Similarly, one of the respondents to another blog said it was

---

23. Stephenson, 'Fury Over BBC's Nativity Insult' (my emphasis).

24. A. Hopkins, 'Christians Outraged with BBC Nativity Drama', 2010, *The Way*, http://www.theway.co.uk/news-8303-christians-outraged-with-bbc-nativity-drama.

25. Ibid., comment posted by Andrew on 21 December 2010.

lovely to see it without the usual assumption that everyone blithely accepted the child was the son of God, except Joseph for the space of about five verses. I really like the way that Mary is portrayed as a real person, rather than the very separate superhuman perfect mother figure we often get, who is difficult to identify with. There is a lot to like here, particularly the way people's likely reactions have been thought through.[26]

Moving on to *The Ark*, there were a number of comments regarding the addition of a fourth son for Noah; not all of these seemed aware that this plot-line came from the Quran although there was an acknowledgement that it presented a number of dramatic opportunities, not least bringing home the loss of life to Noah's close family.[27]

Responses to These Perceived Disagreements with the Bible

As noted by W. Barnes Tatum, '[a]ny perceived departure by a film from the written New Testament text can bring condemnation and protest'.[28] For some viewers, whether the programme portrays the Old or New Testament, every detail is up for scrutiny. However, given that, in any production, there will inevitably be discrepancies between the production and some viewers' understandings of how the texts should be portrayed, the comments surveyed here indicate a range of different responses of Bible-users to the Bible on the small screen, many of which were very positive.

Rejection or Acceptance of the Secular Context

At the extreme negative end of the range are those who see the BBC as actively hostile to faith, especially Christianity; such responses sometimes focus more on criticism of the Corporation as a whole rather than detailed critique of particular features of the programme. One reviewer began their comment on *The Ark* by quoting the 'TV blurb': '"Epic one-off drama telling the story of Noah: a man who risks every-thing to save the people he loves. A retelling of the classic tale, fusing elements from the Bible and Qur'an." There you have it in a nutshell.

---

26. Comment 5, by 'Jon of Kent', on M. Page, 'TV Review: BBC1's The Nativity', *rejesus*, http://www.rejesus.co.uk/blog/post/tv_review_bbc1s_the_nativity/.

27. See, for example, S. Tomkins, 'Rain of Terror', *Reform*, 2010, http://www. reform-magazine.co.uk/2015/04/reviews-april-2015/.

28. W. B. Tatum, *Jesus at the Movies: A Guide to the First Hundred Years* (Santa Rosa, CA, Polebridge, 1997), 11.

Typical BBC hatred for the genuine biblical message and an insult to genuine Christians.' They later went on: 'As usual, then, the BBC got it wrong (I believe deliberately so)! Perhaps they wanted just to annoy Christians, or to dismiss their claims, by mixing it and diluting it with Islam.'[29] However, much more common in the sources I examined were responses accepting that the programmes are not made by Christian organisations and accepting the consequences of biblical portrayal by a secular organisation; with reference to *Miracles of Jesus*, a Pathfinder focus group member commented that 'for the BBC, and for that sort of secular production, it was, on the whole, fairly true to scripture, although understated in many places, and some key facts may have been omitted'. Similar responses could be found to the negative headline for *The Nativity* on 'The Way' website discussed above: one said '[i]t is probably exactly the reaction from the crowd then as it would be today ... It may not have been EXACTLY Scripturally correct but it was on BBC tv [*sic*] ... and may have got the message of the Light into a heart of just one person ... Is this not a good thing?'[30] Another respondent suggested that '[o]nly the churlish or ideologically grumpy would attack the BBC for producing this excellent piece of prime time TV'.[31]

Dramatic License

A number of scholars have noted the problem facing a dramatic writer who is trying to use biblical narratives as their source material. Tatum cites Moira Walsh, reviewing *The Greatest Story Ever Told* in 1965: '"Shall we write 'additional dialogue' for Christ? What kind of small

---

29. K. B. Napier, 'The Ark: BBC 1 (30 March 2015)', 2015, *Christian Doctrine: Bible Theology Ministries*, http://www.christiandoctrine.com/in-the-news/arts-and-media/1379-the-ark-bbc-1-march-2015. This extreme response may be seen as a caricature reflecting some real changes at the BBC. In their examination of religious literacy in the context of the Corporation, Wakelin and Spencer note that, while the BBC was initially 'married to religious broadcasting' it subsequently had a 'more self-consciously secular leadership'; indeed, a more recent survey suggested that BBC staff were half as likely to be religious as their audience; M. Wakelin and N. Spencer, 'Religious Literacy and the Media: The Case of the BBC', in *Religious Literacy in Policy and Practice*, ed. A. Dinham and M. Francis (Bristol & Chicago, IL: Polity, 2015), 227, 229, and 231.

30. 'Mike', 24 December 2010, commenting at Hopkins, 'Christians Outraged with BBC' (emphasis original).

31. 'Simon Jones', 26 December 2010, at Hopkins, 'Christians Outraged with BBC'.

talk did He make, for example, at the marriage feast of Cana? Shall we provide motivation where none exists specifically, e.g. for Judas' betrayal?"[32] Similarly, Richard Walsh notes the strategy employed by some writers who use new plots or characters in order to 'smooth out literary and cinematic problems in the rather episodic Gospels'.[33]

There seems to have been an awareness of this issue among some of the comments I surveyed here. Several responses variously referred to what they termed poetic, dramatic, artistic or literary license, or merely acknowledged necessary additions to the biblical narrative. One of them, Peter Malone, noted that the phenomenon is not new: 'As the early Christian communities did, the film-makers omit, add, create dialogue and incidents. They interpret.'[34] In most but not all cases I surveyed, while the examples of dramatic license were recognised and acknowledged, they were viewed as being of value or at least acceptable.[35]

For example, with regard to *The Nativity*, Mike Meynell acknowledges the necessity of imagination to make televisual sense of the short texts but 'what was so stunning was that it never felt contrived. And I found myself reflecting on the theological significance of the drama all the more as the result.'[36] Another viewer agreed: 'Sticking to the Gospel narratives in a very strict manner would actually produce a very short and somewhat empty story ... very little is said of the birth and early life of Christ'.[37] In contrast, the reviewer noted above, who saw *The Ark*'s departure from the biblical text as an example of 'BBC hatred', considered that there was 'nothing biblically' to justify the dramatic interchanges among Noah's family.[38] However, Hazel Southam, reviewing the same production, for Bible Society, found

---

32. Cited by Tatum, *Jesus at the Movies*, 7.

33. R. Walsh, *Reading the Gospels in the Dark: Portrayals of Jesus in Film* (Harrisburg, PA: Trinity, 2003), 96.

34. Malone, *BBC's 'The Passion'*.

35. See, for example, responses 85 and 134 to Maslany, 'Tony Jordan's Nativity' and 'Bruce', 23 December 2010 at Hopkins, 'Christians Outraged with BBC'. An exception was an American website commenting on *The Ark*, which liked the idea of including a non-biblical storyline where Noah was a ship-builder but also noted 'glaring errors': 'The key in using artistic license is to make sure that one's story does not end up contradicting God's Word' (Chaffey, 'Movie Review: Noah's Ark').

36. Quaesitor, 'What Tony Jordan's Nativity Got So Right', *Quaerentia*, 2010, https://markmeynell.wordpress.com/2010/12/29/what-tony-jordans-nativity-got-so-right/.

37. Comment 8, from 'Geoff' at Page, 'TV Review: BBC1's The Nativity'.

38. Napier, 'The Ark: BBC 1'.

believable characterisation, great dialogue and a sense (towards the end) of imminent peril ... The characters could all have come out of EastEnders: the loving father who apparently goes off the rails; the supportive mother; the teenage son yearning for a more racy life in the city; and young couples trying to work out how and where you have sex in a busy household. Most of the story isn't set on the ark at all, and there are very few animals. There are characters who haven't walked out of the biblical text. Does it matter? Not one jot. This is a film. It tells a great story.[39]

The positive responses to dramatic licence that I found sometimes focused on the effects of modernising and rephrasing biblical speech. In his review of *The Nativity*, Charlie Peer thought that '[i]t was nice to see some of the Bible's classic lines rendered in the modern idiom of the script, such as; Elizabeth: "my baby gave such a kick when I heard your voice"'.[40] Similarly, Matt Page notes that *The Passion*'s script 'breathes new life into some of Jesus' best known soundbites. As with *The Last Temptation of Christ* before it, *The Passion* rephrases classic lines, enabling us to hear them again as if for the first time. They sound like things someone might actually say, rather than something from a holy book.'[41] Also commenting on *The Passion*, Brendan O'Regan acknowledges the tension between using the familiar lines straight from the Bible and adapting them for modern viewers:

There is plenty of Jesus' teaching, not always exact quotes from scripture. The fresh wording does grab the attention, as we can get too familiar with the well known sayings, but there's always a danger with people taking liberties with scripture. Yet, when only the words of scripture are used, as say in the Matthew series, when Bruce Marchiano played the warmest Jesus I've seen yet, it comes across as stiff and stilted in film terms.[42]

A few comments took exception to one particular dramatic license taken by Tony Jordan in *The Nativity*, and often taken by nativity plays every Christmas, namely, what Charlie Peer called a 'cheerful mishmash of Matthew and Luke',[43] where the Magi arrive at the birth scene soon

39. H. Southam, 'The Ark – Review, 2015, *Bible Society*, https://www.biblesociety. org.uk/latest/news/the-ark-review/.

40. C. Peer, 'Review – The Nativity', *Always Hope*, 2010, http://charliepeer. blogspot.co.uk/2010/12/review-nativity.html.

41. Page, 'Drama Goes the Extra Mile'.

42. O'Regan, 'Reviews of The Passion'.

43. Peer, 'Review – The Nativity'. See also Anonymous, 'Good Reception for BBC's "The Nativity"', *CT e-news*, 2011, http://www.cte.org.uk/Publisher/File.

after the shepherds.[44] Other viewers noticed this but found it unprob-
lematic, sometimes responding to these complaints:

> I also noticed the Magi anachronism thing, but I really don't think it matters
> in any way, does it? Biblical truth is important, but if this serves to make the
> important Biblical point (that the Magi did come) then I think the usefulness
> of complaining about the inaccuracy is limited.

Comments on the dramatic presentation and acting generally did not
involve specifically biblically related comments. However, one minor
item did arise in this connection and serves to illustrate how some
responses to the Bible on screen are driven as much by taste and personal
preference as by concern for the parent texts. Michael Barnes's review of
the first part of *The Passion* speaks of its 'brilliant story-telling, carefully
plotted and visually superb. One shot, in which Jesus is showered with
blood-red poppy petals scattered from windows above, makes for a
perfect counterpoint to the traditional waving of palms.'[45] In contrast, this
one feature was mentioned by one of the Pathfinder focus groups as a
non-textual 'distraction'.

The Value of Bible on the Small Screen for Bible-users

One positive feature of these programmes, noted in a number of comments
by Bible-users, was their realism, both in terms of their context –
historical flavour and religio-political background – and in the sense that
they 'brought the story alive'.[46] This is often associated with an affective
response to well-known biblical texts and was most obvious in responses
to *The Nativity*. One reviewer feels that those involved in production 'take
familiar words, read so many times, and turn them into living, breathing,

---

aspx?id=64419, 'DevonMaid' respondent at M. Page, 'Review: *The Nativity* (BBC1)'
and comment 1, 'Bible Believer', at Page, 'TV Review: BBC1's The Nativity'.

44. Comment 5 by 'Jon of Kent' responding to Page, 'TV Review: BBC1's
The Nativity'. See other examples of toleration of the discrepancy, or praise despite
it: comment 8, 'Geoff', on the same site; BBC blog respondents 113, 178, 197 at
Maslany, 'Tony Jordan's Nativity'.

45. M. Barnes, 'The Passion, Part One: "An Almost Unanswerable Question"',
Thinking Faith, 2008, http://www.thinkingfaith.org/articles/20080316_1.htm.

46. Comment by 'felicity' on 22 December 2010 responding to Hopkins, 'Christians Outraged with BBC'. I did find one reviewer who questioned the historical
accuracy: '*The Passion* struggles to be historically authentic' (G. O'Collins, 'The
Passion, Part Four: "Does This Resurrection Work?"', *Thinking Faith*, 2010, http://
www.thinkingfaith.org/articles/20080323_1.htm).

feeling people'.[47] Similarly, respondents to the BBC blog note that they were 'mesmerised and moved' by the programmes, which 'allowed a greater empathy with the main characters and to consider their own feelings'.[48] Another wrote of being 'sucked in', of its 'reality', and of it increasing their faith[49]. And Mark Meynell suggests that Jordan 'has made the people and world into which God's son come [*sic*] thoroughly recognisable and normal – which in turn has made the miracle of the Incarnation seem far more wonderful and ... well ... miraculous'.[50] Jesuit priest Jim Conway likens Jordan's *Nativity* to an Ignatian interaction with biblical texts and notes the way in which the dramatic license of the extra-biblical character, Thomas the shepherd, enables the viewer to make connections with the story:

> Thomas's situation may well resonate with some viewers who, at this time of year, find themselves debt-ridden or living in the shadow of redundancy and unemployment. It raises ethical questions about the injustice of systems and structures that keep the poor in their poverty and/or debt, and about what sort of action people in desperate situations – like Thomas – might resort to.
>
> Those who were expecting a Christmas card presentation of the Nativity might have difficulties with these aspects of Jordan's production. They may argue that his 'imaginative contemplation' of Luke's Gospel (the only gospel to mention the shepherds) goes too far and perhaps is manipulative of the text. For others, Jordan's creative interpretation will make all the difference.[51]

Although less numerous, there were similar affective responses to the other programmes under consideration here. One of the Pathfinder participants commented that *Miracles* 'was much more realistic as how they lived and so on. It wasn't all the razzmatazz of a Hollywood movie, it was more down to earth, and it actually brought it home to you exactly how they lived at that time'; another thought that *The Passion* 'did actually bring alive the stories of the crucifixion, because you hear them in church,

47. J. Pollock, 'Review: The Nativity', *Reading Between the Lines*, 2010, http://jenniepollock.com/review-the-nativity/.

48. Respondent 35 at Maslany, 'Tony Jordan's Nativity'.

49. Respondent 87 at Maslany, 'Tony Jordan's Nativity'.

50. Quaesitor, 'What Tony Jordan's Nativity Got So Right'.

51. J. Conway, '"The Nativity", Part Four: A Gift of Imaginative Contemplation', *Thinking Faith*, 2010, http://www.thinkingfaith.org/articles/20101223_1.htm.

you know, time after time and you think, "Oh I know this," but in fact it made it a bit more vivid really'.[52]

In a few cases Bible-users found themselves informed or provoked to deeper engagement with the parent texts or theological issues raised. One of the Pathfinder groups reported their reaction to *Miracles*' portrayal of Jesus with the Syro-Phoenician woman: 'We were all going, "That's not in the Bible", but that was almost verbatim what's in the Bible, and that was like, "Ooh!"'. Sometimes the effect reported was both affective and cognitive, as testified by a respondent to the BBC *Nativity* blog: 'As someone who has been a Christian all my life, this has brought a very familiar, fundamental part of my faith not just into vivid relief but it has also drawn out new dimensions and meanings, something which even the most skilled clergymen struggle to achieve in Sunday services'.[53]

There were a few cautions expressed considering the ways in which the biblical texts may be misrepresented and consequently misunderstood to those unfamiliar with them: 'if you're using that material with a group of either people who aren't Christians yet, or new Christians, there's a real risk that they go away with what's on the film, rather than what's in the Bible'.[54] And one of the few negative remarks I could find concerning *The Nativity* wondered 'why not produce a show that is thoroughly orthodox and thereby explodes erroneous modernist notions that so many members of the BBCs audience risk internalizing by watching its programs?'[55] The irony is, that respondents desirous of a television presentation which sticks closely and literally to the text (and did not, as this viewer expressed it, take 'unwarranted liberties with the facts'), are themselves taking a literalist approach towards the texts that is commonly perceived as modernist.[56]

---

52. See also the response/review comment on *Miracles* by a Reader Training group on Amazon (*The Miracles of Jesus DVD*, 2009, https://www.amazon.co.uk/Miracles-Jesus-DVD-Region-NTSC/dp/B000FQIRWW) and a review of *The Ark* by David Winter, reproduced in several church magazines ('The Ark', St Ternan's Scottish Episcopal Church, Muchalls, Magazine, 2015, http://www.stternans.co.uk/Magazine%20-%20May%202015.pdf).

53. Response 21, 'Mathilda', to Maslany, 'Tony Jordan's Nativity'; for other examples see also response 35, 'charlotterosewright', and Winter, 'The Ark', St Ternan's Scottish Episcopal Church.

54. Pathfinder focus group response to *Miracles*.

55. Comment by Sean Romer on Stephenson, 'Fury Over BBC's Nativity Insult'.

56. See, for example, M. J. Borg, *Reading the Bible Again for the First Time: Taking the Bible Seriously but Not Literally* (New York: HarperCollins, 2001), 5; H. Cox, *Fire From Heaven: The Rise of Pentecostal Spirituality and the Reshaping of Religion in the Twenty-First Century* (London: Cassell, 1996), 303; C. Smith,

In contrast to those concerned that non-Bible-users might be led astray, some other responses expressed the idea that the Bible on the small screen could be a valuable means of disseminating more widely a knowledge of and appreciation for the Bible's stories, for 'enlightening a society of non believers and making them think':[57] 'It is a chance for many who would not normally go to Church and who do not know much about Christianity to learn about the birth of Our Lord in a way that makes the story relevant and touching'.[58] What these comments share is an appreciation that television is a powerful medium for communicating (adequately or inadequately, depending on one's view of the production) the narratives central to the Christian faith.

Conclusions

Although this sampling of online comments to the Bible on TV is very limited in scope and size it has been sufficient to demonstrate the variety of responses from those contributors who appear to be users of the Bible. While it is inevitable that viewers who value and are familiar with the Bible will often find television adaptations fail to meet their expectations, either in narrative or theological terms, it would also seem that many Bible-users not only enjoy but find value in watching the Bible on the small screen. There are some for whom anything less than a literal acting out of the full text, with nothing added, will fail to please. However, while many others take note of what they perceive to be discrepancies between the Bible on the page and that on the screen, these differences are often tolerated as necessary in a secular production or in balance against what they feel the production gets right. Some see the Bible on television as a means by which its narratives may be communicated to those who do not use or value the Bible. Furthermore, the very dramatization process may provide Bible-using viewers with what is in some cases a profound encounter with the biblical narratives; this may be as a result of them learning something new but, more often, is a result of the production evoking an affective response, allowing viewers to find fresh

---

The Bible Made Impossible: Why Biblicism Is Not a Truly Evangelical Reading of Scripture (Grand Rapids, MI: Brazos, 2011), 150; K. J. Vanhoozer, *Is There a Meaning in This Text? The Bible, the Reader and the Morality of Literary Knowledge* (Leicester: Apollos, 1998), 424–6.

57. 'Geoff' at Page, 'TV Review: BBC1's The Nativity'.

58. Mbololwa responding to Hopkins, 'Christians Outraged with BBC Nativity Drama', on 25 December 2010.

meaning in, or be provoked to renewed consideration of, the texts in which they place value. Although this was a strictly qualitative exercise, the sampling surveyed would suggest that those who found value in the four productions considered here outnumber those who merely offer critique on the basis of a supposed discrepancy between the Bible on the page and that on the screen. Producers of such programmes should find this encouraging!

Chapter 10

PLUNDERING EGYPT:
EXODUS DOCUMENTARIES
AND THE EXPLOITATION OF HISTORY

Mark Harris

'And so they plundered the Egyptians' (Exod. 12:36)

This chapter will examine Exodus documentaries of recent years, arguing that many adopt a sensationalist agenda where historical and biblical scholarship is demonized as sceptical, but which is then 'plundered' haphazardly in order to legitimate literalistic readings of the text. I will also suggest that the plundering strategy involves the construction of historical models that are fraught with inconsistencies upon close examination.

There is no shortage of Exodus documentaries: I have found fourteen from the past two decades, along with a further three that explore the oft-linked eruption of the Aegean volcano Thera.[1] One trend stands out straightaway: the wealth of Exodus documentaries is not matched by a corresponding wealth of interests therein. Indeed, Exodus documentaries are for the most part decidedly one-track, fixated with the question of whether the events narrated in the text actually happened or not. This is a rather limited focus when one considers the enormous wealth of alternative themes that Exodus offers to the aspiring documentary maker, themes that have inspired generations for more than two millennia. In narrative terms alone, Exodus has a lot going for it, as probably the most

1. A list of all of these documentaries is given at the end of this chapter.

ripping of all biblical yarns, and the archetypal story of liberation from grinding tyranny. Its call of 'Let my people go!' has resounded down the centuries in contexts of oppression, notably in the slave trade which eventually led to the American Civil War, and in the speeches of Martin Luther King. A liberating, but also 'a potentially dangerous book' (on account of the divergent ways that it can be interpreted),[2] Exodus still has live political repercussions in today's crisis-torn Middle East. And finally, the status of Exodus as a foundational narrative in both Judaism and Christianity – and one of the sources of the Ten Commandments – means that it is of almost unparalleled religious significance in the Hebrew Bible, holy ground for billions worldwide.

Many of these themes surface in the Exodus documentaries, but all too often in passing as the historical question of whether we can trust the biblical account is prioritized again and again (and answered usually in the affirmative). And this leads on to a second trend: the ambiguous relationship that many Exodus documentaries possess with professional Exodus scholarship. The documentaries often feature individual scholars and archaeologists giving expert opinion, but when the documentaries speak of the scholarly field as a whole it is almost invariably to dismiss it as so much scholarly scepticism. It is true that biblical scholarship has raised many historical questions about the biblical text (and Exodus is a particularly fierce battleground in that regard), but there is a wide spectrum of expert views on the historicity of the Exodus, ranging from the fully affirming to the deeply sceptical.[3] However, the documentaries mostly

---

2. S. M. Langston, *Exodus Through the Centuries* (Victoria: Blackwell, 2006), 7.

3. The most basic problem is that there is no direct archaeological or textual evidence (apart from the biblical text itself) to support the story told by Exodus. What extra-biblical evidence there is, is usually of a plausibility/circumstantial kind. Some scholars are convinced by this, others not. A further basic issue is that the story relies on many miraculous happenings, which are technically beyond the competence of historical enquiry to be established one way or another (unless one calls upon naturalistic explanations, as in many of the Exodus documentaries). And yet another basic issue is the problem of dating: there is no great consistency in the various biblical notices which indicate a possible date for the Exodus, meaning that dates between the sixteenth and twelfth centuries BCE are possible (although many scholars work with a thirteenth century, Ramesside date). In any case, every single postulated date meets with historical problems of one kind or another (D. A. Garrett, *A Commentary on Exodus* [Grand Rapids: Kregel, 2014], 101). As a result of this complex of issues, some scholars are highly doubtful that any reliable history can be salvaged from Exodus, regarding the narrative largely as a myth of origins (e.g., W. G. Dever, *Who Were the Early Israelites and Where Did They Come From?* [Grand Rapids: Eerdmans, 2003],

show little interest in the subtleties or deep questions here.[4] The emphasis is instead on the resolution of 'ancient mysteries' by new artefactual and scientific discoveries,[5] and especially on the presentation of scientific 'explanations' of the big catastrophe and miracle stories of Exodus: the plagues of Egypt (chs. 7–12) and the sea crossing (chs. 14–15). Indeed,

232); 'overall … fiction – the stuff of legend' (Dever, 'The Exodus and the Bible: What Was Known; What Was Remembered; What Was Forgotten?' in *Israel's Exodus in Transdisciplinary Perspective: Text, Archaeology, Culture, and Geoscience*, ed. T. E. Levy, T. Schneider, and W. H. C. Propp [Cham: Springer, 2015], 399–408; here 406); or as 'historical fiction' (Langston, *Exodus*, 150–1). The 'revisionism' of Philip Davies and associated figures goes even further still, to suggest that the whole pre-exilic history of ancient Israel is fictional/ideological, and is therefore of little or no historical value (see E. Nicholson, 'Current "Revisionism" and the Literature of the Old Testament', in *In Search of Pre-exilic Israel: Proceedings of the Oxford Old Testament Seminar*, ed. J. Day [London, New York: Continuum, 2004], 1–22 for a critical review of this school of thought). On the other hand, other scholars are more positive that an historical Exodus is plausible (e.g., K. A. Kitchen, *On the Reliability of the Old Testament* [Grand Rapids: Eerdmans, 2003], 259), even if much of what is related by the text is regarded as being beyond historical verification. A few scholars are certain that it all happened just like the text – compiled by Moses himself no less – says it did (e.g., Garrett, *Commentary*, 20, 46). If there is any kind of dominant view here, it is probably the belief that some distant historical memories lie behind Exodus (e.g., J. J. Collins, *Introduction to the Hebrew Bible* [Minneapolis: Fortress, 2014], 110–13), such as the escape of some Semitic slaves from Egypt. In this model, the escaped slaves settle in Canaan among indigenous Canaanites who are forming new settlements in the central hill country. In time, the slaves' story becomes important in the formation of an 'Israelite' identity for this new community (e.g., A. J. Frendo, 'Back to Basics: A Holistic Approach to the Problem of the Emergence of Ancient Israel', in Day, ed., *Search*, 41–64, here 61; Dever, 'The Exodus', 406; A. Faust, 'The Emergence of Iron Age Israel: On Origins and Habitus', in Levy, Schneider and Propp, eds, *Israel's Exodus*, 467–82, here 478). A recent playing-out of the historicity debate between 'liberal' and 'conservative' scholars can be seen in the 'Was There an Exodus?' essay and responses, published in the March 2015 edition of *Mosaic* magazine (http://mosaicmagazine.com/essay/2015/03/was-there-an-exodus/; accessed 26 May 2017).

    4. That there are many such 'deep questions', actively discussed in contemporary scholarship, is amply illustrated by the state-of-the-art collection of papers published in Levy, Schneider and Propp, eds, *Israel's Exodus*, gathering together perspectives on Exodus from biblical scholarship, archaeology, Egyptology and the natural sciences.

    5. Most of which discoveries turn out not to be so very new after all, nor even accurately reported at times, which is especially the case with the Thera theories, as I will discuss later.

the catastrophe and miracle traditions of Exodus are extraordinarily visual, and documentary makers have not been slow to exploit the latest computer animation technology here. Several documentaries revel in the visual dimension to such an extent that they create virtual apocalypses:[6] the sensationalist elements of the narrative are amplified while being simultaneously legitimated (as if 'proven') by sober scientific research.

Interestingly, this strategy of sensationalizing the text is far from unique to Exodus documentaries. There are numerous books (many at the popular level), documentaries, websites and scientific articles that claim to provide the definitive explanation for 'what really happened' in the Bible's miracle and catastrophe stories (for example Noah's flood, or the destruction of Sodom and Gomorrah) by calling upon spectacular natural phenomena such as earthquakes, volcanoes and asteroid/comet impacts. However, the professional guild of biblical scholarship has tended to exercise caution, and sometimes even downright disdain.[7] Scholarly commentaries on Exodus, for instance, conspicuously avoid prioritizing the naturalistic explanations of the plagues of Egypt and the sea crossing which the documentaries revel in, preferring instead to examine the complex human (social, political and religious) factors standing behind the text, including its many historical difficulties. But, in contrast, few of the Exodus documentaries show any interest in promoting caution; the reservations of biblical scholars about the speculative nature of many of these hypotheses are swept aside.[8] Most Exodus documentaries display the rather unfortunate tendency (as seen from the perspective of critical scholarship) that they tell a one-sided story that hardly reflects the full significance of the book, nor of the range of expert opinions on it.

In order to demonstrate what I have begun to argue here, and to move beyond it, I will now present a brief analysis of each documentary that I have studied, approximately in chronological order, and seen from my perspective as a natural scientist-cum-biblical scholar with a special

---

6. In biblical scholarship 'apocalypse' and 'apocalyptic' are technical and highly nuanced terms. Here I will simply use the words in the popular sense of referring to a horrifying catastrophe that has 'end of the world' overtones.

7. Garrett, for instance, in his recent commentary on Exodus, warns of the 'amateurs and quacks' who publish 'peculiar theories about the time and circumstance of the Exodus' (*Commentary*, 81). By 'peculiar theories', he clearly has in mind those which focus on naturalistic explanations of the miracles of Exodus, such as those featured heavily in the documentaries I examine in this chapter.

8. E.g. J. M. Miller and J. H. Hayes, *A History of Ancient Israel and Judah* (London: SCM, 1986), 64–5.

interest in the ways that *popular* and *scholarly* assessments of biblical texts are so often at odds with each other.[9]

The Documentaries

Mysteries of the Bible: Moses at Mount Sinai (1994)

This, the earliest documentary that I shall examine, was also the first in an extended series of some 45 documentaries entitled *Mysteries of the Bible*.[10] *Moses at Mount Sinai* adopts a format that is common to most of the Exodus documentaries analysed here, whereby the historical questions are introduced at the outset (in this case 'Who was Moses?' and 'What happened on Mount Sinai?') and are then developed in the context of a telling of the story of the biblical text. This means that, in spite of its title (*Moses at Mount Sinai*), the documentary spends a third to a half of its time covering episodes not located at Mount Sinai. In common with other Exodus documentaries, this storytelling is interspersed with short contributions from various historical and archaeological experts, as well as short readings from the biblical text, often given by a disembodied third voice in highly exaggerated dramatic fashion. Visually, the documentary relies on long sweeping shots of the appropriate scenery shot on location, together with frequent use of artistic renderings of the Exodus. Footage of archaeologists going about their work and the 'talking heads' of the experts provide contemporary visual variety.

'The historical evidence of this incident [the giving of the law at Sinai] seems to have been blown away by the sands of time', summarises the narrator at the beginning of *Moses at Mount Sinai*. The many archaeological and historical difficulties behind this statement are then immediately underscored by short comments from leading experts such as archaeologist William Dever and biblical scholar Carol Meyers. But since the documentary proceeds thereafter by a heavy reliance on straightforward narration of the Exodus storyline, the historical doubts are marginalized, and the overall feel of the documentary is a cautious affirmation of the authenticity of the biblical text. There is, however, some

9. M. Harris, 'How Did Moses Part the Red Sea? Science as Salvation in the Exodus Tradition', in *Moses in Biblical and Extra-Biblical Traditions*, ed. Axel Graupner and Michael Wolter (Berlin: de Gruyter, 2007), 5–31; and 'The Thera Theories: Science and the Modern Reception History of the Exodus', in Levy, Schneider, and Propp, eds, *Israel's Exodus*, 91–9.

10. Full details on the Internet Movie Database, www.imdb.com; accessed 26 May 2017

refreshing theologizing by experts towards the end of the documentary, demonstrating that there is more to Exodus than questions of history and authenticity.

Mysteries of the Bible: The Ten Commandments (1997)

The Ten Commandments was made towards the end of the *Mysteries of the Bible* series. The format is similar to *Moses at Mount Sinai*, although the historical issues surrounding the figure of Moses are less the focus of attention than are his core teachings, a focus which makes this unusual among Exodus documentaries. Consequently, the documentary spends much of its time discussing the theological and ethical relevance of the Ten Commandments in their historical context; the documentary is open to the scholarly questions concerning historicity, but balances them with analysis of meaning and significance.

All of this is not to say that *The Ten Commandments* is wholly unlike its predecessor: this later documentary adopts a similar strategy of foregrounding scholarly doubts about the historical authenticity of the narrative, and then subtly silencing those doubts by propounding the narrative as given. A strange degree of naivety surfaces in places, especially where the Ten Commandments are elevated to almost mystical status as unlike any law code given before or since, and most especially at two points in the documentary (close to the very beginning and the end) where the discussion strays into *Indiana Jones* territory by entertaining the idea that the Ark of the Covenant may one day be recovered, along with Moses' stone tablets of the Ten Commandments. Suffice it to say that, although some of the other Exodus documentaries that I examine in this chapter treat the Ten Commandments with a degree of reverence, this documentary provides far and away the most exalted view of them.

Who Was Moses? (1998); Moses (2002)

Who Was Moses? compares closely with the later BBC production *Moses* (2002), and so they are considered together here. Both documentaries were produced and directed by Jean-Claude Bragard, and both make similar claims about Exodus, putting forward a historically rather conservative approach which is sensationalized so that the impression is given that it represents a major advance in understanding. One prominent motif (which also features in other documentaries that I shall examine later) is that the plagues and sea event are explained naturalistically by the Minoan eruption of the Thera volcano (modern day Santorini).

Who Was Moses? begins with the familiar device of a string of rhetorical questions, all relating to the historicity of the Exodus: 'What caused the ten plagues? Did the parting of the Red Sea leave any traces behind? Where exactly is Mount Sinai? And who was Moses?' The narrator then goes on to claim that new evidence is coming to light about 'the real places, the actual events, and the very people behind the earliest chapters of the greatest story ever told'. This new evidence is clearly a game changer, the documentary implies, because it is to be contrasted with the fruitless explorations of the past century, which found no evidence to support the biblical account. In light of this absence of evidence, the narrator continues, 'sceptics' (who are rarely identified by name in Exodus documentaries) had come to the conclusion that ancient Israelites had never been in Egypt in the first place.

By way of presenting the new evidence, *Who Was Moses?* follows Egyptologist James K. Hoffmeier[11] to the Serabit el-Khadim turquoise mine in Sinai (which contains Semitic inscriptions from mine workers), to the archaeological site of Raamses at Qantir in the Nile Delta (potentially one of the store cities mentioned in the biblical account, Exod. 1:11), and to Amarna (the city of Akhenaten, the uniquely monotheistic pharaoh of the fourteenth century BCE). Hoffmeier explains that all of these contribute to a plausible case in support of the biblical Exodus story. Significantly, the placing of this material in the sequence of the documentary suggests that it is these clues that constitute the 'new' evidence which is confuting the sceptics. In fact, all of these clues have been known in scholarly circles (and beyond) for decades (and in some cases a century),[12] and were by no means 'new' when the documentary was made.

A similarly disingenuous move is made by *Who Was Moses?* in its treatment of the plagues and sea event. Again implying that the biblical specialists are going to be shown up as wrong, the documentary explains that some scholars doubt that these things ever really happened, because the texts represent them as supernatural acts. So the documentary proceeds to demonstrate how the plagues and sea event *could* have happened naturalistically. Hoffmeier re-appears, and explains that it is possible to interpret the plague narratives as amplifications of phenomena that are

---

11. The author of two authoritative treatments of the Exodus which seek to establish the historical authenticity of the biblical account: J. K. Hoffmeier, *Israel in Egypt: The Evidence for the Authenticity of the Exodus Tradition* (New York, Oxford: Oxford University Press, 1996); and *Ancient Israel in Sinai: The Evidence for the Authenticity of the Wilderness Tradition* (Oxford, New York: Oxford University Press, 2005).

12. See, for instance, Hoffmeier's discussion of the history behind the deciphering of the Semitic inscriptions at Serabit el-Khadim (*Ancient Israel*, 178–9).

known to occur naturally in Egypt.[13] The documentary does not make it clear, but this thesis has been in currency for a century or more,[14] and has been well known since at least the oft-cited papers of Greta Hort.[15] In other words, it is hardly a new idea. And neither is the next move made by the documentary, where it asks what kind of 'natural power' could have sparked off the natural disasters of the plagues.

At this point, *Who Was Moses?* conflates Hoffmeier's explanation of the plagues with another explanation, calling upon the famous 'Minoan' eruption of Thera in the second millennium BCE. Since Thera was probably the largest volcanic eruption to occur in the last few thousand years, reconstructing it certainly makes for good TV, and the documentary provides stunning shots of the highly photogenic caldera of Santorini, together with computer animation of the blast, and footage of more recent volcanic eruptions such as Mount St Helens in 1980 for comparison. The documentary explores the idea that the ash plume from the Minoan eruption would have darkened the skies over Egypt (the ninth plague), and that the fallout of ash might explain the other plagues (but without providing any details). Dating the eruption at around the mid-sixteenth century BCE, the documentary quickly moves on to suggest that the ash plume rising above Thera could have been the 'pillar of fire and cloud' (Exod. 13:21) which guided the Israelites out of Egypt. The documentary then slows to consider the sea event in detail, beginning with the familiar warning that the Bible experts are about to be proved wrong: 'Most biblical scholars dismiss the episode [the sea event] as a myth', we are told. But the documentary attempts to vindicate the story of the sea event, by locating it at the Mediterranean coast of Egypt, where the tsunamis generated by the Theran eruption provide a spectacular natural-istic explanation. Here, the sea withdraws for the Israelites (crossing a shallow lagoon/Sea of Reeds at the coast), only to come crashing in on the pursuing Egyptians minutes later.

13. As in his 1996 book (*Israel in Egypt*, 149).

14. Sir Flinders Petrie, originally writing in 1911, claimed that, 'The order of the plagues was the natural order of such troubles on a lesser scale in the Egyptian seasons, as was pointed out long ago' (W. M. F. Petrie, *Egypt and Israel* [London: Forgotten Books, 2013], 35–6). This quotation has found its way into prominent naturalistic discussions of the plagues as evidence that this is a very old approach to interpretation of the plagues (Hoffmeier, *Israel in Egypt*, 146; C. J. Humphreys, *The Miracles of Exodus: A Scientist's Discovery of the Extraordinary Natural Causes of the Biblical Stories* [London, New York: Continuum, 2003], 113).

15. G. Hort, 'The Plagues of Egypt', *Vetus Testamentum* 69 (1957): 84–103; 70 (1958): 48–59.

This episode in *Who Was Moses?* might have been designed as a spectacular vindication of the biblical account of the sea event, but it is another spectacularly disingenuous strategy on the part of the documentary makers, since the documentary does nothing to suggest the complexity and controversy surrounding the Thera theories of the plagues and sea event. For one thing, these theories have been around for some time, since at least the 1960s, and they are by no means unknown to biblical scholars. Biblical scholars, however, have not generally been convinced by the Thera theories, for the simple reasons that they are regarded as unrealistically speculative, and require highly selective (and therefore artificial) readings of the biblical text.[16] Perhaps the most significant problem is that the Thera theories introduce more historical difficulties than they solve. One of those historical difficulties is the date of the eruption, which has been shrouded in controversy in the scientific and archaeological literature since the 1980s, and shows no sign of being resolved. On the one hand, radiocarbon dates for the eruption tend to cluster around 1620 BCE, while on the other hand dates from conventional archaeological methods can fall considerably later, perhaps even to 1525 BCE.[17] The documentary is totally silent on this dating controversy, but the fact that the Minoan eruption occurred *three hundred or more years before the time of Ramesses II* (who tends to be the scholarly favourite for the Pharaoh of the Exodus by scholars, and is the Pharaoh implicated in this documentary) creates serious credibility problems. Put simply, how can the Hebrews have built the store cities of Ramesses if they had been delivered from slavery by the eruption-induced plagues and sea event three or four hundred years earlier? The documentary makes no attempt to solve this problem (nor even to own up to it): it presents evidence consistent with a thirteenth-century BCE date for the Exodus (Qantir, and Akhenaten's monotheism), but explains it by means of a Thera theory which requires a sixteenth- to seventeenth-century date.

But having seemingly established Thera as the explanation behind the plagues and sea event, *Who Was Moses?* rapidly moves on (now in its final ten minutes) to the location of Mount Sinai. The traditional location

16. I have written at length about the Thera theories elsewhere (Harris, 'How did Moses?'; 'The Thera Theories'), and give only a very brief outline of the problems here.

17. The discrepancy here is illustrated well by the conflicting perspectives of M. W. Dee, C. B. Ramsey and T. F. G. Higham, 'Radiocarbon Dating and the Exodus Tradition', in Levy, Schneider and Propp, eds, *Israel's Exodus*, 81–9 and M. H. Wiener, 'Dating the Theran Eruption: Archaeological Science Versus Nonsense Science', in Levy, Schneider and Propp, eds, *Israel's Exodus*, 131–43.

(Jebel Musa in the southern part of the Sinai peninsula) is presented, but the documentary prefers Emmanuel Anati's proposal that Har Karkom, much further north in the Negev, should be regarded as the 'mountain of God'.[18] Dating again turns out to be an issue here: Anati's thesis requires the Exodus to have been in the late third millennium BCE, perhaps six hundred years before the Minoan eruption of Thera, and potentially a thousand years before the late second-millennium BCE date of the Exodus in the Ramesside model. Yet again, the documentary makes no attempt to own up to (let alone reconcile) the enormous historical problems that it has introduced by conflating various Exodus models which are separated by as much as a thousand years; it simply finishes by returning to the question in its title, *Who Was Moses?* Here, in spite of widespread scholarly questions surrounding the historical figure of Moses, his historicity is simply asserted, most likely as a scribe trained in Pharaoh's court, apropos of no evidence whatsoever.[19] This is why, we are told, the Bible got so many of its facts right about the Exodus, because Moses himself recorded the story. Using this point to make a sweeping attack on biblical scholarship, the narrator concludes that Moses' story can no longer be regarded as the product of a much later writer's imagination. And the narrator's final sentence clinches it: 'The modern age is rediscovering it [the Bible] as a tool for understanding history'. The clear implication being made here – breathtakingly misplaced in view of the documentary's circular reasoning, and its creative approach to historical reconstruction – is that the past two centuries of scholarly enquiry into the Bible's historical basis are being largely overturned by such evidence as is presented in the documentary.

The later documentary, *Moses* (2002), follows much the same pattern as its predecessor *Who Was Moses?* but with some significant differences in presentation: rather than relying on the narration of a disembodied voice (i.e. a figure whom we never see), *Moses* is presented in the flesh by Jeremy Bowen, a highly respected Middle East correspondent of the BBC. This is coupled with more impressive use of CGI animation than the previous documentary.[20]

18. See the recent overview in E. Anati, 'Har Karkom: Archaeological Discoveries in a Holy Mountain in the Desert of Exodus', in Levy, Schneider and Propp, eds, *Israel's Exodus*, 449–55.

19. Presumably the documentary makers have in mind the biblical note that Moses was raised by Pharaoh's daughter (Exod. 2:7), but they do not say so.

20. CGI is used especially in this documentary to depict the parting of the *Red Sea*, an episode which, ironically, is dismissed here as historically unlikely compared to the documentary's favoured interpretation featuring a Theran tsunami striking a *Sea of Reeds*.

Bowen begins *Moses* with an even stronger version of the thesis of the previous documentary: 'Modern scholars have claimed that Moses and the Exodus, one of the world's most famous stories, was a fantasy. Until now. New archaeological tools and the latest historical research have uncovered some stunning, fresh evidence.' As with the previous documentary we might wonder who these sceptics are who have such strong opinions, but we are never told;[21] one begins to suspect that such statements (along with other similar statements later in the documentary) are designed to work rhetorically rather than to represent any balanced assessment of the state of Exodus research.

Bowen then proceeds through the biblical story in much the same way as in the previous documentary, again pointing to archaeological evidence which supports the biblical story indirectly (that is, on plausibility grounds), and again calling upon Jim Hoffmeier's expertise. Also like the previous documentary, *Moses* spends some time focused on the plagues, again proposing an explanation that combines natural environmental factors in and around the Nile triggered by the Minoan eruption of Thera. And also like the previous documentary, the tsunami from Thera is called upon to explain the sea event.

One significant difference between *Moses* and *Who Was Moses?* concerns their discussions of *dating* the Exodus. Both documentaries completely ignore the controversy over the dating of the Minoan eruption, but (and unlike its predecessor) *Moses* does at least register that there is a mismatch between the thirteenth-century BCE Ramesside archaeological evidence it uses to build much of the plausibility case for an Exodus, and the Minoan eruption (which requires a sixteenth- or seventeenth-century date).[22] Quite unlike the disingenuousness of the previous documentary,

---

21. Since Bowen precedes this comment with this rhetorical question, 'Did Jewish scribes with vivid imaginations simply make up a dramatic tale to give their people a history?' one wonders whether the sceptical scholars being referred to here belong to the revisionist school of P. R. Davies, Lemche and others, who have proposed that much of the Hebrew Bible was written very late (in the Persian period after the exile) in order to give Persian settlers in the land a sense of communal history and culture. Whether this is what Bowen has in mind is impossible to tell, since he does not say, but it is important to point out that the revisionist school is by no means representative of wider scholarship on Exodus (e.g. Nicholson, 'Current "Revisionism"').

22. A good example of such a mismatch is the documentary's reliance on the archaeological discovery of the large stables of Ramesses II (thirteenth century BCE) in order to support the biblical notice that six hundred chariots chased the Israelites to the sea event (Exod. 14:7). In the very next section of the documentary, the sea event is portrayed, with the Israelites being chased towards it by the aforementioned

Bowen now admits in *Moses* that there is a real problem here, namely the mismatch between the Ramesside date and the Minoan date. However, he has a ready solution to hand, suggesting that perhaps there were two exoduses, in the thirteenth and sixteenth centuries, respectively. Hershel Shanks, editor of *Biblical Archaeology Review*, provides support here, explaining a widespread scholarly conviction that there were many migrations backwards and forwards between Egypt and Canaan, forming potentially many mini-exoduses. Perhaps the most prominent of these was by the Moses group. This suggestion is taken by Bowen as tacit confirmation of Moses' historical existence, and the documentary ends by describing the enduring significance of the Ten Commandments, noting that although we know very little for sure about who wrote them down, Moses is an ideal candidate.

The resounding impression given by *Moses* is that Exodus is a reliable record of historical events. But it is worth noting that, in order to reach this conclusion, the documentary has been forced to introduce multiple exoduses in order to explain away the historical problems which it created for itself by conflating evidence from the thirteenth and sixteenth/seventeenth centuries BCE. In other words, the documentary has argued for the historicity of the Exodus text precisely by undermining that historicity with multiple exoduses. This is not a sound argument.

The documentary's case is further undermined by the fact that, in spite of Bowen's promise at the beginning to offer 'fresh evidence', he delivers precious little.[23] Ziony Zevit, reviewing the *Moses* documentary, is particularly critical on this score, speaking of the documentary's 'content vacuum', and its disingenuous presentation of the Minoan eruption: 'The show leaves the incorrect impression that the Thera hypothesis is new,

---

Egyptian chariots. But the documentary goes on to explain the sea event by means of a tsunami from the Minoan eruption, which puts the event three to four hundred years earlier than Ramesses II and his chariots. The documentary does not draw attention to this massive historical inconsistency.

23. The 1990's discovery of Ramesside stables at Qantir/Pi-Ramesses is perhaps the only 'fresh' evidence on offer, although it had already been featured in the earlier documentary, *Who Was Moses?* (1998). See E. B. Pusch and A. Herold, 'Qantir/ Pi-Ramesses', in *Encyclopedia of the Archaeology of Ancient Egypt*, ed. Kathryn A. Bard (London, New York: Routledge, 1999), 787–90; Pusch, 'Piramesse', in *The Oxford Encyclopedia of Ancient Egypt*, ed. Donald B. Redford (Oxford, New York: Oxford University Press, 2001), 3:48–50; S. Prell, 'A Glimpse into the Workshops of the Chariotry of Qantir-Piramesse – Stone and Metal Tools of Site Q I', in *Chasing Chariots: Proceedings of the First International Chariot Conference (Cairo 2012)*, ed. André J. Veldmeijer and Salima Ikram (Leiden: Sidestone, 2013), 157–74.

when in fact it is not. Few historians, if any, consider it viable nowadays. It remains the plaything of disasterist interpreters of history.'[24] Zevit is absolutely right here: Bowen gives no hint in the documentary that the Theran hypothesis is actually a very old idea, nor that it has long been considered implausible by biblical scholars.

Therefore, summing up *Who Was Moses?* and *Moses* together, they follow the familiar pattern of earlier documentaries in challenging scholarly 'sceptics', so that the integrity of the biblical text might be defended. This defence relies on presenting 'new' evidence (which mostly turns out to be rather old evidence), along with speculative naturalistic explanations of the miracle traditions, all tied together disingenuously by means of a 'fast and loose' approach to historical reconstruction which does not hold together under close examination.

The Exodus Revealed: Search for the Red Sea Crossing (2001)

The Exodus Revealed bears a great deal of similarity to the two BBC productions just discussed, in that it seeks to make a case for establishing the historicity of the Exodus against the usual scholarly scepticism. The documentary begins with the familiar rhetorical questions: 'Did Israel's Exodus from Egypt actually occur? If it did, then why has so little evidence been unearthed? Were the people and events described in the biblical account real, or nothing more than elaborate fiction?' Just like previous documentaries, this one adopts a sensationalist tone, promising 'new evidence and discovery' that will allow us to 'test the biblical record'. In spite of these similarities, however, *The Exodus Revealed* presents four key differences to the previous documentaries.

First, rather than explore the usual Ramesside connections with Exodus (placing the events in the thirteenth century BCE), *The Exodus Revealed* looks earlier in time (perhaps the sixteenth century) to ancient Avaris, and to archaeological evidence that has been uncovered since the 1970s of a Semitic presence in the Nile Delta. This Semitic presence is interpreted by the documentary as evidence for Joseph and the Israelites of the Exodus.[25] In other words, unlike previous documentaries this one makes no attempt to connect the Exodus with the time of Ramesses II. Some later documentaries make a similar move.

---

24. Z. Zevit, 'Moses and the Exodus: A BBC Production Hosted by Jeremy Bowen', *Biblical Archaeology Review* 30, no. 5 (2004): 60–2, here 62.

25. There is good historical precedent for making this connection, since Josephus himself identified the Hyksos of Avaris with the Israelites of the Exodus (*Against Apion* 1.103).

Second, Mount Sinai is identified as Jebel al-Lawz in Saudi Arabia. I will discuss this when I turn to the next documentary shortly (*Mountain of Fire*).

Third, *The Exodus Revealed* is highly specific about the location it proposes for the sea event, and it transpires (in due course) that this is proposed for apologetic reasons. In fact, the documentary resists the widespread modern conviction – reflected in previous documentaries – that the sea event took place at a shallow 'Sea of Reeds' rather than the deep Red Sea.[26] Considering the options, this documentary argues that the usual candidates (including shallow lakes and lagoons in the Isthmus of Suez) simply do not match the biblical account, and are insufficient to explain how the Egyptian host could have drowned. Instead, the documentary focuses on a crossing route at Nuweiba in the Gulf of Aqaba (that is, a branch of the Red Sea) proposed by the medical scientist, Lennart Möller, and the adventurer/explorer, Ron Wyatt.[27] A large part of the documentary is devoted to following a diving expedition to uncover traces of Pharaoh's chariots on the sea floor here where, it is claimed, the shapes of chariot wheels are seen in the coral. These shapes are open to a considerable breadth of interpretations, however, as is clear by the considerable length of time that the documentary devotes to trying to convince the viewer that they truly reflect man-made patterns (rather than being entirely natural and haphazard). To my knowledge, no professional archaeologist or biblical scholar has been persuaded by the 'evidence' or scenario for the sea crossing presented in this documentary.

Fourth, working somewhat counter to this high degree of specificity concerning the location of the sea event (and the use of modern diving technology), *The Exodus Revealed* shows no interest in the work of modern scientists in proposing naturalistic explanations of the sea crossing. On the contrary, the documentary explains that if the sea crossing is truly a miracle then we should not expect it to conform to the laws of nature. Making a clear apologetic move, the documentary concludes by suggesting that reason and faith can support each other: the archaeological evidence of Avaris supports the authenticity of the Exodus (against

26. One of the most celebrated difficulties in determining the geography of the Exodus has been the translation of the Hebrew term *yam suph* (e.g. Exod. 15:4). Biblical scholarship for the past century has often maintained that the Hebrew should be translated as 'Sea of Reeds' rather than its traditional rendering as 'Red Sea'. This suggests that the sea event would be located at a shallow inland lake or lagoon rather than the deep sea.

27. L. Möller, *The Exodus Case* (Copenhagen: Scandinavia, 2002).

scholarly scepticism), it is claimed, which in turn supports faith in the sea crossing as a full-blown miracle.

In short, *The Exodus Revealed* makes plain what might be suspected of previous documentaries, that a biblicist agenda is being promoted to support a conservative faith in the narrative account of Exodus, by means of an argument that makes superficial claims on 'evidence' against anonymous scholarly sceptics. The sceptics are set up as a kind of 'straw man', who can be blown down simply by calling upon reason and 'evidence' of a highly debatable kind.

Mountain of Fire: The Search for the True Mount Sinai (2002)

The first half of *Mountain of Fire* recounts the discoveries of Bob Cornuke and Larry Williams, two 'adventurers' (their own term) who claim to take Exodus 'at face value' and thereby have succeeded where archaeologists have failed: at locating the sea event and Mount Sinai.[28] That said, the documentary does not make a strong polemical case against biblical scholarship or archaeology (as do other documentaries), but it nevertheless advocates a strong biblicism, especially on the part of Cornuke: 'Why aren't we following the clues given us in Scripture?' says Cornuke, 'The Bible is like a road map; it's like a compass that you can open up and find these clues'.

Much of the documentary is taken up with interviews of the various explorers. Having discovered the shallow Straits of Tiran at the southern end of the Gulf of Aqaba as their candidate location for the sea crossing, they smuggle themselves into Saudi Arabia. Avoiding detection by the authorities, they make their way to Jebel al-Lawz, where they appear to find a number of features that match the biblical description of Mount Sinai: the altar of the golden calf at the foot of the mountain (Exod. 32), boundary markers to keep the people away from the mountain (19:12), a blackened top to the mountain (caused by the fire of God, 19:18), the altar of the covenant ritual with twelve stone pillars (24:4) and a cave (as used by Elijah in 1 Kgs 19). The story is then taken up by the Caldwell family, also amateur explorers seeking independently to confirm the Bible. They discover the same features at Jebel al-Lawz, as well as a lone ancient cedar tree which they interpret as the burning bush (Exod. 3:2), quail (16:13) and a massive split rock, which was the rock which Moses struck in order to extract water (17:6).

28. Their story is told in the bestseller by H. Blum, *The Gold of Exodus: The Discovery of the Most Sacred Place on Earth* (London: Hodder & Stoughton, 1998).

At the end of the documentary, and with a surprising degree of circum-spection, Cornuke, Williams and the Caldwells come together to discuss the evidence that Jebel al-Lawz is Mount Sinai. Evidence is not proof, and means nothing without interpretation, Cornuke points out. And Williams explains that, although he believes that the site is the best candidate right now for Mount Sinai, we cannot know for sure until it has been examined carefully by professional archaeologists.[29] And belief – religious belief – is acknowledged by Cornuke and the Caldwells to be an important component motivating their search. The documentary therefore has a clear apologetic motivation.

As a testimony to the power of Exodus to inspire faith and fascination outside of the scholarly guild, *Mountain of Fire* is an effective account. As a balanced and informed discussion of current scholarly positions on Exodus it offers rather little, however. One outstanding problem – which the documentary shares with all of the others I have examined so far – is that it operates by means of an uncritical and speculative optimism that the biblical text is basically authentic as it is, and can be read reliably by means of a selective and uncritical literalism. This allows the documentary makers to assert, for instance, that the black summit of Jebel al-Lawz is evidence for the fire of Yahweh's descent onto the mountain (Exod. 19:18), when there is a perfectly mundane geological explanation at hand.[30] The next documentary that I shall examine is probably the most audacious example of this biblicist hermeneutic by far.

The Exodus Decoded (2005)

The Exodus Decoded was made in collaboration with James Cameron, the producer/director of Hollywood blockbusters such as *Titanic*, and it is certainly one of the most lavishly produced of all documentaries that I have examined. In common with others though, it follows the well-worn path of seeking to establish historicity against scholarly scepticism. The presenter, Simcha Jacobovici, promises that he will solve the puzzle of the Exodus, 'the ultimate archaeological mystery'. His solution is breath-takingly speculative though, involving (at times) highly tenuous links being made across cultures and periods simply by interpreting single

---

29. I am aware of no professional archaeologist or biblical scholars who support the location of Mount Sinai espoused in this documentary. Indeed, few even consider this model seriously. One who does, Hoffmeier, subjects it to a scathing critique (*Ancient Israel*, 132–6).

30. Ibid., 134.

isolated artefacts imaginatively. It also makes heavy use of the Minoan eruption of Thera.

One of the key historical decisions made by the documentary is to move the Exodus away from its habitual timeframe in the thirteenth century (the time of Ramesses II), to the time of the Hyksos in the sixteenth century BCE. According to Jacobovici this means that an abundance of ready material evidence surfaces for the Exodus, if we equate the Israelites with the Hyksos and their expulsion under Pharaoh Ahmose I. Jacobovici does just this, going to the extensive archaeological digs in the Hyksos city of Avaris in the Nile Delta, and claiming even to discover direct material evidence for Joseph himself. In common with earlier documentaries, Jacobovici rarely indicates that there are historical difficulties and scholarly controversies surrounding much of the evidence he cites, but simply sums up what he has found as 'hard evidence for the arrival of the Israelites in Egypt and their rise to power'. In order to demonstrate that the Israelites eventually *lost* power and were enslaved (as in the biblical story) Jacobovici next visits the turquoise mines at Serabit el-Khadim to examine the Semitic inscriptions made by mineworkers there. Jacobovici adds this to his tally of evidence for an exodus around 1500 BCE.[31]

A further reason for Jacobovici's dating of the Exodus to around 1500 BCE becomes clear in the next episode of the documentary. Straightaway we move to Santorini, to a presentation of the Minoan eruption of Thera. Refreshingly, the dating controversy surrounding Thera is acknowledged openly now, but Jacobovici adopts a date of around 1500 BCE, presumably because it coincides so well with the thesis he is developing. At this point Jacobovici develops a novel explanation for the plagues. He speculates that the trigger for the plagues could have been an earthquake storm in the region, which could have released underground gas that then contaminated the Nile, and which could also have triggered the distant Minoan eruption. The plagues might then have been a complex series of environmental disasters caused either by this gas leak or by the ash cloud from the eruption itself. Of the ten plagues, the tenth (the death of the firstborn) is noteworthy since it is so difficult to explain naturalistically. 'No one has ever been able to offer a plausible scientific explanation for the death of the firstborn. Until now', claims Jacobovici. He believes that his postulated gas leak would have affected humans directly, as indeed

---

31. Although these inscriptions are known to be much earlier, nineteenth century BCE; see M. Bietak, 'The Volcano Explains Everything – Or Does It?', *Biblical Archaeology Review* 32, no. 6 (2006) 60–5, here 64.

happened one night in 1986 at Lake Nyos in Cameroon. Those who were
sleeping low down (including animals) were suffocated in their sleep
before the gas dispersed into the atmosphere, while those sleeping on
higher ground were unaffected. According to Jacobovici the Egyptian
firstborn males – occupying privileged places in society – would have
slept on beds close to the ground, while others (including the Hebrews)
would have slept on roofs, which explains why the Egyptian firstborn
died and not the Hebrews. In support, Jacobovici describes a mass grave
found at Avaris containing only male bodies which had been buried
hurriedly, and the mummy of Ahmose's son, who had died young (aged
twelve), but Jacobovici makes no mention of the fact that these archaeological discoveries can be explained in other ways.

In case there is any doubt of the significance of what Jacobovici has just
argued, James Cameron now appears on set, in order to sum up progress
so far: 'It seems that the Bible, geology, and archaeology are all telling the
same story. The sceptics, who would like to regard the Exodus as myth,
might resist the idea that it actually happened, because this would imply
that God does, indeed, exist. Believers, on the other hand, may feel that a
scientific explanation of the biblical story takes God out of the equation.'
Cameron's words here provide perhaps the most explicit admission of a
religious agenda in any Exodus documentary so far: the Exodus 'sceptics'
(presumably including many biblical scholars) must be refuted because
the existence of God is at stake. But Cameron's statement simply reveals
how little he and Jacobovici understand the questions surrounding Exodus
in biblical scholarship. To Cameron and Jacobovici (and other Exodus
documentary makers, it would seem), to doubt the historical authenticity
of the Exodus text is to doubt God's existence. There does not seem to be
room in their view for other (less literalistic) theologies of the inspiration
of Scripture, nor for the fact that scholars may continue to share and
debate questions about the text of Exodus while holding their personal
faith commitments apart (and in fact adhering to a wide spectrum of
religious beliefs and none).

Still, Cameron's admission is not the end of it. Making a further
apologetic move, Jacobovici takes up Cameron's query about science
potentially taking 'God out of the equation' to signal the next episode
of the documentary, saying, 'But in the book of Exodus, God does not
suspend nature, he manipulates it. In other words, according to the Bible
we should be able to understand the science behind the miracles. And the
greatest miracle of them all was the parting of the sea.' This intriguing
comment about the Bible's scientific qualifications is sadly not unpacked
by Jacobovici, but he does go on to put forward a full-blown naturalistic

explanation of the sea event, of a particularly complex kind, involving multiple coincidences and unlikelihoods. As the Egyptians chased the Israelites towards a 'Sea of Reeds' (the Ballah lakes in the northern Delta, according to Jacobovici), the seismic activity which had triggered the earlier plagues and Minoan eruption would have created a mass landslip of Delta sediments into the Mediterranean. This would in turn, he explains, have caused the nearby African tectonic plate boundary to rise catastrophically by a metre or more, effectively 'parting' the Sea of Reeds so that the Israelites could cross. 'At this point', asserts Jacobovici, 'further seismic activity, or another collapse of the Delta would have sent a major tsunami crashing against the coast', which would have travelled inland to Ballah and engulfed the Egyptians as they chased the Israelites. Suffice it to say that Jacobovici does not provide any geological evidence or expert scientific opinion to support this explanation:[32] articulated in supreme confidence, it is presumably pure speculation.

And as if this development was not imaginative enough, Jacobovici goes on to suggest that some of the Israelites who crossed the parted sea with Moses did not go to the Promised Land, but made their way to Greece. For sure, traces of Minoan art have been found in excavations at Avaris, suggesting contact between Egypt and the Aegean in the second millennium, but Jacobovici implicates this contact directly in the Exodus. Of course, the Bible is entirely silent on the possibility of Greek contact with the Exodus. So, to demonstrate that some of the Israelites in the Exodus went to Greece (and not Canaan), Jacobovici travels to Mycenae and suggests that the famous hoard of gold and swords found by Schliemann here around 1873 actually came from the spoils of the Israelites plundering their Egyptian neighbours after the death of the firstborn (Exod. 12:35-36). For confirmation of this Israelite–Mycenae link Jacobovici examines a grave stele from Mycenae, and interprets it as showing an Egyptian charioteer pursuing Moses, and then being engulfed by waves at the sea event. Jacobovici seeks the expert opinion of a Greek archaeologist at this point, who provides a totally different (and much more mundane) interpretation of the stele. Not to be deterred, Jacobovici simply uses this incident as a demonstration of how far off-track the experts really are from the truth. Of course, this incident may be interpreted differently, as evidence for the fantastic nature of Jacobovici's theories. It does, at least, demonstrate Jacobovici's pattern of working: he

32. Apart from that of Charles Pellegrino, described here as an 'author'. Pellegrino is well known for promoting controversial solutions to longstanding historical questions.

tends to create speculative patterns across periods and cultures by linking together isolated details and artefacts that happen to catch his eye, while he ignores their wider cultural contexts and histories, along with their established scholarly fields.

The final episode of the documentary concerns Jacobovici's search for Mount Sinai. In common with previous documentaries, Jacobovici points out that the experts have never managed to locate the mountain with confidence, and he casts doubt on the traditional location at Jebel Musa in southern Sinai. Instead, and with the same overflowing optimism that he has displayed throughout the documentary, Jacobovici explains how his own solution – Hashem el-Tarif in eastern Sinai – matches the biblical text uniquely well. This leads Jacobovici into his final discussion, a re-construction of the tabernacle which God commanded Moses to build in the wilderness, and of the ark of the covenant. And here we are treated to perhaps the most outrageously tenuous series of connections in the whole documentary. Jacobovici explains that the tribe of Dan (the 'Danites') helped to make the ark of the covenant.[33] And since, Jacobovici explains, Homer refers to those buried at Mycenae as the 'Danoi', perhaps these are the Israelites who migrated to Greece after the Exodus. In other words, Jacobovici believes that those who made the ark of the covenant then went on to Greece. Since the biblical text is silent on this, Jacobovici must find support elsewhere. He goes back to the artefacts found in Mycenae. There he finds a small golden design which reminds him of the altar and the ark of the covenant described in the Bible (but only when the altar and the ark are imagined in his mind's eye from a particular angle, so that they effectively merge into one shape. Jacobovici helpfully provides a graphical demonstration to explain to the mystified viewer how this unique perspective can be achieved). Needless to say, none of the experts has noticed the relevance of this piece to the Exodus (nor its supposed likeness to the altar and ark), but to Jacobovici it is a stunning find, and with breath-taking confidence he proclaims: 'At last, we know what the ark of the covenant looked like'.

And here the documentary ends. James Cameron summarizes by declaring that the Exodus is 'an historic fact': evidence has been shown for the first time, he claims, that features of the story like the plagues actually occurred, that the 'real Mount Sinai' has been discovered and that

---

33. It is unclear from where Jacobovici gains this piece of knowledge. If he has the biblical text in mind, only one of the people commissioned to build the ark, Oholiab, was from the tribe of Dan (Exod. 31:6); the main portion of the work (37:1) appears to have been done by Bezalel (from the tribe of Judah, 31:2).

'the discovery of the millennium' has been made, namely 'a gold image of the ark of the covenant'. Jacobovici re-appears, to add one final (faith inspired) rhetorical question: 'Did all this happen as a result of massive geological events triggered by nothing more than nature? Or, were the earthquakes, volcanoes and the tsunamis caused by divine intervention when God decided to free a nation from slavery, and forge a new covenant with humanity?' This theological rhetoric goes even further than anything Jacobovici has claimed so far in the documentary, but it demonstrates that the real motivation for his incredible theories – in common with a number of the Exodus documentaries – is not to investigate history but to promote a biblicist/literalist apologetic.

Clearly, *The Exodus Decoded* is nothing if not ambitious, making an apologetic case for the historicity of the Exodus (and for faith in God) based on a highly imaginative treatment of the Exodus story combined with poorly understood smatterings of ancient history and the natural sciences. There is much in common with the methodology and content of earlier documentaries, especially with *Who Was Moses?* and *Moses*, but the extraordinary degree of selectivity in the way that the biblical text and historical artefacts are used here (and the lack of engagement with expert opinion at key points) sets this documentary even further out on a limb.[34] *The Exodus Decoded* gives the impression that it provides ground-breaking and solid new evidence to support Exodus, but any positive message here is completely undermined by the documentary's reliance on unfounded speculation and a poor grasp of historical research. *The Exodus Decoded* is, in many ways, the strongest example of the trend that I identify in this chapter: the haphazard plundering of history and biblical study in order to promote a reactionary agenda.

Walking the Bible with Bruce Feiler: Parts Two and Three (2005)

These two documentaries take a very different tone to those examined so far: they show much less concern with historical questions, but instead describe a kind of travelogue or pilgrimage as Feiler sets out to discover the places of Joseph, Moses and the Exodus. There is no concern to refute scholarly scepticism, nor is there much interest shown in naturalistic

---

34. Indeed, one expert who was featured in the documentary, Manfred Bietak, was so disappointed at both the tendentious treatment that he received in the documentary's final edit, and the many historical blunders that were made, that he published a spirited attack on the documentary, criticising it at almost every point (Bietak, 'The Volcano').

explanations of the plagues or sea crossing. In fact, such niceties are regarded as rather irrelevant to the Exodus story, even to the extent that they might undermine it. Adopting a strongly faith-based tone, the power of the story is said to be in what it tells us about its central character, God, rather than what nature can do.

Feiler tells the Exodus story in a straightforward, unquestioning way as he proceeds on his pilgrimage, mentioning historical questions only rather rarely, such as (for instance) the debate over whether the sea event took place at the Red Sea or a Reed Sea (Feiler adopts the latter). There is little by way of special effects, animation, expert interviews or historical reconstructions, but since the documentaries are so taken up with Feiler's personal reactions to what he encounters they contain a great deal of human appeal and charm. Thus, by means of a kind of homespun theological wisdom, Feiler has an ability to conjure extra layers of meaning from the narrative in ways that the historically fixated documentaries cannot. Summing up his journey at the end of the two documentaries, Feiler goes to Mount Nebo, the end of Moses' pilgrimage (Deut. 34), and says, 'When I first started on this journey I was interested in scientific and archaeological questions. By the end, I had a much more spiritual journey, drawing closer to the Bible, and entering the story myself.' Feiler's aim seems to be to encourage viewers to take their own inner pilgrimage into the biblical text.

Riddles of the Bible: Exodus Revealed (2006)

With this National Geographic documentary we return to the perennial theme of history. Thera features yet again. However, unlike previous documentaries this one is rather sceptical that science has anything to add to our appreciation of Exodus. The point is made at the end of the documentary that we do not need the evidence of science to believe in Exodus, but rather faith.

The narrator begins in time-honoured fashion by asking whether the story is historically credible, and makes an unusual emphasis on the miracles: 'A biblical tale of miracles, catastrophes, history changed by the hand of God. From the burning bush to the death of the firstborn, scholars and enthusiasts pursue natural explanations for supernatural events, in laboratories, in desert sands and on volcanoes. Will these theories provide proof that the miracles actually happened? What's the real story of Exodus? Is it possible that it never happened at all?' This documentary appears to regard the miracle narratives of Exodus as the lynchpin on which the whole story stands or falls; skirting over the archaeological questions that occupy the attention of so many of the other documentaries, this one lingers instead on scientific treatments of the plagues and sea crossing. The documentary features a number of natural scientists explaining their ideas, but at key points the narrator concludes the discussion by throwing cold water on their models. For example, Cambridge scientist Colin Humphreys[35] is featured demonstrating a naturalistic explanation for the burning bush, but the narrator is unimpressed: 'Plausible perhaps, but hardly proof. When it comes to the miracles of Exodus, explanations abound from the sublime to the ridiculous.' As if to indicate how we should understand 'the ridiculous', the documentary instantly moves into scientific studies of the plagues, where they are presented as a chain reaction of environmental disasters. Again, the narrator is unimpressed: 'Using science imaginatively does produce some possible, if slightly far-fetched, natural scenarios for the supernatural plagues. But did they happen at all?'[36]

Therefore, unlike the majority of Exodus documentaries, this one shows little interest in establishing the historicity of the narrative by means of 'evidence' or scientific 'explanations'. In fact, this documentary entertains genuine doubt as to whether we can judge the authenticity of the Exodus by such means at all, and towards the end it offers the widespread scholarly view that the Exodus story may well have coalesced gradually from the memories of many escapees from Egypt.

As regards the naturalistic explanations of the plagues and sea event, the documentary seems to collect together so many explanations precisely to illustrate how little they tell us in the final analysis. The documentary concludes with this final statement, suggesting that an apologetic message should be drawn from the questions and doubts: 'Scientific explanations offered for the many miracles of Exodus, though intriguing, take us no closer to proving it happened, and the archaeological and historical records remain resolutely silent about these epic events … The truth of this story can only be answered in the heads and hearts of each individual. But surely the questions are worth asking. Ultimately the power of Exodus lies more in faith than in science.' Hence, despite the doubts aired earlier in the documentary as to whether any of this actually happened in the first place, it is clear that, in the final analysis, we are expected still to harbour a basic trust in the happenstance of the Exodus story. Therefore, the doubts are used positively to establish a tacit apologetic

35. Humphreys is author of *The Miracles of Exodus: A Scientist's Discovery of the Extraordinary Natural Causes of the Biblical Stories* (London, New York: Continuum, 2003).

36. The documentary directs even greater scepticism towards the tsunami model of the sea event.

agenda: naturalistic explanations of the miracles are undermined by the documentary precisely in order to prompt the viewer to take the existential decision of faith based on the Exodus narrative alone.

The Bible's Buried Secrets (2008)

This American documentary (not to be confused with the BBC documentary of the same name) does not look at the Exodus in detail, but it is significant in offering a far more positive assessment of contemporary scholarly views of the Exodus than any other. The documentary focuses especially on the development of monotheism as a religious system, which necessitates taking a long view across the whole Hebrew Bible. In discussing mainstream scholarly views of the birth of Israel as a nation, the point is made that the proto-Israelites were most likely indigenous Canaanites who had settled in the central hill country around the thirteenth century BCE. In other words, the documentary promotes the gently minimalist line taken by many critical scholars towards the Exodus: there is no evidence of the Bible's story of a mass migration from Egypt to Canaan, but it is quite possible that the text reflects memories of small groups of escaped slaves, especially if those slaves had been exposed to the historical Yahweh cult located in Midian in their travels, and had then brought it to the proto-Israelites.

This documentary is therefore a refreshing exception to the otherwise universal rule that Exodus documentaries show no great interest in engaging with the currents of mainstream biblical scholarship.

Secrets of the Bible: Parting of the Red Sea (2014) and Secrets of the Bible: The Staff of Moses (2014)

This series of documentaries focuses on some of the more sensational 'mysteries' of the Bible, and features a number of documentaries on Exodus.

Parting of the Red Sea has a connection with earlier Exodus documentaries through its Executive Producer, Jean-Claude Bragard. Like Bragard's Exodus documentaries for BBC (*Who Was Moses?* and *Moses*) – and indeed, like the majority of Exodus documentaries – scholarly scepticism is flagged up here early on, only to be swept aside in favour of amateur affirmation. So, archaeologist Eric Cline appears declaring that searching for an historical Exodus is an 'exercise in futility', but his damning indictment is soon forgotten as the documentary turns to recount the personal stories of police officer-turned-adventurer Bob Cornuke, and software engineer Carl Drews. Both men seek to establish the plausibility of the Red Sea crossing, Cornuke by exploring the Straits of Tiran as the crossing location (as mentioned above in *Mountain of Fire: The Search for the True Mount Sinai*), and Drews by creating computer simulations of a 'strong east wind' (Exod. 14:21) over a shallow sea of reeds.[37] Both men are portrayed as wholly convinced by the results of their investigations, Cornuke that the crossing really must have taken place at the Straits of Tiran, Drews that the crossing was really facilitated by a strong wind exposing a crossing point across a shallow lake in the northern Delta. The documentary does not attempt to judge between these geographically incompatible explanations, but rather offers them up as examples of personal faith triumphing in the face of scholarly negativity. As the documentary closes, the narrator tells us: 'Professional archaeologists insist that finding the location of the Red Sea parting is futile. But amateurs Carl Drews and Bob Cornuke each think they have solved the mystery. If, as they believe, God has left his fingerprints on the earth, it cannot be long before the truth is revealed.' We are left wondering whether this is a prediction that archaeology will soon discover evidence that Cornuke and Drews were right all along, or whether it is a dire apocalyptic warning that Jesus will soon return to judge the archaeologists for their disbelief!

The Staff of Moses (2014) can be treated very briefly, not least because it is the most *Indiana Jones*-like of all of the documentaries examined here. It concerns the search by 'historical detective' Graham Phillips for the real staff of Moses. This staff, the 'most powerful artefact in history', and Moses' 'supernatural weapon', was the very same staff that Moses used to bring down the ten plagues upon Egypt, and to part the Red Sea, according to the literalistic reading employed by Phillips and the documentary makers. By drawing a highly optimistic but incredible sequence of historical conjectures, Phillips discovers that the staff has been underneath his nose for decades, lingering in a display cabinet in Birmingham Museum (UK). The trouble is that none of the experts believe that this piece is the very staff of Moses, even accusing Phillips of making evidence up. The documentary ends by expressing the usual trope of one lone man's heroic faith in the literal authenticity of Exodus against the united but negative axis of sceptical scholars.

---

37. C. Drews and H. Weiqing, 'Dynamics of Wind Setdown at Suez and the Eastern Nile Delta', *PLoS ONE* 5:e12481 (2010); C. Drews, 'Could Wind Have Parted the Red Sea?' *Weatherwise* 64 (2011): 30–5.

Patterns of Evidence: Exodus (2015)

This, the most recent documentary, is the flagship of a wider media initiative (www.patternsofevidence.com), which supplies books, updates on archaeological research, merchandise (for children as well as adults), material for religious ministry (including sermons), and which has begun a fundraising campaign to create more documentaries. The overall aim of this initiative appears to be to promote religious faith by advocating the historical reliability of the Bible. To illustrate, the publicity for the documentary features prominent quotations from its producer, Timothy Mahoney, such as, 'You never know where a crisis of faith will lead you', or, 'I spent 12 years asking "Is the Bible true? If not what should I put my faith in?"' Of all Exodus documentaries, this one is perhaps the most upfront about the existential religious agenda behind its historicism.

When evaluated within the canon of Exodus documentaries, *Patterns of Evidence* is also perhaps the one most guilty of painting mainstream scholarship in a negative light. The documentary opens with the familiar motif of scholarly scepticism: 'For over 1500 years, Western civilization accepted the Bible as being true. But after the 1950s scepticism grew when archaeologists found mounting evidence contradicting the early history of the Bible. Today that scepticism has only increased.' Finding an alternative to that scepticism provides the driving force behind the documentary: Mahoney immediately describes how he felt compelled to travel around the world to find 'the truth about the Exodus ... taking on the giants of archaeology, religion and tradition.' And take them on he does: leading archaeologists (Israel Finkelstein and Norma Franklin) and a rabbi (David Wolpe) are interviewed explaining the mainstream historical questions about the Exodus story, but the documentary portrays these experts as opponents of religious faith by picturing them alongside well-known atheists such as Richard Dawkins and Christopher Hitchens, and by accusing the experts of making the Bible out to be false, a 'fairy tale', so that Christianity and Judaism are 'based on a gigantic lie'. It matters little that several of the Exodus experts explain their own religious beliefs and practices in positive terms along the way: the documentary only appears to be interested in maintaining a polarised view, where the historicity of the biblical account – and the impact of that historicity on religious faith – is an all or nothing affair; there is no room for the more nuanced view of biblical history adopted by many scholars, as presented in *The Bible's Buried Secrets*, for instance.

Having made its point so starkly, *Patterns of Evidence* then proceeds by adopting the strategy widespread among Exodus documentaries, where a plausibility case (a 'pattern of evidence') is assembled to support the veracity of the biblical account in the face of alleged scholarly scepticism.

As in the earlier documentaries, *The Exodus Revealed* and *The Exodus Decoded*, this particular plausibility case is built around archaeological evidence from Avaris, which suggests a flourishing Semitic presence in the seventeenth and sixteenth centuries BCE. Unlike the previous documentaries though, *Patterns of Evidence* simultaneously attacks the thirteenth-century BCE Ramesside date. The suggestion is that this latter date is not only erroneous, but is maintained by scholars largely in order to discredit the authenticity of the Bible.

In order to substantiate its chronological case, *Patterns of Evidence* makes heavy reliance on the historical author David Rohl. who has done much to argue for a drastic revision to the current consensus in ancient Egyptian chronology.[38] However, it is not too much to say that Rohl is fighting something of a lone battle against the weight of scholarly consensus. Rohl's 'New Chronology' would push the dating of many significant periods in Egyptian history (including the period of occupation of Avaris by Semitic peoples) forward, perhaps by more than three centuries after the conventional date, a revision which most Egyptologists regard as so enormous as to be implausible. Significantly, Rohl has championed the Bible's Exodus story in his revisionist case. Such is his confidence that the Semites of Avaris are the Hebrews described in the biblical book of Exodus, that Rohl believes he has identified archaeological evidence for the existence of Joseph in Avaris, for the enslavement of the Hebrews, and even for Pharaoh's killing of the Hebrew infant boys. Much of *Patterns of Evidence* is spent presenting Rohl's arguments, alongside other supporting experts such as John Bimson. And although space is given to some dissenting voices – with Mahoney admitting that Rohl's scheme is widely regarded as controversial – the documentary does so little to present the mainstream side of the argument, and so much to present Rohl's case as stunningly successful, that one would easily be left with the impression that Rohl has won the argument resoundingly. The truth is, however, that Rohl's revised chronology has not won over many followers in mainstream academia. On the contrary, even Egyptologists who advocate an historical Exodus much as described in the biblical text, Kenneth Kitchen and Hoffmeier, in particular, have argued against Rohl's chronology, and both cautiously support a thirteenth-century (Ramesside) date for the Exodus.[39]

---

38. See, for example, David Rohl, *A Test of Time: Volume I. The Bible – From Myth to History* (London: Century, 1995).

39. See, for example, K.A. Kitchen, review of D. M. Rohl, *A Test of Time, Volume I. The Bible – From Myth to History*, *Palestine Exploration Quarterly* 129 (1997): 172–4; Kitchen, *Reliability*, 310; Hoffmeier, *Israel in Egypt*, 126.

But the academic details of this argument are of less interest to *Patterns of Evidence* than is the question of whether the Bible is to be believed or not, which, for Mahoney, is *the* critical question for religious belief. As Mahoney explains at the end of the documentary, 'It's startling to think how significant [the disagreement over Exodus dating] could be. Because chronology, the dates assigned to these events, is the thing being used to convince the world that the Bible is just a fairy tale.' In other words, *Patterns of Evidence* suggests that the chronology disagreement is not just an academic debate, but is the result of a conspiracy against the (religious) truth of the Bible. Although most of the other Exodus documentaries make similar implications by highlighting scholarly 'scepticism', *Patterns of Evidence* does more than many to present this as a do-or-die faith issue.

Minoan/Thera Documentaries

Three final documentaries should be mentioned briefly, since although they do not discuss the Exodus, they explore the Minoan eruption of Thera, and the idea that Thera provided the historical root of Plato's legend of Atlantis. These documentaries are all British productions (Channel 4 or BBC): *The Minoans* (2004), *Timewatch: The Wave That Destroyed Atlantis* (2007) and *Timewatch: Atlantis the Evidence* (2010). There is a large degree of overlap between them, since they all set out to explore the demise of Minoan civilization a century or more after the Minoan eruption, and the eruption's role in this. There are also several parallels with the Exodus documentaries, not only in the way that both kinds of documentary revel in the great visual spectacle provided by the volcano, but also in the way that bridges must be built between the scientific picture of the eruption and what archaeology might reveal of the human response to the eruption. Building these bridges necessarily involves a certain amount of speculative reconstruction, although the case for Thera's role in the downfall of Minoan civilization is aided by the fact that there is at least some material evidence that Theran tsunamis swept the coast of Minoan Crete,[40] while there is none at all that they reached Egypt. A third parallel between the Minoan and Exodus documentaries is that they display a similar degree of disingenuousness in promising brand new evidence to solve old mysteries, when the Thera theories which they offer have actually been around in their current format as solutions to the Minoan problem and the Exodus since the 1960s.

---

40. This is the subject particularly of *The Wave that Destroyed Atlantis.*

The most recent of the Minoan documentaries, *Atlantis the Evidence*, provides the clearest comparison with the Exodus documentaries, since it concerns the interpretation of a similarly ancient story (Atlantis), which is fraught with a similar degree of controversy to Exodus. Like the Exodus, many have claimed that the legend of the destruction of Atlantis reflects a genuine happening in history (and many explanations have been proposed down the ages), but also like the Exodus many (especially scholars) have urged caution or outright scepticism.[41] In *Atlantis the Evidence*, the presenter Bettany Hughes adopts a similar strategy to that of most Exodus documentaries: she begins by introducing the idea that Atlantis is a myth that no reasonable historian would accept as credible, but then promises 'brand new scientific evidence' to demonstrate traces of a real historical story underneath the legend. But as the documentary unfolds into a presentation of the Minoan eruption of Thera, it quickly becomes clear that we are being treated to a rehash of Thera theories that have been in circulation for decades, much as with many of the Exodus documentaries. In spite of this, Hughes concludes the documentary with an assertion as strong as any in the Exodus documentaries: 'Surely, this is the root of Plato's Atlantis legend'. We therefore see that, in spite of the long-running scientific and archaeological controversies surrounding the Minoan eruption (and especially regarding its dating), and in spite of our almost complete ignorance of the effects that it had on neighbouring civilizations (for example Crete), Thera provides a highly malleable solution to any number of ancient mysteries. Rather like second-millennium Egyptian history, Thera can be easily plundered for convenient answers to outstanding problems, even to the extent that myths and legends can be transformed into history.

Discussion

Looking across the various Exodus documentaries surveyed here, some common threads emerge.

First, the Exodus documentaries are overwhelmingly concerned with the historicity of what is related in Exodus, usually to support it, or to advance it in the face of perceived scepticism.[42] The documentaries almost invariably do so by means of a more or less conservative literalism

41. R. Ellis, *Imagining Atlantis* (New York: Knopf, 1998).

42. Those few documentaries which are not overwhelmingly concerned with historicity (such as those by Bruce Feiler) are the welcome exceptions that prove the rule.

concerning the text, all too often backed up by poor historical arguments and misunderstood theories which are, in any case, presented disingenuously as state-of-the-art.

Second, biblical scholars and archaeologists are often used individually as expert commentators in the documentaries, but when they are referred to *en masse* they are usually said to be sceptical. Natural scientists, on the other hand, often appear as enthusiastic advocates for the historicity of Exodus. This means that a not-so-subtle divide between the theologians/ biblical scholars and the scientists is communicated, perpetuating (but ironically, also subverting) the popular motif of conflict between science and religion. In the Exodus documentaries the professional religious scholars (biblical scholars especially) are seen to be the sceptics, while the natural scientists are the believers.[43]

Third, it is rarely explained why biblical scholars might question many aspects of the Exodus story in historical terms, except that it is something to do with a lack of extra-biblical evidence. This shows how poorly the documentary makers understand the field. The lack of evidence is certainly a part of what informs the scholarly caution, but the documentaries do little to represent the much more sophisticated understanding of the Exodus text which forms the context to this scholarly caution, an understanding which introduces many relevant historical questions quite apart from the point about extra-biblical evidence.[44] In other words, the documentaries rarely suggest that there are other ways of interpreting the text historically than a simplistic 'did it happen or not' polarization.

Fourth, the documentaries so often promise new evidence to overturn the old mysteries and scholarly scepticism, when what they actually deliver turns out to be recycled ideas that have been in circulation for decades. The Thera theories are common examples of this, used in both the Minoan and the Exodus documentaries.

Fifth, there is a fascination with promoting *material* artefacts (from archaeology and the natural sciences) over promoting a deeper understanding of the *textual* artefact at our disposal, namely the text of Exodus itself. Naturalistic studies from the sciences of what may have been behind the plagues and sea event are highlighted as being particularly attractive, presumably because of their imaginative and visual 'apocalyptic' appeal.

---

43. A point that I also argue in more general studies of the miracle stories of Exodus in Harris, 'How did Moses', 25–8.

44. And here *The Bible's Buried Secrets* is the exception that proves the rule.

The fact that these studies invariably entail a selective reading of the text (where naturalistic elements in the text are taken literally insofar as they fit the model being proposed, while other details are largely overlooked) is never mentioned, nor are the reasons why biblical scholars might object to such a selective approach.

Sixth, while the issue of history is of near-ubiquitous interest in Exodus documentaries, a great deal of variety is shown in the ways that the documentaries negotiate the religious dimensions of Exodus. Some make no explicit religious claims about what they present (for example *Who Was Moses?* and *Moses*), while others mix their focus on history with an approach that includes theological interpretation (for example *The Ten Commandments*). Yet others have clear apologetic motives (for example *The Exodus Revealed*), while a handful adopt a more spiritual tone altogether (the Bruce Feiler documentaries). But every documentary maker (with the possible exception of Bruce Feiler) appears to regard the historical issue as of paramount importance.

Seventh, those documentaries that promote the historical authenticity of Exodus on apologetic grounds (for example *The Exodus Decoded*) rely on a more-or-less literalistic/biblicist theology of Scripture. Scholars are demonized as 'sceptics', sometimes with the clear implication that this scepticism is based on anti-religious grounds (for example *Patterns of Evidence*). In other words, the existence of God, and the validity of the Bible as a source of religious truth, are seen to be at stake in the debate about whether these things happened or not. There is rarely any acknowledgment of other theologies of Scripture, such that it might be possible to maintain theistic beliefs while also holding more nuanced views of the Exodus than a simple true/false binary regarding its historicity. In other words, the documentaries often stray into theological territory but rarely display any understanding of it.

My preliminary conclusion from this is to expand upon what I said at the beginning. Exodus, the second book of the Bible, is of enormous fascination to documentary makers. However, the great wealth of Exodus documentaries is not matched by a corresponding wealth of interests explored therein. Instead, the focus is almost invariably on history, and on a limited range of approaches to that history, which the majority of documentaries keep re-packaging and re-branding as though they are presenting ground-breaking, fresh and novel evidence. One has to question why so many documentaries are made that cover essentially the same ground, and all too often inaccurately, disingenuously and with a poor understanding of historical and biblical research. This leads me directly to my conclusions.

Conclusions

Why, then, are documentary makers so single-minded about the historicity of Exodus, and why do so many of them seek to establish it against
a perceived threat from biblical scholarship? For sure, the historical
authenticity of the Exodus has been a key apologetic battleground for
Judaism and Christianity since the earliest times,[45] and some of the
Exodus documentaries are clearly motivated in this direction (notably
Patterns of Evidence). Also, fundamentalist Christianity has long had a
difficult relationship with critical biblical scholarship, often seeking to
defend biblical literalism against the creeping dangers of 'liberalism' and
relativism. But many documentaries do not take an explicitly apologetic
line, and none appears to defend a full-blown fundamentalist literalism
(although some veer in this direction, *The Exodus Decoded* notably). So
why might supposedly 'secular' documentaries, such as the BBC productions, promote the historicity of the Exodus by attacking professional
scholarship? One explanation is that perhaps the documentary makers are
attracted by the prospect of challenging the hegemonic establishment of
biblical scholarship, so that they may promote other kinds of specialisms,
the natural sciences in particular. And it certainly seems that the ever-
topical science–religion debate might have a part to play in this.

It is fair to say, though, that those documentaries that affirm the historicity of the Exodus in the face of scholarly caution are still playing into
the hands of religious conservatives who have a theological stake in the
literal accuracy of the text. It is quite possible then that the documentaries
were deliberately constructed to be attractive to a particular consumer
market. In which case, the very sizeable evangelical Christian population
of the United States provides an obvious potential market, and one which
is (presumably) more likely to welcome a documentary that confirms
a conservative biblicism than one that challenges it. A complementary
market to this is provided by the widespread public fascination with
'ancient mysteries', and with the attempts of modern science to resolve
them. Ancient Egypt and the Bible have long been seen as rich store-
houses of such ancient mysteries, with the added attraction for Exodus
that key parts of its narrative lend themselves to being realized on the
screen (thanks to CGI) in spectacular and catastrophic terms. Biblicist
concerns to strengthen historical authenticity, and a fascination with the
scientific resolution of ancient mysteries, are augmented by the visually

---

45. One only has to read Josephus's lengthy historical defence of the Exodus in
Against Apion to see that this was an issue even two thousand years ago.

mesmeric properties of the apocalypse. We therefore find that, although the humble Exodus documentary may appear at first sight to fall into the genre of 'TV historical documentary', it has overtones of 'conservative apology', and 'apocalypse' too. Therefore, depending upon how we might identify the motivational factors behind the making of these documentaries, we are likely to place them in different (not altogether complementary) genres.

Scholars such as myself might hope that Exodus documentaries are primarily made for educational purposes, to explain and promote a serious field of historical, textual and theological enquiry accurately. That is, at least, how they almost invariably sell themselves in the opening few minutes, as offering new light on old problems. It is sobering then to realize that education appears to be rather low on the list of the documentary makers' priorities compared to consumer demand, sensationalism and entertainment. As regards the *accuracy* of the material presented in the documentaries, in the shifting sands of the Exodus it is perhaps an issue that is open to interpretation in any case. However, Manfred Bietak, the leading archaeologist of Avaris, had strong words to say about the accuracy of *The Exodus Decoded*: 'If this film were presented as a work of fiction, it would be engaging and entertaining. But it is not presented as a work of fiction. It makes the public believe it is based on a serious investigation.'[46] Zevit, reviewing *Moses*, makes much the same point: 'The program neither tackles complex historical matters seriously nor presents them in a responsible way. It either does not take its viewers seriously or assumes that its viewers are not serious people.'[47] Bietak and Zevit lay serious charges at the feet of the documentary producers, but charges that are fully justified in my opinion.

TV documentaries are made for many reasons, and to serve many audiences, but they are invariably marketed as representing an issue as accurately as possible, with the purpose of informing and stimulating. But with many of the Exodus documentaries, it seems to me that information has too often been sacrificed to stimulation: stimulation of a target audience which (the documentary makers assume) is incapable of dealing with difficult and complex issues. It is one thing, it seems to me, to misrepresent scholars who have spent many years working on these problems with patience and integrity, but it is quite another to treat one's audience with contempt.

---

46. Bietak, 'The Volcano', 65.
47. Zevit, 'Moses', 62.

Documentaries Cited

On Exodus:

1994   Mysteries of the Bible: Moses at Mount Sinai. Multimedia Entertainment, FilmRoos, and A&E Networks. Produced by Lionel Friedberg, David M. Frank.

1997   *Mysteries of the Bible: The Ten Commandments*. FilmRoos/A&E Network. Produced by William Kronick.

1998   *Who Was Moses?* BBC for Discovery Channel. Produced and directed by Jean-Claude Bragard.

2001   *The Exodus Revealed: Search for the Red Sea Crossing*. Discovery Media Productions. Produced and directed by Lad Allen.

2002   *Mountain of Fire: The Search for the True Mount Sinai*. Dean River Productions. Directed by John Schmidt; produced by John Shepherd and Jason Behrman.

2002   *Moses*. BBC Manchester/TLC/Jerusalem Productions. Presented by Jeremy Bowen; produced and directed by Jean-Claude Bragard.

2005   *The Exodus Decoded*. The History Channel and Discovery Channel Canada. Presented by Simcha Jacobovici and James Cameron; produced by Felix Golubev and Simcha Jacobovici.

2005   *Walking the Bible with Bruce Feiler*. Part 2. TMC Entertainment. Presented by Bruce Feiler. Directed by David Wallace; produced by Rebecca Dobs.

2005   *Walking the Bible with Bruce Feiler*. Part 3. TMC Entertainment. Presented by Bruce Feiler. Directed by David Wallace; produced by Rebecca Dobs.

2006   *Riddles of the Bible: Exodus Revealed*. National Geographic. Produced by Anna Fitch.

2008   *The Bible's Buried Secrets*. Providence Pictures, NOVA, National Geographic. Directed and produced by Gary Glassman.

2014   *Secrets of the Bible: Parting of the Red Sea*. World Media Rights and IMG. Executive producer, Jean-Claude Bragard; produced and directed by John Blystone.

2014   *Secrets of the Bible: The Staff of Moses*. World Media Rights and IMG. Executive producer, Jean-Claude Bragard; produced and directed by Charlie Clayton.

2015   *Patterns of Evidence: Exodus*. Thinking Man Films. Directed and produced by Timothy P. Mahoney; executive producer David Wessner; co-producers Peter Windahl and Diane Walker.

On the Eruption of Thera:

2004   *The Minoans*. Lion Television for Channel Four. Presented by Bettany Hughes; produced and directed by Melanie Archer and Tim Kirby.

2007   *Timewatch: The Wave That Destroyed Atlantis*. BBC. Produced and directed by Harvey Lilley.

2010   *Timewatch: Atlantis the Evidence*. BBC. Presented by Bettany Hughes; produced and directed by Natalie Maynes.

Chapter 11

THE HISTORY CHANNEL'S *THE BIBLE*,
AN EPIC...?

Meg Ramey

What do you get when an ex-angel marries the king of reality television, and they decide to make a miniseries capable of competing with *The Walking Dead* for top ratings in a prime-time spot?

A drama about the Bible, of course. What else?

An Epic in the Making

When husband and wife team Mark Burnett, of *Survivor*, *The Apprentice* and *The Voice* fame, and Roma Downey, main protagonist in the *Touched by an Angel* series, began to discuss the development of a 'positive-message project', their shared faith and Catholic upbringing led them to consider doing something with the Bible.[1] Soon they were working in collaboration with the History Channel to produce a series that condensed the Bible into ten 44-minute episodes. Though such a challenge might seem daunting, Burnett says that he 'never thought for one millisecond about not doing it' once he had set his mind to the task.[2]

---

1. T. L. Stanley, 'Mark Burnett and Roma Downey Put Faith in "The Bible" for History', http://articles.latimes.com/2013/mar/03/entertainment/la-et-st-the-bible-history-survivo-20130303.

2. Ibid.

The Bible on Television

The couple soon enlisted the aid of experts, and consulted with roughly forty religious leaders and academics from around the world and from various denominations to make the script as historically and scripturally accurate as possible.[3] By 2012, filming had started on location in Morocco with an international cast and crew of hundreds. In 2013, the finished episodes aired in pairs over the course of five Sunday nights from 3–31 March, with the final instalment coinciding with Easter Sunday.

The show was a hit! On its first night, the miniseries drew 13 million viewers and consistently attracted 10 million on each of the four following nights.[4] *The Bible* was rated 2013's number-one new series on American cable[5] and was nominated for the 'Outstanding Miniseries or Movie' Emmy award that year.[6] The astonishingly fast DVD release of the series, only two days after the last episode aired, was timed to capitalize on the show's momentum and publicity, a strategy that worked well. It became the fastest-selling TV-to-DVD title since 2008 as well as the top-selling miniseries ever in its first week release.[7]

The impact of the series rippled over into other genres as well. A book entitled *A Story of God and All of Us* based on *The Bible*, which itself, ironically enough, was based on a book, opened at the #6 spot on the *Publishers Weekly* Hardcover Fiction list and at #27 on the *New York Times* Hardcover Fiction list.[8] The show also spawned the 2014 major motion picture *Son of God* that culled scenes from the last five episodes

3. Notable names from the field of biblical studies included Professor Helen Bond, Professor Craig Evans, Rabbi Josh Garroway, Professor Mark Goodacre, Dr Paula Gooder and Professor Candida Moss – all of whom are thanked in the closing credits of each episode.

4. Josh Sandburn, 'Behind the Hit *Bible* Miniseries: The Man Who Helps Hollywood Get Religion', http://business.time.com/2013/04/01/behind-the-hit-bible-miniseries-the-man-who-helps-hollywood-get-religion.

5. Lightworkers Media, 'Roma Downey and Mark Burnett's #1 New Cable Series THE BIBLE Is Also A New York Times Best Seller, Dominating Amazon and Is #1 On iTunes And #1 On Twitter', http://www.prnewswire.com/news-releases/roma-downey-and-mark-burnetts-1-new-cable-series-the-bible-is-also-a-new-york-times-best-seller-dominating-amazon-and-is-1-on-itunes-and-1-on-twitter-199936641.html.

6. Television Academy, 'Mark Burnett', http://www.emmys.com/bios/mark-burnett.

7. Erik Hayden, '"The Bible" Earns Emmy Nomination', http://bibleseriesresources.com/press-release.

8. Shanon Stowe, 'Book Based on "The BIBLE" Miniseries Becomes National Bestseller on the Heels of Telecast Success', http://www.breakingchristiannews.com/articles/display_art_pf.html?ID=11201.

and reformatted them into a two-hour feature film released to audiences worldwide. The condensed movie version of the television series garnered almost $60 million (USD) in gross revenue and three Emmy nominations.[9]

And just in case anyone was wondering, *The Bible*'s resurrected Christ overtook *The Walking Dead*'s revivified zombies in the Sunday night ratings race ... just barely though.[10]

An Epic Reception of the Bible

Jaroslav Pelikan once wrote that the key to understanding any age is to examine its portrayals of Jesus.[11] How the Bible is handled in art can serve as a barometer for epochs and cultures, especially when artists produce work that is intentionally targeted for mass consumption by appealing to a particular society's preferences, and Mark Burnett is certainly someone who has proven himself capable of understanding the zeitgeist of an age. Though British by birth, he has his finger on the pulse of the American public and gives his audiences what they want. His ability to produce record-setting and award-winning shows alone proves that fact.[12]

Other essays in this volume discuss the usefulness and success of Bible documentaries in conveying biblical scholarship to the general public. Since, however, Burnett states clearly in the DVD extras that creating a Bible documentary was never the purpose, this essay will focus more on the reception of the Bible in *The Bible*. After a brief examination of the motivating factors behind yet another dramatization of the Bible, it will focus on the series' interpretation of the Bible by discussing what it transmits to its audience and what it might imply about the culture for which it was produced.

9. 'Son of God', Internet Movie Database (IMDb), http://www.imdb.com/title/tt3210686/?ref_=nv_sr_1; cf. Hayden, 'The Bible'.

10. Lisa King, 'Sunday Night TV: The Bible and The Walking Dead Continue Ratings Race', http://communities.washingtontimes.com/neighborhood/tv-den/2013/mar/23/tv-tonight-bible-and-walking-dead-continue-ratings.

11. Jaroslav Pelikan, *Jesus Through the Centuries: His Place in the History of Culture* (New Haven, CT: Yale University Press, 1985), 2–3.

12. His list of accolades included six Emmy awards, four People's Choice awards, one PGA award and a star on the Hollywood walk of fame. His productions have garnered a collective total of 112 Emmy nominations. America's *TV Guide* magazine named him the 'Producer of the Year' while TIME Magazine named Burnett one of the world's most influential people (Wikipedia, 'Mark Burnett', http://en.wikipedia.org/wiki/Mark_Burnett).

Why Another Bible Epic?

Whether one calls it a representation, retelling, remake, rewrite or something else, what all artistic receptions of the Bible have in common is that they adapt, or as Roma Downey puts it, they breathe 'creative expansion into' the stories.[13] Such a practice is not novel given that the Bible itself contains adaptations from earlier biblical material in which the same stories are retold in different ways,[14] and that's even before we begin discussing the numerous ways in which these stories were retold within post-biblical Jewish literature.[15] Let's face it, sometimes modern artists do a lot less 'adapting' of their source material than some of the ancient editors themselves did.

That being said, any dramatization of the Bible is almost guaranteed to generate controversy or criticism even when the work is a mere parody of the original material.[16] It takes *hutzpah* to do any remake of the Bible, and the producers should be commended for even attempting it. The effort, time and expense that they spent on the project are obvious and impressive. So given the scope of the project and the scrutiny it was bound to face, it is worth asking what stimulated Burnett and Downey to take on this challenge in the first place.

When one attempts to understand any artist's intent, there are many clues available for consideration. Titles, introductory notes, external packaging, advertising, promo material, endorsements, press releases and, of course, interviews with the artists or producers all contribute to

13. Stacy Jenel Smith, 'Roma Downey, Mark Burnett: Bible Series Profound Experience', http://www.creators.com/lifestylefeatures/fashion-and-entertainment/hollywood-exclusive/roma-downey-mark-burnett-bible-series-profound-experience-royal-pains-paulo-costanzo-makes-good-on-high-school-goal.html.

14. Enns makes this same point in his review of the series and offers the standard example of David in the Deuteronomistic Historian's narrative versus the rewrite of David in the Chronicler's version (Peter Enns, 'Q: What Do Roma Downey and Writers of the Bible Have in Common? A: Neither Sticks to the Script', http://www.patheos.com/blogs/peterenns/2013/03/q-what-do-roma-downey-and-writers-of-the-bible-have-in-common-a-neither-sticks-to-the-script.

15. Iterations on biblical stories found in the Talmud, the pesher from Qumran or Josephus's works are all good examples of this practice. Geza Vermes first labels their retellings as the 'Rewritten Bible' (*Scripture and Tradition in Judaism* [Leiden, Netherlands: Brill, 1973], 67–126) while James Kugel simply calls them 'narrative expansions' (James L. Kugel, *In Potiphar's House: The Interpretive Life of Biblical Texts* [Cambridge, MA: Harvard University Press, 1994], 6).

16. Diane Winston succinctly summarizes, 'It's a minefield' (Stanley, 'Mark Burnett').

understanding the purpose behind the product. In a survey of this material, a few of Downey and Burnett's reasons for remaking the Bible stand out.

Perhaps the strongest, and certainly the most personal, motivation for the project stems from the couple's own professed Christian piety, their love for the book and its 'main character'. Journalists reviewing the miniseries frequently refer to the series as a 'labor of love' and one undertaken in prayer.[17] In one interview, Downey announces, 'I've loved Jesus all my life'.[18] Likewise Burnett explains, 'To us, as a family, we love the Bible. This is not a TV show to us. It's images and sound and sacred text that people will still watch, way after our grandchildren are old people.'[19] He calls the Bible 'a grand narrative, but it tells a pretty simple story about God's never-ending love for all of us'.[20] Though some have questioned the commercialization of the Bible and the couple's professional advancement from the series,[21] Downey and Burnett come across in interviews as sincere in their faith and genuinely motivated by personal piety.[22]

17. Cf. Downey who notes, 'Casting began with prayer' (Robert Lloyd, 'Review: History's "The Bible" an Epic, Epically Overwrought, Tale', http://articles.latimes.com/2013/mar/02/entertainment/la-et-st-history-the-bible-review-20130302) and Burnett who admits, 'I knew it was a huge undertaking, but I'd prayed about it' (Stanley, 'Mark Burnett').

18. Lloyd, 'Review'.

19. Bill Keveney, 'Sneak Peek: Bible Stories Come to Life on History', http://www.usatoday.com/story/life/tv/2012/12/16/history-bible-docudrama-mark-burnett-roma-downey-sneak-peek/1771069.

20. Stanley, 'Mark Burnett'.

21. In the 25 March 2013 episode of *The Colbert Report*, Stephen Colbert with his characteristic satire alludes to these possible motivations when he jokes about who Downey had to sleep with to get the part of the Virgin Mary, and in reference to Burnett's grandiose claims about *The Bible*'s impact, he remarks, 'As the Bible says, "Pride cometh before giant TV ratings"'. Colbert also draws attention to a possible commercial motivation when discussing the franchise merchandise the series spawned: 'If you enjoy watching *The Bible,* you want to explore the source material'. At this point, instead of pulling out a Bible, he draws out a copy of the book and says, 'I speak of course of the *Story of God and All of Us: A Novel Based on the Epic TV Series "The Bible"*. All the biblical stories you love from the miniseries, finally assembled into one book' (Stephen Colbert, 'History Channel's "The Bible"', http://thecolbertreport.cc.com/videos/t23n7e/history-channel-s--the-bible-).

22. If, as Jesus taught, where one's treasure is tells where one's heart is, then one of the couple's latest financial endeavours reveals a great deal about their desire to find practical outlets for expressing their Christian faith. They have recently donated $1 million (USD) to start the International Global Engagement's 'Cradle of

Also like many artists before them, Downey and Burnett started with a desire to modernize the Bible.[23] The impetus to do so surfaced while watching Cecil B. DeMille's *The Ten Commandments*, a film each loved as children while their own teenagers seemed unable to connect with it, finding it 'dated'.[24] By putting a fresh face on these age-old stories, they hoped to generate a buzz about the Bible that could inspire conversations about it,[25] help viewers to connect emotionally with the characters[26] and ultimately inspire them to read the good book itself.[27]

As Brits who now live in the States, Burnett and Downey admit to being 'stunned' that the Bible is not part of the public school curriculum in the US as it often is in European countries.[28] They argue that regardless of one's view on the sanctity of the text, the Bible is still a centrepiece of the Western canon just as much as Shakespeare.[29] Burnett partly blames the biblical illiteracy that he sees in America on the public school system's 'literary malpractice', and hopes that their miniseries will reach America's 'underserved audience'.[30]

The series, however, was not just made for the scripturally illiterate. In fact, it appears that the audience targeted most by the show's publicity campaign was the more conservative wing of American Christianity, a fact that is shown in many ways even if one does not believe that the

Christianity' fund to help Middle Eastern Christians as well as other religious and ethnic groups displaced by ISIS (Jeremy Weber, 'Winter Is Coming: Mark Burnett, Roma Downey Launch $25 Million Plan to Help Christians in Iraq and Syria', http://www.christianitytoday.com/gleanings/2014/october/winter-is-coming-mark-burnett-roma-downey-iraq-syria-ige.html?paging=off).

23. Burnett states, 'It was time for an updating. Adding fresh visual life to a sacred text' (Eric Marrapodi, 'Reality TV Goliath takes up Bible miniseries challenge, hopes for better outcome', http://religion.blogs.cnn.com/2013/03/02/the-reality-of-the-bringing-the-bible-to-life/?hpt=hp_c1).

24. Stanley, 'Mark Burnett'.

25. Burnett: 'We hope that on Monday mornings people will talk about *The Bible* they saw the night before' (Monica Graham, 'Graham: Bible series has N.S. connection', http://thechronicleherald.ca/religion/753909-graham-bible-series-has-ns-connection).

26. 'We tried to make it emotionally connective', Downey said. 'We want viewers to walk through the pages of the Bible in the footsteps of these characters' (Stanley, 'Mark Burnett').

27. Roma Downey on the DVD extras says, 'My best hope is that we will tell these stories in an exciting way that will draw people back to the book itself'.

28. Marrapodi, 'Reality TV Goliath'.

29. Graham, 'Graham: Bible series'.

30. Ibid.; Stanley, 'Mark Burnett'.

casting of an Obama-look-alike in the role of Satan was intentional.[31] From the opening prelude montage of quotes by American presidents and leaders about how the Bible is the 'foundation of our laws', the 'blueprint' and 'guide' for our nation, the intended demographic is quite obvious.[32]

Additional analysis of the advertising, promo material and early endorsements of the film also suggests that Downey and Burnett targeted a conservative American evangelical audience. The couple travelled across the country for months screening parts of the miniseries at venues such as religious conventions, prayer breakfasts, churches and Christian news stations.[33] Their proactive campaign garnered endorsements from big names in the American evangelical world, including Orange County mega-church pastor Rick Warren, Texas health-and-wealth televised pastor Joel Osteen and multi-media platform evangelist T. D. Jakes, while also snagging a seal of approval from *Focus on the Family* and *Answers in Genesis*.[34] The producers also worked with Outreach, a Christian marketing firm that provided publicity material, such as tune-in posters as well as sermon and study guides to tens of thousands of American churches and pastors.[35]

The producers, however, did not want to reach Americans only. In an interview on ABC News, Burnett offers his prediction on the impact of the series: 'I'm telling you, millions will either open the Bible or reopen the Bible, millions and millions and millions, maybe a billion'. To this projection his interviewer responds somewhat sceptically saying, 'Millions of new people may open the Bible?' Burnett responds optimistically by claiming, 'I think, to be honest with you because I'm a very blunt person, I think a billion's a low number'.[36]

---

31. A media storm was created when Right-wing commentator and talk show host Glenn Beck tweeted about the resemblance (#Anyone else think the Devil in #TheBible Sunday on History Channel looks exactly like That Guy?), a claim that the producers fervently denied. The controversy, however, led them to cut Satan out of the 2014 film version *Son of God* (Roma Downey, 'Producer: Why We Cast "Obama" Devil out of "Son of God"', http://www.usatoday.com/story/opinion/2014/02/17/television-god-devil-obama-movie-roma-downey-column/5560379/.

32. In an interview on ABC news, Burnett states, 'The Bible Is the Foundation of this Nation' (28 February 2013 interview, http://abcnews.go.com/Nightline/video/bible-remaking-oldest-stories-told-18614821).

33. Stanley, 'Mark Burnett'.

34. Ibid.; Elizabeth Mitchell, 'The Bible on the History Channel: A Review', https://answersingenesis.org/reviews/tv/the-bible-on-the-history-channel-a-review.

35. Stanley, 'Mark Burnett'.

36. 28 February 2013 interview on ABC news; cf. Keveney, 'Sneak Peek'.

While it would be hard to ascertain whether Burnett's prediction came true, one Gallup poll taken after the series concluded reported that 11% of American adults surveyed about their Bible reading credited *The Bible* miniseries with inspiring them to read Scripture more.[37] If that poll is at all accurate, then the producers should be congratulated for encouraging biblical literacy in America. The question remains, however, as to what sort of Bible they have given to their audience.

The Reception of the Bible in a Television Epic

The Bible: An Epic Story but Is It Historical?

Given that the series aired on the History Channel, one might be forgiven for expecting the series to place a premium on historicity. Then again with shows entitled *Pawn Stars* and *Swamp People*, perhaps the channel has not been too concerned with 'history' of late, prioritizing drama over documentary. Therefore, even though broadcast by the *History Channel* and screened by clergy and academic consultants to help 'ensure the show's historical and scriptural accuracy',[38] the end product demonstrates that reconstructing the past as factually as possible was not the producers' primary concern. Far more important for them was depicting the biblical stories as they appear in the Bible.

In an interview with CNN, Rabbi Joshua Garroway, one of the academic consultants for the series, revealed,

> One of the issues that came up frequently in the comments was the goal of the production was to remain faithful, or at least as faithful as possible, to the narrative and text of the Bible, *as opposed to a historical critical approach* … The series is not meant to be a historical feature but as a representation of the biblical narrative which is at times historical and at times not.[39]

Likewise in an article for *The Daily Beast*, Candida Moss, another of the series' academic consultants, discussed how scholars wrangled to retain some measure of historical integrity for the show while also respecting pious sensibilities. 'The space between historical accuracy and

---

37. Barna Group, 'The State of the Bible: 6 Trends for 2014', https://www.barna.org/barna-update/culture/664-the-state-of-the-bible-6-trends-for-2014#.VLH3TabWqdd.

38. Graham, 'Graham: Bible Series'.

39. Marrapodi, 'Reality TV Goliath' (italics mine).

religious fidelity is pretty narrow indeed – might as well make it look as good as you can',[40] Moss added.

The producers' approach towards the Bible's historicity is not surprising given that both regard the Bible as 'the absolute truth'.[41] On the DVD extras, Burnett states, 'The only way to approach this project was to treat the sacred text as a fact. Otherwise, you'd be making a documentary where you'd have academics saying, "Well, in the Bible it says this, but historically we're not sure". We don't even want to be doing that. That's a different project. We have to take the story as a fact.'[42]

Faithful to this stated objective, *The Bible* presents historically controversial biblical events with no hint of questioning their historical veracity as one might do when making a documentary. In the series, the world is created in six days instead of evolving over eons; Adam and Eve are real individuals rather than figurative representatives of humanity; Satan is a real character; Noah's family and an ark full of animals escape a worldwide flood destroying the rest of creation; the Red Sea miraculously parts for Israelites to walk across on solid ground; the city of Jericho, which in the show is definitely occupied during the conquest period, has walls that supernaturally come tumbling down before Joshua's army rushes in to destroy what remains; Shadrach, Meshach and Abednego escape the fiery furnace without a singe while Daniel walks out of the lions' den without a scratch; Jesus performs miracles, walks on water and is resurrected bodily; the disciples speak in tongues at Pentecost; and Saul is blinded by a vision of the resurrected Jesus on his way to Damascus.

Enhanced with CGI effects, the miraculous elements of the Bible are given centre stage and depicted in a way that intends to make them look historically plausible, though the end result is less than convincing.[43] In fact, the historical portrayal of the supernatural is one of the aspects that

40. Candida Moss, 'Diogo Morgado Puts the Carnal in Incarnate, but Was Jesus Really a Babe'? http://www.thedailybeast.com/articles/2014/03/04/diogo-morgado-puts-the-carnal-in-incarnate-but-was-jesus-really-a-babe.html.

41. Stanley, 'Mark Burnett'.

42. *The Bible*, DVD extras.

43. Genzlinger's assessment was correct, though marginally overstated, when he warns potential viewers, 'And those thinking that the ancient miracles might be better served by the special effects available in 2013 than they have been in previous versions should prepare for disappointment. The Red Sea parts no more convincingly here than it did for Charlton Heston in 1956' (Neil Genzlinger, 'God's Word', http://www.nytimes.com/2013/03/02/arts/television/the-bible-mini-series-on-history-channel.html?_r=1&).

the producers promoted most. On ABC news, Downey claims, 'We have brought miracles to life on the screen'.[44]

Since the biblical events and miracles are presented as factual history, there is very little here that a conservative Christian would find objectionable. Take, for example, the glowing reviews from conservative Christian news outlets, such as *The Christian Post*,[45] or this endorsement found on the apologetic *Answers in Genesis* website:

> *The Bible* presents biblical history *as real history* in graphic, interesting, and memorable ways ... Today, many people in the world are biblically illiterate even where the Bible enjoys wide circulation and despite the comparatively high rate of literacy. Though many reasons could be cited for this tragic situation, one major problem is that the *historicity of the biblical narratives* has been increasingly downplayed by those who claim the accounts are allegorical or metaphorical ... [B]y eroding people's faith in the *Bible's history*, this approach actually drives people from its truth and makes the Bible seem irrelevant and not worth their time. Thankfully, *The Bible* allows *the plain truths of biblical history* from the time of our origins to speak ... [E]ven as a stand-alone production, *The Bible* will likely lead many to Christ. Why? Because it presents the Bible's history *as real history* – instead of eroding trust in God's Word from the very first verse.[46]

Taking events from the Bible and presenting them unquestioningly as accurate history will not score many points in the academy, but it does appeal to the conservative Christian demographic of *The Bible*'s audience.[47]

44. ABC News, '"The Bible" Cast: "Hot Jesus" Responds to Twitter Nickname', http://abcnews.go.com/GMA/video/bible-miniseries-cast-finale-sneak-peek-hot-jesus-18829901.

45. Tunnicliffe writes, 'Burnett and his wife have produced a mini-series that is not only "not disappointing," but actually rises to the top of the "Wow" scale ... For someone that has read and taught the Bible for most of his life, I had a remarkable spiritual and emotional experience. The theme of God's love and hope for all humanity is the thread that holds the entire series together. I received a fresh new perspective on many of the famous Bible stories ... [T]he Burnetts – with an impressive list of over 40 advising scholars – have been faithful to the spirit of the text and at the same time provided a television series that is compelling, gritty at times and spiritually moving' (Geoff Tunnicliffe, 'Review: "The Bible" – This Time, Hollywood Got it Right', http://www.christianpost.com/news/review-the-bible-this-time-hollywood-got-it-right-90992).

46. Mitchell, 'The Bible' (italics mine).

47. Even with the producers' prioritization of scriptural fidelity over historical accuracy, Christian tradition tends to trump the actual Scriptures in *The Bible* when the two are at odds. E.g., traditional mistranslations take precedence over the original

The Bible: Recreating an Epic Historical Context

While *The Bible* may not be concerned with investigating and presenting scholarly findings regarding the historicity of biblical events, what it does well is recreate the socio-political context surrounding the New Testament stories.[48] Depicting the historical backdrop to biblical events is one of the most important functions, in my opinion, that fictional rewrites and film remakes can perform. By incorporating extra-biblical scenes culled from Josephus's writings into a timeline of Gospel events, *The Bible* provides a more coherent and consistent plotline running across the Jesus episodes (6-9) than it offers in the OT episodes, a plotline that revolves around the establishment's growing concern about Jesus, which ultimately climaxes with Jesus' death. That is the story that the producers have chosen to tell and around which the action revolves.

To frame the Jesus episodes for the audience within that particular narrative, each of those episodes opens with the montage of previously and not-yet-seen scenes that are edited together and narrated in a way that presents the upcoming events as an inevitable collision course of powers. The second half of the series begins by depicting a land in turmoil full of various pressures that could rupture the fragile peace in Israel. Its

languages when Moses parts the *Red*, not *Reed*, Sea (cf. *yam-sûp* in Exod. 13:18) and Jesus is born in the traditional Western stable rather than in a guest room (cf. *kataluma* in Lk. 2:7). Likewise, the typical Christian solution of harmonizing the differences in the Gospels is preferred to preserving the actual gospels' distinctive details. That is why at Jesus' birth Magi from Matthew (2:1-12) appear side by side with the shepherds from Luke (2:8-20) and why at his death Jesus utters the seven traditional sayings rather than either the cry of derelection as portrayed in the Gospels of Matthew and Mark (Mt. 27:46/Mk 15:34), three sayings that are unique to Luke (23:34, 43, 46), or those unique to John (19:26-27, 28, 30). Also, following Catholic tradition, the producers combine the two distinct persons of Mary Magdalene (cf. Mt. 27:55-56, 61; 28:1; Mk 15:40-41, 47; 16:1-8, 9; Lk. 8:1-3; 24:10; Jn 19:25; 20:1-18) and Mary of Bethany (cf. Lk. 10:38-42; Jn 11:1-33; 12:1-8) into one character in the series. On a more positive note, however, they do forego the traditional portrayal of Mary Magdalene as a repentant prostitute (cf. Lk. 7:36-50) and do not conflate her character with the woman caught in adultery (cf. Jn 8:1-11). For a more detailed analysis of the series' positive portrayal of Mary Magdalene, see Mark Goodacre's blog post on that topic ('A Celebration of Mary Magdalene in *The Bible* Series', http://ntweblog.blogspot.com/2013/03/a-celebration-of-mary-magdalene-in.html).

    48. Cf. Peter Enns 'Getting Jesus Right: 2 Quick Comments on Week 4 of "The Bible" on the History Channel', http://www.patheos.com/blogs/peterenns/2013/03/getting-jesus-right-2-quick-comments-on-week-4-of-the-bible-on-the-history-channel.

scenes focus on different characters' reactions to that impending threat so that the audience witnesses not only the tensions between the Israelites and their Roman rulers but also those among the Israelites themselves caused by their divergent approaches to dealing with Roman occupation. Nationalistic Jews actively antagonize the Romans and long for the arrival of their messianic warrior-king to crush the empire. Conversely the temple establishment and the Herodians, though they use disparate methods, both try to quell conflicts before they erupt into outright rebellion.

For example in episode 6, while Herod tries to please his 'Roman friends' by decorating the temple with a golden eagle, another group tries to purify the temple by taking down the unclean image (cf. *Antiquities* 17.149-67), an act that will undoubtedly antagonize their overlords. Though Herod's methods of control are depicted in this episode as deplorable,[49] the uprisings that ensue after his death (cf. *War* 2.55-56; *Antiquities* 17.269-77) suggest that only a heavy hand like Herod's can hold down the nationalistic fervour and religious zealotry simmering and threatening to boil. The grisly scene of 2,000 bloody, blackened and decaying figures on crosses (cf. *War* 2.72-75; *Antiquities* 17.295-98) that Jesus' family witnesses on their return from Egypt to Galilee makes the might of Rome abundantly clear and serves as a warning against any future rebellion. The scene also foreshadows Jesus' own future when he himself will run afoul of the Roman government.

The way is thus paved for the audience to better understand the choices that Israel's leaders, such as Caiaphas, Antipas and even the Roman procurator Pilate, make in order to secure the peace and to keep Caesar's wrath from descending on them. No doubt the scene of those crucified Galileans is vivid in Caiaphas's memory when in episode 7 he hears that people have taken to the streets to protest against the use of Temple funds to build the aqueduct (cf. *War* 2.175-77, *Antiquities* 18.60-62). As the high priest surveys the slaughtered men, women and children lying in the streets after the protest, he muses, 'Pilate's keeping us in our place. Imagine what he could do at Passover.' The narrator's voiceover in episode 6 reminds the audience that for these leaders 'any gathering of people is a threat', and thus any charismatic leader who could draw such crowds would be seen as a security risk. This observation helps to explain to a modern audience

---

49. Herod slits the throats of those who tried to remove the eagle; he murders a town full of baby boys in order to eliminate the one who might become a threat to his dynasty (cf. Mt. 2:16-18); and he even has his own son executed (cf. *Antiquities* 17.182-87).

why even non-militaristic leaders, such as John the Baptist and Jesus, presented a dangerous challenge to the establishment's authority.[50]

Now gospel events portrayed in the series, such as Jesus' drawing a crowd of 5,000 who after being miraculously fed begin to shout 'Messiah', his triumphal entry into Jerusalem like a conquering king, his cleansing of the Temple and prophesy of its destruction, all take on greater significance. Add the powder keg of crowds at Passover, and it is no wonder Caiaphas is afraid. At the beginning of episode 8, Caiaphas declares that Jesus 'must not interfere with Passover. God will bring his wrath down upon all of us, and who knows what Pilate will do if the crowds run out of control.' Later in the same episode, Caiaphas asks, 'If the Romans step in, can you imagine the slaughter? It will mean the end of the Temple, the end of our faith, the end of our nation.'

The miniseries' depiction of the justifiable fears of these leaders explains the extreme measures taken against Jesus. The audience can simultaneously disagree with the leaders' decisions while also understanding the intense pressure under which they live. Viewers can see how desperation to preserve a nation could drive Caiaphas to decide: 'We remove this man or the Romans destroy everything ... The life of one peasant for the future of God's nation.' Likewise, they can understand why Pilate, faced with a mob crying out for Jesus' death, feels powerless to stop Jesus' execution. Characters that have been portrayed traditionally as one-sided villains are, to some measure, rehabilitated into complex men placed in unenviable situations.

Here, the medium of film has a distinct advantage over text because it can visually transport viewers back in time, so to speak, where they can watch the political manoeuvrings and machinations play out. Viewing facial expressions and hearing a tone of voice can enable audiences to empathize with characters' fears. Film can also humanize characters and their contexts in another way that text cannot – through simple film editing. *The Bible* does this effectively in episode 8 when during the Passover celebration the scene of Jesus praying in the Garden of Gethsemane is cross-cut with scenes of Caiaphas and Jewish officials praying in the Temple and Pilate and his wife praying to their ancestors in front of a shrine. The technique of cross-cutting is used not only to show concurrent events but also to demonstrate their interconnectedness. These characters are depicted as people all seeking divine guidance, asking for blessing and trying their best to survive in difficult situations.

---

50. Another voiceover by the narrator in episode 7 reminds the audience, 'Jesus is a savior to some but a potential threat to Rome'.

The Bible: A Christian Epic

Every episode of *The Bible* begins with the following caveat: 'This program is an adaptation of Bible stories that changed our world. It endeavours to stay true to the spirit of the book.' So how well does *The Bible* reflect the 'spirit' of the Bible?

First of all, the answer depends on whose Bible you are talking about – a Christian Bible or the Hebrew one. A Jewish viewer watching *The Bible* might take offense to the Christianization of the first testament, and – make no mistake – when the producers entitled the project *The Bible*, they were definitely referring to a *Christian* Bible.[51] From the show's strategic promotion among selected audiences to even its film editing, this series was clearly targeted for a Christian audience and tells a Christian metanarrative.

For example, for the promotion of the series, Downey and Burnett not only hired Outreach, the Christian marketing firm mentioned earlier, but also partnered with Jonathan Bock and his Grace Hill Media group, 'a public-relations and marketing firm that acts as a middleman between Hollywood and the country's faithful'.[52] Bock marketed the series to churches, Christian organizations and faith-based news outlets, and according to *Time* magazine, his concern was to make sure 'church-goers would find the miniseries to be an accurate representation of what *Christians* believe to be the word of God'.[53]

From the first to the last episode, the events are seen through a decidedly 'Jesus gaze' as even the film editing makes clear. The miniseries begins with an overview of *The Bible* by splicing together scenes from its episodes. That synopsis ends with a scene in which Jesus falls while carrying his cross. The camera zooms in for an extreme close-up on Jesus' face and continues moving in until his iris fills the entire screen. The editor uses a dissolve effect so that the shot of Jesus' eye morphs into a swirling universe of galaxies and star clusters until there is only blackness. The scene then transitions seamlessly into the beginning of the first episode in which light breaks forth from darkness while a voiceover utters the opening words of the Bible – 'In the beginning' – and continues to narrate the rest of creation that the audience sees depicted on screen. As the New Testament does, the producers have tied creation, not to mention the entire series, to Christ (cf. Jn 1:1-18), and presented him as the one

---

51. Lloyd states, 'Theirs is a Christian view, in which the Old Testament is a prophetic prelude to the New' (Lloyd, 'Review').

52. Sandburn, 'Behind the Hit'.

53. Italics mine (ibid.).

through whom 'all things in heaven and on earth were created' (cf. Col. 1:15-20).

Likewise, the series ends with a final shot of the resurrected Jesus on the isle of Patmos. Again the camera zooms in for an extreme close-up shot until his iris is the entire *mise en scène*. This shot once more dissolves into another of a silhouetted earth. The camera pulls back so that we see the world with a ray of light shining on it. The camera work and editing suggest not only that Jesus holds the 'light of the world' in his eye, both in this ending scene and in the opening one, but also that Jesus is the Alpha and Omega of *The Bible* series and of its interpretation of the Bible itself.

Besides these bookend appearances, 'Jesus' also appears a great deal in between and not just in the five episodes devoted to the New Testament. Diogo Morgado, the actor who plays Jesus, first appears in episode 1 as one of the three guests called 'Lord' by Abraham (cf. Gen. 18:1-15). Unlike the two angels accompanying him in their *Twilight* wanna-be red cloaks, Jesus wears a beige cloak very similar in appearance to the one he dons in the New Testament episodes. Morgado continues to function in a divine role when Abraham bargains to save Sodom and Gomorrah from destruction (cf. Gen. 18:16-33). In episode 2, his voice is again used for God's when speaking to Moses from the burning bush (cf. Exod. 3:1-22) and then at the giving of commandments on Mt. Sinai (cf. Exod. 20).[54] Finally in episode 5, though intentionally blurry, he appears to be the one with Shadrach, Meshach and Abednego in the fiery furnace, the one before whom Daniel falls to his knees and whom he calls 'Lord' (cf. Dan. 3).

Though *The Bible* offers a Christian metanarrative for the Bible, there was surprisingly little character development of its central character – Christ. Sure there was plenty of swelling background music and crowds clamoring to touch him whenever he made an appearance, but it was almost as if he was only famous for being ... well, famous. Perhaps given the series' targeted demographic audience, the producers did not feel the pressure to develop Jesus' character in a way that explains his uniqueness or creates emotional ties for the audience.[55]

---

54. Admittedly, one would need to have already watched the New Testament episodes to recognize Morgado's voice since the character remains hooded the entire time.

55. The same has been said for the entire series: 'The result is a mini-series full of emoting that does not register emotionally, a tableau of great biblical moments that doesn't convey why they're great. Those looking for something that makes them feel the power of the Bible would do better to find a good production of "Godspell" or "Jesus Christ Superstar"' (Genzlinger, 'God's Word').

While it may be too much to ask, a well-done dramatization of Jesus should have the audience falling in love with his character not because of his stunning good looks but because of who he is and what he does. *The Bible*'s portrayal of Jesus left me personally feeling unconnected, uninspired and frankly bored.[56] It did not adequately portray what is so great about Jesus and why this character has continued to inspire billions over the last two millennia. When Jesus first calls Peter in episode 6 to come and be a fisher of men, Peter asks what they are going to do. Jesus responds by saying, 'Change the world'. By the end of the series, I was still waiting to learn how.

The Bible: A Sanitized but Still Sensual Epic

A reviewer for the *Pittsburgh Post-Gazette* quipped that the miniseries should have been titled '"The Bible's Greatest Hits" (Sanitized for Your Protection)'.[57] Another wrote, 'With the pace of a music video, the characterizations of a comic book and the political-correctness quotient of a Berkeley vegetarian commune – laughably, the destruction of Sodom is depicted without the faintest hint of the sexual peccadillo that takes its name from the city'.[58]

The critics are right, of course. The producers have removed aspects from the biblical stories that might be deemed less 'family friendly' by a more conservative American viewership. For example, Noah never gets drunk and naked (cf. Gen. 9:20-27); Abraham never pimps out his wife to save his own skin … twice (cf. Gen. 12:10-20; 20:1-20); and Lot never sleeps with his daughters (cf. Gen. 19:30-38). And yes, the men in Sodom never try to rape Lot's angelic visitors (cf. Gen. 19:1-11).

One could argue though that none of the above details are essential to the narratives themselves. The producers do, for example, retain David's affair with Bathsheba, which is more integral to the overall plot of the Davidic narrative. Yet even when a reference to sex could not be removed, they refrained from depicting the act itself.

56. Likewise, Keene observes, 'Perhaps the strangest thing about this adaptation of The Bible is how slow and tedious it can be' (Keene, 'The Bible').

57. Rob Owen, 'TV Review: "The Bible" a proverbial action film', *Pittsburgh Post-Gazette*, http://www.post-gazette.com/ae/tv-radio/2013/02/28/TV-review-The-Bible-a-proverbial-action-film/stories/201302280468.

58. Glenn Garvin, 'Reviews of "The Bible", "Red Widow" and "Vikings"', http://www.miamiherald.com/2013/03/03/3261342/reviews-of-the-bible-red-widow.html.

Maintaining a 'family friendly' feel, however, did not stop the producers from infusing a heavy dose of sensuality into the series and from viewing the female characters through a decidedly 'male gaze'. Virtually every female role was played by incredibly attractive actresses over whom the camera liked to linger. The audience is given a tantalizing glance of lovely Hagar's naked backside after she sleeps with Abraham, of beautiful Bathsheba as she takes an incredibly sensual bath and of naked Eve sucking seductively on a juicy fig.

Lest the female viewership feel cheated, the producers cast a Portuguese model and telenovela star in the role of Jesus who inspired the viral tweet #HotJesus. Many quips have been made about Morgado's appearance, which put the 'sin' in sensuality, 'the carnal in incarnate'.[59] Stephen Colbert even advised the show to 'lose the Aber-Christy & Fitch model' because 'it does not project holiness when you cannot look at him without saying, "God damn!"'[60]

That television shows tend to cast attractive actors and include sensuality on screen is not a ground-breaking observation, but when such things are needed because the biblical stories themselves are not enough to hold a modern audience's attention, what does that say about society? Moss also pondered this question when in a review of *The Son of God*, the film remake of the series, she wrote,

> In the absence of any real evidence for the appearance of the historical Jesus it says a great deal about *us* that we assume that Jesus must be attractive to be appealing. Christians may be shooting themselves in the foot when it comes to casting Jesus. When Jesus is made all sexy for the screen, doesn't it suggest that his words and deeds aren't powerful enough on their own? They seem to have been for Paul. And Jesus himself doesn't seem to have wanted to get us hot under the collar. But as long as beauty is linked to power, success, and moral goodness, silver-screened Jesus will continue to lead us into temptation.[61]

Also intriguing was the series' sanitization of Old Testament characters, at least of the males. *The Bible* presents a 'Sunday school' version of these characters by removing most of their foibles and turning them into flat, one-sided Bible heroes. This is true for Abraham, Moses, Joshua and even Samson to some extent. For instance, throughout the Abrahamic storyline in episode 1, the series portrays Abraham as a strong man of faith who

59. Moss, 'Diogo Morgado'.
60. Colbert, 'History Channels "The Bible"'.
61. Moss, 'Diogo Morgado'.

follows God unswervingly. He first appears as the starry-eyed dreamer who believes that God will provide his family with land and descendants 'as numerous as the stars', while his relatives, including Sarah, are doubtful. Sarah tries to talk Abraham out of his attempt to rescue Lot while Abraham exemplifies his faith by leading his men in a battle charge cry of 'Trust in God'. Because Abraham is held up as a paragon of faith in the series, it is Sarah alone who doubts God's promise of a child and who laughs at the thought of an old woman giving birth. Gone are the doubts of the biblical Abraham and the fact that he laughs first (cf. Gen. 17:17-18).

The Bible's Abraham also appears rather conservative in his sexual mores because how could he be a Bible hero and good example for American evangelicals today if he were not? He is properly appalled by Sarah's plea for him to have sex with and impregnate Hagar and at first refuses (which I am *sure* is exactly what Abraham would do in his highly patriarchal and polygamous culture). Even the look on his face after sleeping with Hagar is one of guilt. Sarah's jealousy eventually leads to the cruel banishment of Hagar and Ishmael. While Abraham stands weeping at their departure, Sarah coldly watches. The only arguably shining moment for Sarah is when she rushes to save Isaac from being sacrificed.

The pattern, as seen in the above example and throughout the Old Testament portion of the series, is that the male characters are fairly consistently held up as exemplary, laudable heroes of faith while the women are quite simply not. Instead, they tend to be foils for the men's faithfulness, serving as temptresses to sin, doubters who distract their husbands or at best lukewarm participants in Israel's community: Sarah is doubtful and jealous; Lot's wife, who the audience is probably happy to see turned into a pillar of salt, is never anything but cantankerous and disagreeable; Rahab, the prostitute, helps the Israelite spies not because she has chosen to be on the side of Israel's God but because a spy holds a knife to the throat of her son;[62] Delilah is Samson's downfall; and Bathsheba's beauty turns David to the dark side.[63] As Glenn Garvin, *Miami Herald*'s reviewer of *The Bible* miniseries, opined, 'I don't know if men

---

62. This depiction misses the theological point of the story – that even foreigners who side with God can be included in Israel – which is a perfect foil to the story of Achan, an Israelite who receives the same fate as the Canaanites because by keeping loot from their city, he has identified himself with them rather than being obedient to God.

63. This issue too is much better handled in the New Testament episodes. In fact, the way the show handles Mary Magdalene's role is quite refreshing. Again for a more in-depth discussion, see Mark Goodacre's New Testament blog (Goodacre, 'Mary Magdalene').

are conducting a war on women, but television certainly is – if Sunday night is any indication'.[64] Though 'war' is an overstatement, the series certainly possesses a 'male gaze' that offers a derogatory and sensual portrayal of Old Testament women while sanitizing and idolizing the men.

While it is true that sanitization takes place in the Bible itself,[65] more often than not the Old Testament writers were raw in their retelling of Israel's history precisely when one would expect them to create mythic leaders with almost divine perfection. Such whitewashing of the Old Testament's male characters therefore diminishes the authenticity of the narratives themselves. The reviewer for the *New York Times* says something similar: '[T]he approach here actually shows a lack of faith in the power of the biblical stories. The real Bible is a layered, often lyrical epic in which personal journeys are intertwined with collective ones, and human failings bump up against human strivings.'[66] One of the best aspects of the actual Bible's Old Testament stories is their honest portrayal of humanity – flawed, messy, broken, yet beautiful humanity. People can relate to complex characters that struggle in discerning and doing what is right, and *The Bible* is most successful with its character portrayals when it actually honors the Bible by retaining the complexity of its characters. As with most aspects of the show, the New Testament episodes do a much better job of this than the Old Testament episodes.[67]

The Bible: Epically Scary Scriptures

Given the show's willingness to airbrush so many of its male characters' flaws, it is somewhat surprising that the same cleanup job was *not* done for the character of God himself.[68] The Bible itself contains many troubling, or at least confusing pictures of God, and over the course of the series, *The Bible* depicts several of these stories during which God

a. commits mass genocide by almost wiping out the entire human race in a flood (episode 1; cf. Gen. 6:9–7:24);
b. rains down fire and sulphur to burn entire cities and turns a woman into a pillar of salt simply for glancing back at the cities (episode 1; cf. Gen. 19:1-29);

64. Garvin, 'Reviews'.
65. The Chronicler's rewriting of the Deuteronomistic History is again a classic example.
66. Genzlinger, 'God's Word'.
67. Caiaphas and Pilate are good examples of more complex characters rather than simplistic caricatures placed in binary categories of good or evil, hero or villain.
68. God is consistently referred to with masculine pronouns throughout the series.

c. commands a father to sacrifice his own son as a loyalty test (episode 1; cf. Gen. 22:1-19);
d. sends an angel of death to destroy all the firstborn sons in Egypt (episode 2; cf. Exod. 12:29-30);
e. destroys the entire Egyptian army in the Red Sea (episode 2; cf. Exod. 14);
f. has his followers commit some mass genocide of their own against the Canaanites (episode 3; cf. Josh. 6);
g. tells Samson to destroy all the Philistines, and himself consequently, by collapsing a stone theatre (episode 3; cf. Judg. 16:25-31);
h. sends the Babylonian army to burn Jerusalem and destroy its people (episode 5; cf. 2 Kgs 24:22; 2 Chron. 36:17).

I do not know about others' reactions, but I imagine that if I were seeing those events for the first time enacted in all their violent and bloody glory then, contrary to the producers' intentions, I would *not* be inspired to open the Bible or to learn more about the God depicted in it.

While it is true that *The Bible* pictures God favourably when God is credited with saving Noah's family; guiding Abraham's family to a new land; freeing the Israelites from slavery and giving them land; saving Shadrach, Meshach and Abednego in the fiery furnace; delivering Daniel from the lions' den; and bringing the Israelites back from exile, several of these positive actions come at the cost of extreme violence toward other groups as well. Without more explanation, the picture that emerges of God is, to say the least, confusing. Is God as capricious, chaotic and vindictive as these collective scenes would suggest? Does God really desert Samson because of a haircut? Why does Saul lose the throne simply for flubbing a sacrifice and delaying an execution while David gets away with murder and adultery and then, instead of being punished, is blessed with an everlasting dynasty?

One of the main techniques that is often used to great effect in films and fiction that rewrite the Bible is that of gap filling.[69] In places where the motivation of a character is not clear or where there are holes in the plotline, artists connect the dots for their audience and usually do some of their most creative work there. *The Bible* does not do this well with the troubling scenes mentioned above but plays them 'straight' and so leaves the audience scratching heads and wondering why any of these characters really would want to worship and follow this God in the first place.

69. For further discussion on this topic, see Chapter 1, especially pp. 21 and 48 of my book *The Quest for the Fictional Jesus: Gospel Rewrites, Gospel (Re)Interpretation, and Christological Portraits within Jesus Novels* (Eugene, OR: Pickwick, 2013).

Inclusion of *so many* of these scenes may have done more damage than good to God's reputation. After watching the series, one of my students commented, 'You'd think if they were going to whitewash anyone, they would've whitewashed God'.[70] Indeed!

People of faith have struggled for millennia with how to incorporate those troubling biblical images into a theology of God's character. While some prefer to ignore the issue, it is more difficult to do so with dramatizations than with descriptions on paper. As Dorothy Sayers once wrote, '[T]here is no more searching test of a theology than to submit it to dramatic handling; nothing so glaringly exposes inconsistencies in a character, a story, or a philosophy as to put it upon the stage and allow it to speak for itself'.[71] The same can be said for the dramatic handling of Bible stories. How does one, for example, reconcile the image from episode 1 of Jesus/God standing over Sodom and watching it burn with the Jesus in episode 9 who from the cross prays for forgiveness for those watching him die? Dramatization of these events brings an audience literally face to face with them and forces it to grapple with their implications for any theology of God.

The inclusion of so many violent stories of God, however, is simply one aspect of the series' ode to violence. If a biblical story selected for the series contained violence, then that aspect was sure to be included. Even minor events that do not advance the plot and are unessential to the narrative arch, such as Abraham rescuing Lot, are included to add more fight scenes.

Certainly the Bible itself contains violence, as the above list of divine acts attests, but biblical stories have been portrayed on television and in the cinema for years without being as brutal. In the past, even scenes of violence that are integral to the narrative and impossible to remove, such as Jesus' crucifixion, have been done in ways that minimize the amount of blood and guts displayed. Just watching either version of DeMille's *King of Kings* or *The Ten Commandments* and comparing it with *The Bible* immediately highlights the different approaches.

Instead of downplaying the gruesome nature of such events, the miniseries made them even more graphic. It added savage touches, such as eyeballs being poked out with the squishy sound effects, samurai-sword-wielding angels hacking and slicing their way through a crowd with sounds of flesh ripping and blood splattering, scenes of cannibalism

70. Thanks to Kelsey Kreider for faithfully watching each of the episodes with me and for providing her own insights.

71. Dorothy L. Sayers, *The Man Born to be King: A Play Cycle on the Life of Our Lord and Saviour Jesus Christ* (San Francisco: Ignatius, 1990), 13.

with even children gnawing on human bones and Paul using the ancient equivalent of waterboarding to torture Christians. How such portrayals could be considered appropriate for a 'family friendly' show is puzzling.

Not only is it the graphic nature of the violence displayed but also the amount of screen time dedicated to violence that is unsettling.[72] One of the times that I watched the series, I kept track of the amount of time given to scenes of violence in *The Bible*. Out of the 440 minutes of the series, I counted 181 minutes spent on violence. In other words, if all those scenes were placed together, then approximately four out of the ten episodes would be devoted to violence.

If the amount of violent biblical scenes chosen to be included and the brutality of their portrayal were not enough, the producers used their artistic license to add additional violent scenes not found in the biblical narratives. Perhaps *The Bible* is just keeping in step with other recent dramatizations of literature, such as *The Hobbit* trilogy, that add a substantial heaping of gruesome scenes not found in their original source material. Maybe that is what the producers meant when they said that they needed a fresh, relevant updating of the Bible.

Fifty years of research on the effect of television violence has demonstrated that there is a correlation between viewing media violence and heightened levels of aggression in those who watch it.[73] So what does it suggest about our society when one compares the violence in a biblical epic from fifty years ago with those produced in the last decade, such as Gibson's *Passion*, the BBC's *Passion* or the *History Channel*'s *The Bible*? The difference is noticeable, striking and disturbing.

Conclusion

The Bible miniseries is an epic born out of piety and the excellent intentions of promoting biblical literacy. Like all presentations of the Bible though, this one too brings its own lens through which the biblical material is understood, a lens which ultimately mirrors more one's own society, or at least one segment of it.

The miniseries reflects a culture that wants to be entertained with sensational spectacles – the bedazzlement of CGI-enhanced miracles, the adrenaline rush of battle scenes and the titillation of the sensual – rather than delving into character development. Since ambiguities make many

---

72. Cf. Lloyd, 'Review'.

73. John P. Murray, 'Media Violence: The Effects Are Both Real and Strong', *American Behavioral Scientist* 51, no. 8 (2008): 1212–30.

people uncomfortable, escape into the binary categories of hero and villain are preferable to the Bible's own presentation of the complexity within characters and its multiplicity of voices and viewpoints.

Making the Bible 'fresh' and 'engaging' to a society entertained by bloodshed and battle has resulted in some of the most violent Old Testament stories taking centre stage in the series. The accentuation of those events created a common theme throughout the Old Testament episodes – most likely one that the producers never intended – of 'Bible heroes' expressing their fidelity to God through the exclusion and destruction of other ethnicities, presented in the miniseries as uniformly immoral and wicked enemies of God and Israel. Thankfully, the New Testament episodes humanized the opposition more and explored their sides of the story.

Although the Bible itself can glorify violence and dualistically divide people groups into good or bad, perhaps this aspect of the series is more a reflection of our modern world. Sometimes the instinctual reaction to the increasing multiculturalism and pluralism that come with globalization is the dehumanization of other ethnicities in tandem with the zealous protection of one's own religious traditions.

Since, however, we see a similar type of situation manifesting itself in the New Testament world as a result of the globalization brought about by the Roman Empire, perhaps an exploration of New Testament responses would be instructive. One way of counterbalancing the extremism portrayed in the Old Testament episodes would have been a stronger juxtaposition of Jesus' peaceful model of establishing God's kingdom with Israel's earlier violent conquest and destruction of nations. Also since the Old Testament episodes portray more ethnocentrism with the advancement of Israel, often at the expense of other people groups, the New Testament episodes would have done well to emphasize more the inclusive nature of the early Jesus movement, which brought together different ethnicities, social groups and genders based on the principle of loving one's neighbour as one's self.

To be fair, the New Testament episodes do give a nod in that direction by highlighting the inclusion of Mary Magdalene and by showing more of the multicultural composition of the early church in the final episode. Also the series' sequel, *A.D. The Bible Continues*, which aired on NBC in Spring 2015, made ethnic diversity a priority.[74] However, simply recruiting an ethnically diverse cast, as Burnett and Downey have done

74. David Bauder, 'Diversity Important for Follow-up to the Bible', http://abcnews. go.com/Entertainment/wireStory/diversity-important-follow-bible-28286063.

for the sequel, will not be enough to help an audience understand the radical notion of peacefully establishing an empire through love of others rather than through violent exclusion.

So long as society prefers the brutality and gore of television shows like *The Walking Dead*, then maybe this type of kingdom and its king has no chance of being dramatized with depth and substance. Unless the new sequel uses violence to compete, perhaps its resurrected Christ will fail epically in holding its audience's attention and winning another ratings race against the revivified zombies.

Chapter 12

WHEN THE RESURRECTED BIBLICAL EPIC
TRANSFERRED TO THE SMALL SCREEN …
AND PROMPTLY DIED AGAIN: A CRITICAL
AUTOPSY OF THE 2016 ABC SERIES
OF KINGS AND PROPHETS

David Tollerton

Introduction

'An epic biblical saga of faith, ambition, and betrayal', the television series *Of Kings and Prophets* (hereafter *OKP*) was intended as a treatment of the reigns of Saul and David that lucratively tapped into the 2014 cinematic impact of *Noah* and *Exodus: Gods and Kings* (hereafter *Exodus*).[1] With ancient battles, political and sexual intrigue, lavish production and a well-known lead actor, such ingredients were anticipated to add up to a commercial success. They did not. In March 2016 the American ABC network broadcast two episodes of *OKP* before cancelling future airings. After a lengthy delay, the remaining episodes eventually appeared via video-streaming on Amazon Prime, but have received little attention.

This chapter will explore the causes of this failure, focusing particularly on the period of its initial broadcast. In all likelihood *OKP* will itself be largely forgotten (indeed those involved may actively want us

---

1. ABC, 'About *Of Kings and Prophets*', 2016, http://abc.go.com/shows/of-kings-and-prophets/about-the-show (accessed 31 August 2018).

to forget it) and given its poor viewing figures and curtailed television run it is difficult to see what direct cultural impact its content will have. Nonetheless, the story of *OKP*'s cancellation provides valuable insights into the commercial fragility of small screen representations of the Bible, especially when taking on controversial sections of the canon. I will argue that, while the series did consciously attempt to address some of the difficulties flagged up among receptions of *Noah* and *Exodus*, it then faced other problems more specific to the economic and narrative demands of television.

OKP and the 2014 Biblical Epics

Dubbed 'the year of the Bible Movie', 2014 saw a dramatic big-budget return of the biblical to mainstream Hollywood cinema, with the most prominent examples being *Noah*, directed by Darren Aronofsky, and *Exodus*, directed by Ridley Scott.[2] Previously considered to have died out in the 1960s, the return of the 'Bible epic' genre had an array of possible explanations.[3] Twenty-first-century computer-generated imagery offered dramatic new scope for depicting the miraculous, Scott's own commercially successful revival of the classical historical epic with *Gladiator* (2000) showed the potentials of resurrecting epic genres long considered defunct and the ongoing financial travails of the cinema industry may have encouraged a return to Hollywood glories of the past.[4] But however we unravel the origins of the Bible epic's 2014 return, the outcome was two relatively successful commercial ventures. Aronofsky's film was the more unequivocally profitable of the two, *USA Today* declaring only three days after its American release that '[b]y almost every measure, *Noah* is

2. Variations of this phrase appear among a range of sources. For example: Tom Shone, 'A Movie Miracle: How Hollywood Found Religion', *The Guardian*, 31 July 2014, https://www.theguardian.com/film/2014/jul/31/-sp-faith-films-hollywood-religion-christian-noah-heaven-is-real-bible; Nick Allen, 'Biblical Films' Hollywood Comeback', *The Telegraph*, 25 December 2013, http://www.telegraph.co.uk/news/worldnews/northamerica/usa/10537680/Biblical-films-Hollywood-comeback.html.

3. See Adele Reinhartz, *Bible and Cinema: An Introduction* (New York: Routledge, 2013), 4; Catherine Wheatley, 'Can Religion Sell? Noah and the Search for an Audience', *The Conversation*, 4 April 2014, https://theconversation.com/can-religion-sell-noah-and-the-search-for-an-audience-24384.

4. On the role of visual effects and the Bible epic, see Samuel Tongue, 'Picturing the Plagues and Parting the Waves: The Biblical Effect in *Exodus: Gods and Kings*', in *Biblical Reception 4: A New Hollywood Moses: On the Spectacle and Reception of* Exodus: Gods and Kings, ed. David Tollerton (London: Bloomsbury, 2017), 113–35.

an unmitigated hit'.[5] Within a month, media outlets reported that it had made over \$300 million globally, with its production budget being around \$125 million.[6] *Exodus* had a more uneven reception at the American box office, but when viewed internationally it far surpassed its reported \$140 million production costs.[7]

That *OKP* was meant to be a small screen continuation of this success is clear when we note the various overlaps between *Noah*, *Exodus* and *OKP*. The relationship between *Exodus* and the television series is particularly clear-cut through the involvement of Adam Cooper and Bill Collage. Described as the two 'developers' of *OKP*, they were also co-writers of Scott's film.[8] The title elements 'Kings and Prophets' and 'Gods and Kings' were clearly intended to echo one another, and even typefaces used in marketing material closely align.[9] But if *OKP* might reasonably be described as a small screen spin-off of *Exodus*, its attempts to evoke memories of *Noah* are also evident, particularly through its most high-profile casting choice. By some margin the most recognisable actor in the series is Ray Winstone, playing Saul. Some reviewers queried his casting, Robert Bianco, for example, offering the following critique:

> The problems [...] start with Saul himself. In the Bible, he's the ancient uniter of Israel and Judah. In the hands of British actor Ray Winstone, he's more like a London mob boss who's losing control of the family business while fighting off attacks from the rival Philistine gang. Winstone is a fine actor but an odd choice.[10]

5. Scott Bowles, '*Noah* Is a Hit, Yet Film Fans May Not Believe in It', *USA Today*, 31 March 2014, http://www.usatoday.com/story/life/movies/2014/03/31/noah-box-office/7122211/.

6. Nancy Tartaglione, '*Noah* Crosses \$300M in Global Box Office', *Deadline*, 22 April 2014, http://deadline.com/2014/04/noah-crosses-300m-in-global-box-office-718036/.

7. Brent Lang, 'Box Office: *Exodus: Gods & Kings* Tops Charts with \$24.5 Million', *Variety*, 14 December 2014, http://variety.com/2014/film/news/box-office-exodus-gods-kings-tops-charts-with-24-5-million-1201379097/; Phil Hoad, 'Global Box Office: Exodus Grapples with Noah for Top Prophet Margins', *The Guardian*, 10 December 2014, https://www.theguardian.com/film/2014/dec/10/global-box-office-exodus-gods-and-kings-noah-ridley-scott.

8. ABC, 'About *Of Kings and Prophets*'.

9. Compare ABC, 'About *Of Kings and Prophets*' and Fox Movies, 'Exodus: Gods and Kings', 2014, http://www.foxmovies.com/movies/exodus-gods-and-kings.

10. Robert Bianco, 'Review: ABC's *Of Kings and Prophets* is an Epic Fail', *USA Today*, 8 March 2016, http://www.usatoday.com/story/life/tv/columnist/2016/03/07/review-abc-of-kings-and-prophets-robert-bianco/81263938/.

What Bianco overlooks is that Winstone was also one of the lead actors in *Noah*, playing the villainous Tubal-Cain. Saul and Tubal-Cain indeed bear similarities in their presentation, both portrayed as undone by hubris and defiance against divine will. It is overwhelmingly likely that, regardless of how well he functions in *OKP* itself, Winstone's central appearance in this small screen representation of the Hebrew Bible is purposefully meant to associate *OKP* with memories of *Noah*. But there are also stylistic links between *Noah* and *OKP*, particularly between the very first scene of the ABC series and the revelatory visions received by the title character of Aronofsky's film. The viewer of *OKP* episode one is confronted immediately with a rapidly edited, violent and purposefully disorientating sequence that is far more reminiscent of Noah's visions than anything seen in the more conventionally staged *Exodus*. While it does share with *Exodus* a propensity for epic, aerial shots of ancient cityscapes, *OKP* appears to have also mined Aronofsky's more visceral and unsettling style.

For these reasons (and others that will be addressed below), it seems clear that *OKP* should be understood as the small screen outcome of both *Noah*'s and *Exodus*' commercial successes at the cinema. Yet what went so catastrophically wrong for this television production? I will leave aside straightforward judgements as to its quality as a drama, partly because these are so subjective, but also because even if we were to declare that *OKP*, *Noah* and *Exodus* were all equally 'good'/'bad' in terms of their artistic merit, I suggest that *OKP* faced specific problems. These related to its confrontation with difficult biblical material and dynamics specific to the very medium of network television. To address them it is useful to begin with aspects of the series' reception.

OKP vs. The Parents Television Council

Despite their relative commercial successes *Noah* and *Exodus* were controversial films. One high-profile element of this was the accusation of 'whitewashing' in their casting, with fuel added to the fire by less-than-ideal responses from key individuals associated with each of the productions. Ari Handel, the co-writer of *Noah*, failed to diffuse the issue when remarking that '[a]t the level of myth, and as a mythical story, the race of the individuals doesn't matter', while Scott, in an interview in *Variety*, argued that it would not have been viable to tell financial backers of *Exodus* 'that my lead actor is Mohammad so-and-so from such-and-such'.[11]

---

11. Handel is cited in Nick Clark, 'Racism Storm as *Noah* Writer Denies All-White Cast is "Racist"', *The Independent*, 17 April 2014, http://www.independent.co.uk/

The creators of *OKP* were at pains to avoid a repeat of these controversies, co-author Adam Cooper reflecting of his earlier experiences with *Exodus* that '[w]e were pretty bruised by how that came out, the criticism about whitewashing is something that matters to us very much'. The television production was consequently cast 'with an eye toward diversity', and subsequent media reviews made reassuringly little reference to issues of the ethnicity of the actors involved.[12]

OKP may have avoided the controversies regarding ethnicity and casting that arose in response to *Noah* and *Exodus*, but its reception was nonetheless troubled. The first episode, aired on 8 March 2016, received a raft of negative media reviews with a recurring theme being unfavourable comparisons with the vastly more successful HBO series *Game of Thrones*.[13] But by this point the tone had already been set through opposition from the Parents Television Council (hereafter PTC), a development worth considering in depth.

The PTC was founded in 1995 as a movement to preserve 'family values' on American television and by the 2000s was viewed as the preeminent national organisation to lobby on this issue.[14] Working with conservative politicians, press outlets eager for stories of controversy and the Federal Communications Commission, the PTC has become a familiar voice in public media commentary. In January 2016 it began to take aim at the sexual and violent content of *OKP*, prompted into doing so by the online release of a trailer for the series and executive producer Chris Brancato's

arts-entertainment/films/news/racism-storm-as-noah-writer-denies-all-white-cast-is-racist-9268130.html; Scott Foundas, '*Exodus: Gods and Kings* Director Ridley Scott on Creating His Vision of Moses', *Variety*, 25 November 2014, http://variety.com/2014/film/news/ridley-scott-exodus-gods-and-kings-christian-bale-1201363668/.

12. Cited in Kevin Porter 'ABC's Biblical "Soap Opera" *Of Kings and Prophets* Blasted as "Extraordinarily Violent", "Sexual"', *Christian Post*, 4 March 2016, http://www.christianpost.com/news/of-kings-and-prophets-blasted-as-extraordinarily-violent-sexual-158905/.

13. For example, Emily Yahr, '*Of Kings and Prophets* Tried to be *Game of Thrones* and Failed. What Went Wrong?', *The Washington Post*, 9 March 2016, https://www.washingtonpost.com/news/arts-and-entertainment/wp/2016/03/09/of-kings-and-prophets-tried-to-be-game-of-thrones-and-failed-what-went-wrong/; Neil Genzlinger, 'Review: In *Of Kings and Prophets*, Biblical Tales Retold', *The New York Times*, 7 March 2016, http://www.nytimes.com/2016/03/08/arts/television/kings-and-prophets-tv-review.html?_r=3.

14. James Poniewozik, 'The Decency Police', *Time*, 20 March 2005; Kathleen Lowney, 'Wrestling with Criticism: The World Wrestling Federation's Ironic Campaign Against the Parents Television Council', *Symbolic Interaction* 26, no. 3 (2003): 434.

(in retrospect rather misjudged) boast that 'we'll be fighting with broadcast standards and practices ... [W]e're going to go as far as we can.'[15]

Viewed at face value the PTC's opposition could initially be understood in largely secular terms, and indeed the organisation's stated mission 'to protect children and families from graphic sex, violence and profanity in the media' is, like almost all of its website content, devoid of any explicit religious positioning.[16] But the background of its relationship with *OKP* is more complex than this. The founder of the PTC, Brent Bozell, is also involved with the Catholic League for Religious and Civil Rights, an organisation that has lobbied on an overtly confessional basis against media output deemed offensive.[17] And at times faith-based commentary can be clearly discerned amidst the PTC's argumentation regarding *OKP*. Specifically, it is apparent in a suggestion that the series is problematic not merely because it includes sexual and violent content, but because it does so in relation to the Bible. On 11 January 2016 Christopher Gildemeister, the PTC's Head of Research Operations, published a lengthy warning about *OKP*, featuring a passage (worth citing at length) in which substantial presumptions about the Bible are at play:

[T]he point of the Bible's stories is almost comically missed by *Of Kings and Prophets'* producers and writers, the ABC network, and most of Hollywood – the fact that they serve as lessons in morality. These stories teach that sinful behavior has negative effects on individuals and society, and that God continues to walk with, care for, and love the Jewish people (in the Old Testament) and all people (in the New Testament). Those are the reasons such stories are still studied by Christians – indeed, the whole reason they're included in the Christian Bible at all ... not because they're filled with salacious sex stories and graphic gore. Yes, some Bible stories contain references to war and adultery; and certainly, some individuals in Biblical history exhibited bad personal behavior, just as some of America's founding fathers did. But just as a story about Thomas Jefferson which

15. Cited in Bryn Elise Sandberg, '*Of Kings and Prophets* Boss Talks Sexually Explicit Bible Series: "We're Going to Go as Far as We Can"', *The Hollywood Reporter*, 9 January 2016, http://www.hollywoodreporter.com/live-feed/kings-prophets-boss-talks-sexually-853669.

16. PTC, 'The PTC Mission', 2016, http://w2.parentstv.org/main/About/mission.aspx.

17. Catholic League, 'Board of Advisors', https://www.catholicleague.org/board-of-advisors/. One of the Catholic Leagues' more high-profile campaigns was against the 1999 film *Dogma*. See Jamie Allen, '*Dogma* Director Faces Down Catholic Criticism', *CNN*, 17 September 1999, http://edition.cnn.com/SHOWBIZ/Movies/9909/17/dogma/.

focused solely on his sexual affairs and ownership of slaves, but ignored his authorship of the Declaration of Independence and role in the American Revolution, would be hopelessly unbalanced, grossly unfair, and miss the entire point of mentioning him, so too is a recounting of Biblical stories that focuses exclusively on its scandalous aspects. At that point, the tale ceases to be either Biblical morality or history.[18]

Leaving aside the suggestions of supercessionism and his reading of American history, the main thrust of Gildemeister's position appears to be that 'the entire point' of making any screen adaptation of the Bible is that it offers 'lessons in morality'. It is to be suspected that, despite appearances, the surface issues of sexual or violent content are secondary, only acting as advance warnings that a more foundational issue of ethos is deemed awry. It is surely not coincidental that Gibson's reverential *Passion of the Christ*, a film by some margin more graphic than *OKP*, received comparatively gentle treatment at the hands of the PTC.[19] Good representations of the Bible on screen should, Gildemeister says, be inherently positive about 'Biblical morality' and serve to reinforce a Christian message. Despite the PTC's self-presentation as a non-religious organisation, it is apparent that such opposition to *OKP* has at least confessional foundations. Interestingly, its views on 'Biblical morality' can be also occasionally detected in later mainstream media reviews. Writing for the widely circulated *USA Today* newspaper, Robert Bianco offers a similar appraisal:

> Historians and theologians may not agree on who wrote the Bible, but they do share a general belief in why it was written: to offer moral guidance and spiritual encouragement. A TV show that uses biblical characters as an excuse for sex and violence while jettisoning the religious intent is not Bible-based in any real sense of the idea. Or worth watching.[20]

Leaving aside the dubiously sweeping assessment of what 'historians and theologians' believe, there is again a clear implication that a screen depiction of the Bible must be fundamentally positive about its content and offer audiences straightforward moral guidance.

18. Christopher Gildemeister, 'ABC Promises 'Violent, Sex-Drenched' Bible Series', PTV, 11 January 2016, http://w2.parentstv.org/blog/index.php/2016/01/11/abc-promises-violent-sex-drenched-bible-series/.

19. Erin Wilhelm, '*The Passion of the Christ*', PTC, 2004, http://www.parentstv.org/ptc/publications/moviereviews/PTC/2004/passion.asp.

20. Bianco, 'Review: ABC's *Of Kings and Prophets*'.

As I will outline below, in the two aired episodes of *OKP* such clear guidance is notably missing. But I suggest this is apparent less with regard to presentational issues of sexual and violent content, and more in relation to its treatment of a deeper thematic concern: God's (non-)ethical nature.

Genocide and the Disturbing Divine

While *OKP* managed to sidestep the 'whitewashing' controversies of its big screen precursors, it entirely embraced their propensities to upset the theological sensibilities of religious conservatives. The two aired episodes of *OKP* cover elements of 1 Samuel 14–17, though as with *Noah* and *Exodus* liberties are taken in terms of material added, subtracted and reordered. But it is the portrayal of divine morality that has most potential to cause disquiet. It is useful to first turn to how this issue emerges in *Noah* and *Exodus*.

In Aronofsky's film God is at times a profoundly troubling off-screen presence. The darkest point arrives when Noah (played by Russell Crowe) comes to believe that he has been commanded to murder his own grand-children. Initially horrified by this prospect, Noah unsuccessfully pleads with God before finally steeling himself for the task ahead:

> Please! Please! Please! I cannot do this. Tell me I don't need to do this. Please. Have I not done everything that you asked of me? Is that not enough? Why do you not answer me? Why? [Silence. Noah descends to his knees] I will not fail you. I will not fail you. I will not fail you. It shall be done.[21]

Coming after scenes of mass-drowning in the flood, by this point in proceedings God appears at best morally tainted, and at worst monstrous. That Noah ultimately fails to kill the children yet is granted divine blessing at the film's close would appear to provide some measure of narrative redemption to God, but Aronofsky nonetheless takes us to very dark places with regard to divine character (and some leaving the movie theatres will have been only partially comforted by its resolution). It is notable that Gildemeister, when forewarning that *OKP* may fail to convey 'Biblical morality', singles out *Noah* as a worrying precursor.[22] A parallel dynamic plays out in Scott's *Exodus*. Here, the divine is repre-sented through a young boy (named as 'Malak' in the credits) who is at

---

21. *Noah*, directed by Darren Aronofsky © Paramount Pictures 2014. All rights reserved.

22. Gildemeister, 'ABC Promises'.

times fervently (even petulantly) intent upon inflicting vengeance on the Egyptians. Moses (played by Christian Bale) shows repeated disquiet, and when told of the plan to kill the firstborn he is forcefully angry: 'No, no! You cannot do this! I want no part of this!'[23] The film closes with Malak and Moses reconciled, but some commentators have justifiably wondered whether *Exodus'* rushed attempts at narrative closure do effectively mitigate the divine horror earlier flagged up so explicitly.[24] *OKP* consequently suffered from confronting a PTC already primed for disapproval by the content of the 2014 epics.

OKP itself very much continues, even extends, these patterns of portraying the divine as morally problematic. The key example is its treatment of 1 Samuel 15, that is, God's command to Saul to destroy the Amalekites. It is a topic that arises immediately upon the viewer's introduction to the prophet Samuel (played by Mohammad Bakri):

[Samuel] Elohim our Lord has commanded that in retribution that you destroy their men, destroy their women and destroy their children.

[Saul] The Amalekites are no threat to us. They are nothing. Our enemies now are the Philistines.

[Samuel] Do you defy Elohim's command?

[Saul] I ask for his blessings for the union of my people.

[Samuel] Slay the Amalekites, and you will have it.

[Saul] Samuel, I am tired, my men are tired. Surely it is more important that first we unite the twelve tribes. And then if it is still Elohim's wish, we then march on the Amalekites.

[Samuel] You are to do it now. Elohim has spoken.[25]

In comparison to 1 Sam. 15:3-4, Saul is here more initially hesitant to follow the divine injunction, and *OKP* later dwells upon its psychological effects in far greater depth. The scene in which the Amalekites are slaughtered is brutal and bloody, with slow-motion violence, a melancholy rather than triumphant soundtrack and extensive close-ups of the

---

23. *Exodus: Gods and Kings*, directed by Ridley Scott © 20th Century Fox 2014. All rights reserved.

24. Jon Morgan, 'Interpreting the Entrails: Religion and Violence in *Exodus: Gods and Kings*', in Tollerton, ed., *Biblical Reception 4*, 57–74.

25. 'Offerings of Blood', *Of Kings and Prophets*, directed by Michael Offer © ABC Studios 2016. All rights reserved.

corpses.[26] At one point Saul pauses at length before a cowering mother and child, only to finally kill them with a dagger. After the event we see Saul in shock, his face splattered with blood. Apparently traumatised, he refuses to finally kill Agag, the captured Amalekite king, defiantly uttering '[p]rophet be damned! Today I am the one who speaks!'[27] The line mirrors Samuel's final utterance above, underlining Saul's defiance of God. But having so graphically visualised the horror of 1 Sam. 15:8 ('[Saul] utterly destroyed all the people with the edge of the sword') it is hard for viewers to see the defiance in wholly negative terms. Such questioning of divine justice (on the part of both Saul and the viewer) is only encouraged during a sequence of dialogue in which Samuel chastises Saul for failing to kill Agag:

> [Saul] Samuel, I have listened to your commands all the years that I have sat on that throne. And not once have I questioned you. But now you sanction murder in the name of Elohim?
>
> [Samuel] In your weakness you put yourself above the Lord.
>
> [Saul] You are not the Lord.
>
> [Samuel] I am the prophet.
>
> [Saul] And I am the king!
>
> [Samuel] You do not question his will.
>
> [Saul] Then, if he cannot be questioned, what is his purpose? The Lord I've revered does not slaughter women and children.[28]

The dialogue between Saul and Samuel contained in the biblical text (15:13-31) is markedly different from this. Where the biblical Saul repents

---

26. A shot of corpses being piled upon one another appears immediately reminiscent of scenes of Hebrew slavery in Scott's *Exodus*. Given the connections in production between *Exodus* and *OKP* this seems unlikely to be coincidental. Some commentators saw in Scott's imagery clear references to documentary footage of the Holocaust. See Nathan Abrams, 'Exodus – Our Verdict', *Jewish Quarterly*, 27 December 2014, http://jewishquarterly.org/2014/12/exodus-verdict/. Another link between Scott's work and the destruction of the Amalekites in *OKP* comes from comparing the attack on the caravan train in his 2005 film *Kingdom of Heaven*. The visual framing of the scene is remarkably similar, the only major difference being that the Templar knights, who shout 'God wills it' as they brutally massacre a group of Muslims, appear less morally conflicted than Saul.

27. 'Offerings of Blood', *Of Kings and Prophets*, directed by Michael Offer © ABC Studios 2016. All rights reserved.

28. Ibid.

for failing to fully annihilate the Amalekites and their livestock, the Saul of *OKP* instead raises stark questions about the morality of God's command. He is portrayed as far more defiant than the biblical Saul, perhaps arrogantly placing his moral judgements higher than those of God. Yet a significant proportion of viewers would likely sympathise with his concerns. They are prompted into doing so by the sombre and graphic staging of the violence, but also because the acts God commands would so easily fall inside a modern definition of genocide.[29] Given contemporary viewer sensibilities regarding acts of genocide (namely that they are unambiguously crimes of upmost horror and seriousness), it seems likely that many would side with Saul in this exchange.

The destruction of the Amalekites in 1 Samuel 15 was never likely to be transferred to the screen in way that could smoothly overcome the discomfort of contemporary audiences, but it is notable that *OKP* actually heightens such discomfort by lingering on the bloody slaughter of innocents and then placing our outrage in the mouth of Saul. 1 Samuel 15 has been considered a problematic text by numerous modern commentators, and attempts to render it morally palatable have on occasion involved significant interpretive gymnastics.[30] John Allister, for example, suggests that because Saul warns the Kenites to 'withdraw from among the Amalekites' (1 Sam. 15:6) he was *implicitly* allowing some Amalekites to leave.[31] Even while we may recognise a measure of desperation in Allister's reading, it does highlight how, by contrast, *OKP* does not even try to mitigate uncomfortable dimensions of the text. Like *Noah* and *Exodus* before it, this small screen representation of the Hebrew Bible actually accentuates the ethical difficulties and forces the viewer to grapple with a morally difficult vision of the divine.

Small Screen Challenges

Noah replaced archetypal children's book images of the Ark with a vision of providential mass death, *Exodus* gave us a portrayal of the divine

---

29. See article 2 of the United Nations' Convention on the Prevention and Punishment of the Crime of Genocide (1948).

30. See, for example, Wes Morriston, 'Ethical Criticism of the Bible: The Case of Divinely Mandated Genocide', *Sophia* 51 (2012): 117–35, and Eleonore Stump, 'The Problem of Evil and the History of Peoples: Think Amalek', in *Divine Evil? The Moral Character of the God of Abraham*, ed. Michael Bergmann, Michael J. Murray and Michael Rea (Oxford: Oxford University Press, 2010), 179–97.

31. John Allister, 'The Amalekite Genocide', *Churchman*, 124, no. 3 (2010): 223.

as petulant destroyer of babies and *OKP* presented a king wrestling with a genocidal command. But while *OKP* was to some extent merely continuing a theme present in the 2014 Bible epics it developed out of, it also faced problems specific to network television.

The first problem is one of narrative structure. *OKP* lost a significant share of viewers between episodes one and two, and while it may be possible that this is due entirely to perceptions of artistic quality, I suggest that the way it was forced to format its tale of ethical ambiguities caused major difficulties.[32] *Noah* and *Exodus* take the viewer to some very dark places with regard to God's relationship with his creation, but by the time they leave the cinema some manner of resolution has been at least offered. Noah does not kill his granddaughters, and the final scene is one in which divine rainbows fan across the heavens atop a world renewed. Moses overcomes his horror at the killing of the firstborn, and in the final scenes of *Exodus* he is able to share a warm relationship with Malak whilst carving out the Ten Commandments. Some may wonder if the resolutions are substantial enough to outweigh the disturbing implications of what has come before, but there is at least a trajectory toward consolation. Perhaps, we are prompted to conclude, it was just about all worthwhile in the end. The first episode of *OKP*, however, ends with the grim dimensions of Amalekites' destruction left wholly unresolved. The moral universe the characters inhabit appears so groundless it is hard to know who to root for as you mull over the programme during the next seven days. It is not clear that the Philistines are actually any worse than Samuel and Saul, and David's rise to prominence in the Lord's favour is rather undercut by heavy suggestions of divine sadism. The inherently episodic nature of *OKP* is essentially equivalent to including a vast intermission midway through screenings of *Noah* and *Exodus* in which the audience is prompted to dwell upon the horror they have witnessed and asked whether they would like to be re-immersed in that world. Even secular viewers might conclude that it is all a little too nihilistic. The creators of *OKP* evidently wanted to replicate the sharp theological quandaries and flawed protagonists presented in *Noah* and *Exodus*, but they may have underappreciated that, this being television rather than cinema, they were asking rather more of their viewers' stamina.

32. See Bill Keveney, 'ABC Cancels *Of Kings and Prophets* After Two Episodes', *USA Today*, 18 March 2016, http://www.usatoday.com/story/life/tv/2016/03/18/abc-cancels-kings-and-prophets-after-two-episodes/81948366/.

But a second television-specific difficulty concerns economics. Network television is reliant not on ticket sales, but advertisers, Harold Vogel dryly remarking that ultimately '[p]rograms are scheduled interruptions of marketing bulletins'.[33] One side-effect is that the PTC were able to not merely publicise pre-airing concerns about *OKP* to a press media habitually eager for stories of religious controversy, but they could also lobby advertisers to pull out of involvement with the relevant segment of ABC's broadcasting. On 1 March 2016, one week ahead of the opening week of *OKP*, the PTC announced that it had contacted 'over 200 of the nation's top TV sponsors' and presented the following warning:

> Recent studies have demonstrated that television advertisers risk harming their brand and their ability to influence buying decisions when they put their sponsorship dollars behind programs saturated in sex and violence. One meta-analysis from Ohio State University found that advertising on such programs decreases advertising effectiveness. Advertisers have a big and important responsibility to the program's viewers: what they sponsor allows programs to remain on the air, for better or worse. Without advertisers, TV shows do not exist. It is our sincere hope that advertisers take heed and choose to put their sponsorship dollars towards programming that isn't saturated with sex and violence and which could harm children. We will let you know which companies are proud to pay for graphic sex and violence as the series unfolds in the coming weeks.[34]

What starts as a comparatively dry commentary on television economics ends, via superficial sarcasm, with a clear threat to name-and-shame companies using *OKP*'s advertisement breaks. Precise information on the effect this threat had is unavailable, but ABC's judgement that *OKP* was, in commercial terms, unviable after only two episodes should be understood in the context of an economic model particularly vulnerable to targeted lobbying. ABC was additionally vulnerable because, unlike streaming services such as Netflix or Amazon, it openly publishes viewing figures, making low ratings clear for all to see. With weak ratings and PTC lobbying, advertising slots during *OKP* would have appeared a notably poor investment.

33. Harold L. Vogel, *Entertainment Industry Economics: A Guide for Financial Analysis*, 9th edn (Cambridge: Cambridge University Press, 2014), 312.

34. Melissa Henson, 'ABC's *Of Kings and Prophets*, Broadcast TV's Version of HBO's Explicit *Game of Thrones*', PTC, 2016, http://w2.parentstv.org/blog/index. php/2016/03/01/abcs-of-kings-and-prophets-broadcast-tvs-version-of-hbos-explicit-game-of-thrones/ (accessed 31 August 2018).

Conclusion

Historically, there have certainly been cinematic representations of the Bible that have commercially benefited from controversy, *Monty Python's Life of Brian* being one especially clear example.[35] *Noah* and *Exodus* both had vocal conservative critics, but as noted above, they proved relatively successful in commercial terms.[36] *OKP*, however, was judged to be unviable even with 8/10 of its filmed episodes unaired. Viewer doubts about its artistic quality may have played some part (though to my own mind it is not markedly worse than *Exodus* – unsurprisingly given that it shares scriptwriters), but other issues appear to have hampered this production.

First, replicating *Noah*'s and *Exodus*'themes of severe moral ambiguity but then necessarily segmenting it across numerous episodes created particular strains. *OKP*, more than *Noah* and *Exodus*, needed to lure viewers *back* on a consistent basis, but the ethically groundless cosmos its characters inhabit presented an unenticing proposition. When it is hard to know whether we want any of Saul, Samuel, David or even God to actually succeed in their ambitions, it is clear that something has been lost in translation during the transfer to the small screen.

But more important was *OKP*'s fragility in the face of sustained PTC campaigning. In January 2016, the ostensibly secular PTC forewarned that *OKP* would run counter to the Christian 'Biblical morality' that they suggested should motivate all screen representations of the Bible. One week before the first episode was aired, the PTC then announced that it was threatening the advertisers vital to ABC's profit-making. The situation was only further exacerbated on the very morning before *OKP* was first shown, when executive producer Chris Brancato invited the PTC to an advance screening of *OKP*, presumably in an attempt to alleviate

---

35. See Robert Hewison, *Monty Python: The Case Against* (London: Methuen, 1981).

36. See, for example, Sean Hannity et al., '*Noah* Faces Storm of Criticism over Religious Merits', *The Sean Hannity Show*, 27 March 2014, http://video. foxnews.com/v/3401163917001/noah-faces-storm-of-criticism-over-religious-merits/?#sp=show-clips; Ken Ham, 'The Noah Movie Is Disgusting and Evil— Paganism!', *Answers In Genesis*, 28 March 2014, https://answersingenesis.org/blogs/ ken-ham/2014/03/28/the-noah-movie-is-disgusting-and-evil-paganism/; Glenn Beck, speaking on *The Blaze* radio on 15 December 2014, available at Erica Ritz, 'Beck: New "Exodus" Movie Makes Moses "Arrogant" Before Turning Him into a Terrorist', *The Blaze*, 15 December 2014, http://www.theblaze.com/stories/2014/12/15/did-exodus-gods-and-kings-turn-moses-into-a-terrorist-glenn-beck-certainly-thinks-so/.

some of their fears. But this backfired when, on 8 March 2016, the PTC president Tim Winter – now able to claim prior knowledge of the series' content – reiterated his opposition to various press outlets.[37] Unable to hide the subsequent ratings failure amidst such negative publicity ABC quickly moved to cuts its losses.

The story of *OKP*'s failure suggests that when representing the Bible on screen the transfer of commercial success from big to small screen faces particular challenges. In 2014 the secular directors of *Noah* and *Exodus* pushed ethical questioning of the divine to remarkable levels, but the gamble largely paid off. Despite all of the controversy, audiences were curious to see what Aronofsky and Scott had done with these familiar biblical tales. *OKP*, however, demanded long-term emotional investment in a morally murky vision of the Bible, and faced revenue collapse from advertisers petitioned by a well-organised and long-established lobbying group.

It is probable that a television drama quite like *OKP* will not emerge again in the near future. An ethos which ran so viscerally counter to a view of Bible stories as morally uplifting appears to create risky ventures. This is an unfortunate state of affairs given that biblical passages such as 1 Samuel 15 are, to my mind, genuinely disconcerting, and might be valuably confronted in the public square via television. *OKP*, alas, never got far enough to provoke such discussions among a large audience. Writing in *The New York Times* Neil Genzlinger reflected that '[i]f you bear with it […] Episode 3 brings things more sharply into focus'.[38] But instead of *OKP*'s third episode being aired ABC replaced it with *Beyond the Tank*, a reality show following the mixed fortunes of aspiring entrepreneurs struggling for investment.[39] This specific outcome, at least, appears curiously apt.

37. Lesley Goldberg, 'Parents Television Council Blasts ABC's Biblical Drama *Of Kings and Prophets*', *Hollywood Reporter*, 8 March 2016, http://www.hollywoodreporter.com/live-feed/parents-television-council-blasts-abcs-873531.

38. Genzlinger, 'Review: In *Of Kings and Prophets*'.

39. Keveney, 'ABC Cancels *Of Kings and Prophets*'.

INDEX OF REFERENCES

INDEX OF AUTHORS

Lightning Source UK Ltd.
Milton Keynes UK
UKHW010909100223
416739UK00004B/571